ID# PEPE ROMERO

PEPE ROMERO

DIALOGUES ON A LIFE'S JOURNEY WITH THE GUITAR

By Pepe Romero

As told to Walter Aaron Clark

Foreword by Philippe Entremont

UNIVERSITY OF ROCHESTER PRESS

© Pepe Romero and Walter Aaron Clark 2025

All rights reserved. Except as permitted under current legislation, no part of this work may be photocopied, stored in a retrieval system, published, performed in public, adapted, broadcast, transmitted, recorded, or reproduced in any form or by any means, without the prior permission of the copyright owner.

First published 2025

University of Rochester Press
668 Mt. Hope Avenue, Rochester, NY 14620, USA
www.urpress.com
and Boydell & Brewer Limited
PO Box 9, Woodbridge, Suffolk IP12 3DF, UK
www.boydellandbrewer.com

Our Authorized Representative for product safety in the EU is Easy Access System Europe - Mustamäe tee 50, 10621 Tallinn, Estonia, gpsr.requests@easproject.com.

ISBN: 978-1-64825-118-4

Library of Congress Cataloging-in-Publication Data

Names: Romero, Pepe, author. | Clark, Walter Aaron, author. | Entremont, Philippe writer of foreword.
Title: Pepe Romero : dialogues on a life's journey with the guitar / by Pepe Romero ; as told to Walter Aaron Clark ; foreword by Philippe Entremont.
Description: Rochester, NY : University of Rochester Press, 2025. | Includes index. |
Identifiers: LCCN 2024051350 (print) | LCCN 2024051351 (ebook) | ISBN 9781648251184 (hardback) | ISBN 9781805436577 (pdf) | ISBN 9781805436584 (epub)
Subjects: LCSH: Romero, Pepe. | Guitarists—United States—Biography. | Flamenco musicians—United States—Biography. | LCGFT: Autobiographies.
Classification: LCC ML419.R6655 R68 2025 (print) | LCC ML419.R6655 (ebook) | DDC 787.87092 [B]—dc23/eng/20241029
LC record available at https://lccn.loc.gov/2024051350
LC ebook record available at https://lccn.loc.gov/2024051351

A catalogue record for this title is available from the British Library.

Cover photo by Paul Carter. All interior photos are courtesy of the Romero family.

Dedicated to Mamá and Papá

With infinite gratitude for the gifts of life, love, and music that they gave me

CONTENTS

List of Figures	ix
Foreword by Philippe Entremont	xiii
Preface: Pepe and I by Walter Aaron Clark	xv

PART I. FORMATION

1.	Early Life	3
2.	Early Education with Mamá	13

PART II. GUITAR

3.	Technique	25
4.	Teaching	34
5.	Guitars and Guitar Makers	

PART III. CONCERTIZING

6.	The Soloist and the Quartet Member	75
7.	Managers	84

PART IV. REPERTOIRE

8.	Premieres	103
9.	Revivals	118
10.	Improviser, Arranger, Composer	128

PART V. CONNECTIONS

11.	Celebrities in Politics, Religion, Science, Arts, Athletics	141
12.	Conductors, Orchestral Musicians, Singers, Pianists	151
13.	Guitarists	171

VI. LOVES

14.	Love of Great Composers	183
15.	Love Relationships	193
16.	Giving 100%	203

Appendix 1. Chronology	215
Appendix 2. Awards	218
Appendix 3. Discography	222
Bibliography	235
Index	237

FIGURES

Figure 1.	Pepe and Walter in Del Mar, 2024	xx
Figure 2.	Pepe's handwritten copy of *Don Quixote,* first page (1951) and last page (1956)	19
Figure 3.	Pepe dancing with Mamá, 1998	20
Figure 4.	Pepe explains some fine points of technique to Mark Switzer, 1988	38
Figure 5.	Pepe conducts a masterclass in Baden, Switzerland, 1983	39
Figure 6.	Pepe (*left*) with German master builder Edmund Blöchinger, 2005	51
Figure 7.	(*Right to left*) Miguel Rodríguez I, Angel, Miguel Rodríguez II, Pepe, 1974	52
Figure 8.	Celin, Hermann Hauser, Jr., Angel, and Pepe, 1970	54
Figure 9.	Pepe Sr. (*right*) and Pepe Jr. in Pepe Jr.'s workshop, 2024	58
Figure 10.	The Romero Guitar Quartet in 2005, after the departure of Angel and the passing of Celedonio: Pepe (*top*), Celin (*center*), Celino (*left*), Lito (*right*)	76
Figure 11.	The original Romero Quartet, in 1963: Angel (above), Celedonio (*center*), Celin (*left*), Pepe (*right*)	86
Figure 12.	Herb Fox (*left*), Mamá, and Pepe when the Romeros received the 1991 Martell Prize	89
Figure 13.	Michael Palmer conducts the American Sinfonietta with Pepe as soloist, 1991	94
Figure 14.	Pepe performs with Vicente Coves at Granada's Auditorio Manuel de Falla, 2003	96
Figure 15.	Pepe signing autographs with Yoon Kwan Park (*rear, with child*), his first manager in Korea, 1985	98

FIGURES

Figure 16.	Pepe consults with composer Loris Tjeknavorian about his guitar concerto, 1990	105
Figure 17.	(*Left to right*) Miguel Barrón, Pepe, Mayita Barrón, and Michael Zearott, 1992	107
Figure 18.	Basque priests of the Residencia Kempis in 1969. Back row (*left to right*), Francisco de Madina, Celedonio, and Angelita Romero. Pepe is in the front row lighting a cigar.	110
Figure 19.	Pepe with producer and pianist Wilhelm Hellweg, 1996	125
Figure 20.	Pepe performing with Iona Brown, 1981	126
Figure 21.	Pepe plays for Joaquín Rodrigo, 1983	
Figure 22.	Pepe (*right*) and his family with Pope John Paul II at St. Peter's, 1982	143
Figure 23.	Lajos Markos painting a portrait of Pepe playing the guitar, 1981	147
Figure 24.	Pepe (*left*) with Rafael Frühbeck de Burgos speaking with Queen Sofía of Spain, 1991	154
Figure 25.	Pepe performs with Victoria de los Ángeles at a concert honoring the centenary of Federico Moreno Torroba's birth, 1991	155
Figure 26.	Pepe (*left*) with Lorenzo Palomo in Berlin before the premiere of *Nocturnos de Andalucía*, 1996	156
Figure 27.	Filming of the documentary *Shadows and Light*, with Neville Marriner conducting, 1991	156
Figure 28.	Conductor Miguel Ángel Gómez Martínez with Pepe, 1983	158
Figure 29.	Pepe performing in Linares, Spain, to honor the centenary of Segovia's birth, with Odón Alonso conducting, 1993	159
Figure 30.	Pepe (*left*) with Morton Gould at Carnegie Hall, 1992	163
Figure 31.	Pepe performing with Mexican tenor Francisco Araiza, 1988	168
Figure 32.	Pepe performing with German bass-baritone Thomas Quasthoff, 1994	170

FIGURES

Figure 33.   Philippe Entremont conducting the Munich Symphony Orchestra in a performance of Rodrigo's *Concierto de Aranjuez* with Pepe as soloist, 2015   170

Figure 34.   (*Left to right*) Pepe, Angel, and Celin Romero enjoy their beloved *puros* in 2000   178

Figure 35.   Jazz guitarist Joe Pass (*left*) with Pepe, 1994   180

Figure 36.   Pepe standing next to the theater door through which Mozart passed at the 1787 premiere of *Don Giovanni* in Prague, 2000   186

Figure 37.   Pepe with his first wife, Kristine, on her birthday in 2024   200

Figure 38.   Pepe with his second wife, Carissa, in Moscow, December 1991   201

Figure 39.   Pepe (*center*) with his children (*left to right*): Pepe Jr., Tina, Angelina, and Susanna, at Christmas 2023   204

Figure 40.   Pepe with his ultimate idol, Celedonio, in 1996, the year of his passing   206

FOREWORD

PHILIPPE ENTREMONT

R EMEMBER . . .
    We first met some decades ago. At that time, I was the music director of the Netherlands Chamber Orchestra. And Pepe was engaged by the NCO management to take part in the annual series in the magnificent Main Hall of the Concertgebouw. As soon as we met, we knew we were on the same wavelength. I had nothing to say to Pepe while rehearsing, as we understood each other without words. . . . I knew immediately that Pepe was an exceptional artist.

When he arrived on stage, he impressed the audience with his elegance, his natural authority. When he started playing the guitar, the whole audience was fascinated. So was I!!! Needless to say, it was an enormous success. I still hear the sound of his guitar that very day when he played the *Concierto de Aranjuez* at the Concertgebouw. I have conducted this very famous concerto many times in my career, but never, ever have I enjoyed it as much as with Pepe as soloist. Never!!!

Life went on, and we didn't give so many concerts together, until the wonderful tour on the East Coast, from Boston to Miami, in November 2015, with the Münchner Symphoniker (Munich Symphony Orchestra). Pepe was there with the Romero Quartet, and we programmed Joaquin Rodrigo's *Concierto Andaluz* for four guitars, as well as his *Concierto de Aranjuez*. I often remember that tour with great joy, as it was one that deeply touched both of us. When I look back, I must admit that it was quite interesting to present such a music program with a German orchestra. Yet, it was a tremendous success!

To finish, I would like to express all my respect and admiration for such a marvelous artist as Pepe Romero. He is the perfect interpreter for this repertoire. Thank you, Pepe. You are really a great master of the guitar. I love you!!!

PREFACE: PEPE AND I

WALTER AARON CLARK

PEPE IS THE SPANISH diminutive of José, and though the subject of this book was named at birth José Luis Romero Gallego, he is universally known as Pepe Romero. Born into a family of guitarists in Málaga in 1944, he was a genuine child prodigy and began appearing in public already in the early 1950s. His career really took off after the family moved to Southern California in 1957, seeking a wider field of opportunity for father Celedonio (b. 1913), his eldest son, Celín (b. 1936), Pepe, and Ángel (b. 1946). (Editorial note: Celin and Angel will hereafter be spelled in the English manner, without accents.) All four were virtuosos, and within a few years they formed the Romero Guitar Quartet, a novel ensemble that took the music world by storm. Pepe maintained dual careers as a quartet member and soloist, and he excelled in the realms of both classical and flamenco guitar, twin peaks rarely scaled by a single guitarist. Since those early days, he has continued to make his mark not only as a leading concert and recording artist, arranger, and composer, but also as a teacher. He is widely and justifiably regarded as one of the leading and most influential guitarists of the past six decades.

His is a life rich with memories, experiences, associations, and insights that have much to offer to a wide range of readers, not just guitarists. As he approaches retirement, he wishes to leave a permanent record of the music he has loved and played and of the people who have touched his life and whose lives he has touched in turn. It has been a rare privilege to assist him in this important task, but one might well ask how I came to merit such an honor. Relating the genesis of this book requires a bit of an autobiographical digression, for which I request the reader's indulgence.

In fact, I have known Pepe Romero longer than any other person in my life, with the exception of my siblings and their offspring. Pepe and I first met in January 1976 when I journeyed from Colorado to

Southern California in order to take some guitar lessons with him. I was 23 years old, and he, 31. Already at that relatively young age, he was an internationally acclaimed performer, and he was also gaining renown as a superb teacher. The seeds of my desire to meet and take lessons with him had been sown about a year and a half earlier, when I was a student at the North Carolina School of the Arts, majoring in guitar and studying with Jesús Silva. A fellow student, Bob Priest, was from the Los Angeles area and had studied privately with Pepe. He continually sang Pepe's praises and encouraged me to pursue studies with him once I had finished my degree at NCSA, which was one of only a small handful of schools at that time to offer a program in classical guitar.

I graduated in May 1975 and moved to Colorado, where my parents had retired to a town called Monument, in between Colorado Springs and Denver. I earned money playing various gigs and giving lessons, and by early 1976, I was able to afford a pilgrimage to Del Mar, north of San Diego, where Pepe lived. His wife, Kristine, picked me up from my hotel and drove me in a Romero-trademark Mercedes-Benz to their spacious home on Biscayne Cove. When I arrived, Pepe was still busy with another student, but I was able to eavesdrop on their session. The student played a passage from Luys de Narváez's *Diferencias sobre "Guárdame las vacas,"* and then Pepe executed the same excerpt, to demonstrate how it was properly to be done. The difference between the two renditions was immediately apparent. Pepe's technique was perfectly fluid, and even in the rapid passages, every note exhibited the same golden luster, round and smooth like a polished gem.

Then my lesson time came, and I recall playing a bit of a flamenco *guajiras* for him, little realizing that this was a personal favorite of the family and formed the basis of his father's delightful *Fantasía cubana*. Pepe seemed satisfied with the level of talent that I demonstrated, but aside from his comments on technique and interpretation, what I most remember is this bit of advice: if I wanted to interpret Spanish music with more than merely technical acumen, if I wanted to understand the Spanish character that underlay it, I should acquaint myself with two great works of art. One was *Don Quixote* by Cervantes, and the other was Mozart's *Don Giovanni*. I already had some passing familiarity with those two masterpieces, but I now set out to deepen and broaden my understanding of them.

There is no doubt that he was right about the importance of steeping myself in that novel and that opera, but I still find his guidance highly idiosyncratic. It was not at all what I expected him to recommend. And despite the fact that I have now known Pepe for almost fifty years, I was repeatedly surprised by the answers he gave to my questions during our interviews for this memoir. His penchant for approaching questions and providing answers in a way that seems to come straight out of left field, so to speak, is no doubt a manifestation of his genius. And that penchant is everywhere on display in this book! If his responses were all perfectly predictable, then there would not be much difference between him and the rest of us. But there is a difference, and a very large one at that. After having written books about great Spanish composers such as Isaac Albéniz, Enrique Granados, Federico Moreno Torroba, and Joaquín Rodrigo, as well as a biography of the Romero family of guitarists, I have concluded that I am not a genius but that I am just smart enough to be able to write usefully about geniuses like them.

Several years would pass between those initial lessons with Pepe and regular studies in the context of a formal degree program. I moved from Colorado to Southern California in 1979 and worked at a variety of jobs in the hopes of making enough money to afford the graduate program at the University of Southern California (USC), where Pepe was teaching. In the meantime, I took lessons with one of his leading disciples, William Kanengiser, who generously taught me free of charge. My finances remained insufficient for studies at USC, a pricy private university, but then I got lucky. Pepe left USC to join his brother Celin on the music faculty of the University of California, San Diego, in 1982, and he invited me to study with him there. With a combination of loans and personal income, I could afford the much lower tuition of UCSD and promptly accepted his invitation. I finished a master's degree in 1984, thereafter spending two years in West Germany studying early music with lutenist Jürgen Hübscher on a Fulbright grant. During that time, I maintained my connection with Pepe and Celin, as they often toured Germany, and I was sometimes able to travel with them to attend their concerts. So, my maestros also became my friends.

I was now in my early thirties, and despite my talent and academic success, it was obvious that, as one German friend gently expressed it, "the train had left the station." I was not going to be a concert artist, and neither did I aspire to become one. However, my travels throughout Europe while on the Fulbright had reawakened an early passion for history, art, and language. The only place where those interests intersected with music was musicology. I applied for and was accepted into the PhD program in musicology at UCLA, and after finishing in 1992, I secured a tenure-track position at the University of Kansas. Over the ensuing decade, my relationship with the Romeros became rather tenuous, as we had little contact. But fate intervened once again when, in 2003, I applied for and was hired as a full professor of musicology at the University of California, Riverside, about fifty miles east of Los Angeles and ninety miles north of San Diego.

I gradually renewed my friendship with Pepe and Celin, not only for pleasure but also with an ulterior motive. My friend and fellow Romero disciple Bill Krause and I were researching an Oxford biography of Torroba, and insofar as Bill lived in Virginia, it fell to me to interview the Romeros about their collaborations and friendship with the Spanish composer, the author of some of the foremost zarzuelas of all time as well as a wealth of works for the guitar, including solo pieces, concertos, and compositions for the Romero Quartet. The book definitely benefited from the insights I gleaned from Pepe and Celin during those interviews, but I was not the only one with an ulterior motive. As the Torroba biography neared completion, Pepe proposed that I write a book about the Romero family. He owned a condominium not far from their spacious home overlooking the Pacific Ocean in Del Mar, and it was used to store the family's vast archive of documents, scores, and recordings stretching back many decades. As I surveyed the archive, it became clear that the history of this remarkable family was a story that needed to be told. I accepted the invitation, and the book finally appeared in 2018, published by the University of Illinois Press in its Music in American Life series.

I was then asked by the daughter of Joaquín Rodrigo to write the first-ever complete biography of her father in English, an offer I couldn't refuse. I joined forces with Rodrigo scholar Javier Suárez-Pajares, and that book has just been published by Norton. Never at a loss for surprises, while I was still working on Rodrigo, Pepe expressed an interest in publishing his own memoirs. He was approaching eighty and knew that the road behind him was much longer than the road that lay ahead. It was now or never. But he would need someone to help him with such a large task, and I seemed to be the logical choice. Again, this was an offer I couldn't refuse.

Our approach has been a simple one. The book consists of a series of interviews, in which I pose brief questions and he expatiates on them. I came up with suggestions for chapter headings and then devised a series of questions relevant to the subject of each chapter. Though I live only about an hour's drive from Del Mar, it proved far more expedient to conduct the interviews via Zoom, after which I would transcribe and edit the material. We customarily converse in English, a language in which Pepe is perfectly fluent, though occasional lapses into Spanish provide special insights when there is no exactly equivalent word or expression in English.

The dialogues presented here are not laid out in chronological order, in the manner of a traditional biography. Rather, the organization is topical in nature, with six major areas each subdivided into two or three relevant chapters (that a typical classical guitar has six strings is not a coincidence). The purpose of this book, therefore, is not simply to provide a more or less permanent record of his life but rather to give readers the benefit of his profound insights into the music he has made and the musicians he has known. Pepe has a very philosophical temperament, and his views on a wide variety of subjects will prove both interesting and useful to a wide readership. Musicians of every stripe and music lovers with various predilections will peruse these pages with increasing appreciation not just for Pepe's genius but also his persistence in the face of obstacles and dangers that would have deterred many another musician. And for that we can be immensely grateful, as his contributions to the world of classical music are in a class by themselves. It has been my privilege to get to know Pepe even better as a result of this collaboration, and it will be the reader's privilege as well.

Walter Aaron Clark
Murrieta, CA 2024

Figure 1. Pepe and Walter in Del Mar, 2024.

PART I

FORMATION

1

EARLY LIFE

Q. You were born in Málaga in 1944, eighty years ago. What are your very earliest memories?

A. Among my earliest memories is of a freak snowstorm in Málaga! But what I remember most is not cold weather but rather the warmth of my family. Our house was a frequent destination of my father's friends, who enjoyed reciting poems, making music, and conversing. But the one memory that stands out is of my mother cooking in the kitchen, fanning the flames in a big coal-fired iron stove. I sat there performing various tasks to help out, one of which was to separate the stones from the lentils. In those days, everybody was trying to make just a little bit more money, and vendors who sold things like lentils would mix in stones so that a "pound" of lentils was actually less than a pound. My mother would give me the job of separating the lentils from the stones. That's an image that has accompanied me through my entire life as a guitarist, because while I am practicing, I am always separating the "lentil" notes from the "stone" notes. And I think that's what we have to do with everything in life, to remove the bad from the good, to separate the stones from the lentils.

When you asked me about my earliest memories, my head was immediately bombarded by some very happy images, especially of my uncles coming over to see Celin and me, even before Angel was born, when I was 2 years old. I was born in March 1944 and he was born in August 1946. But my memories go back before he was there, when it was just Celin, who was often playing the guitar. In that respect, he took after my father, who, no matter what happened, good or bad, was always playing. It seemed as if 100 percent of the time he was playing the guitar or transcribing music for it. He would only stop to write poetry! He was obsessed with the arts, and his closest friends shared that passion. He often performed with a *recitador* (reciter), who would recite poetry while my father played the guitar. But my father also loved to recite poetry, as did his brothers. For example, a very happy memory is seeing my uncle Adolfo come round the corner riding his bike after work. He came directly from his job to visit Celin and me. My other uncle, Maximino, made himself so comfortable at our house that he might have been living with us. At least he seemed to be there most of the time. When Angel was born, I was sleeping with him when my father came into the room and announced that I had a new baby brother.

My uncles had a huge impact on who I am and what I think. Both of them were devoted to Celin and me. At the time he was spending so much time at our house, Maximino was single, but he later married and had five daughters. Adolfo also married, and he eventually had three daughters and a son. My cousin Pepa was just a few months older than me, and my cousin María del Carmen was a couple of years older. So, Celin and I, being boys, were great favorites of both uncles, and they liked to play games with us. Maximino taught me how to play checkers and chess, and then I would play against both him and Adolfo. And what was my father doing all this time? Of course, he was playing the guitar, making transcriptions, and composing. What was he doing when the house got flooded during an inundation? He was playing the guitar and making transcriptions. So, making music was a constant. It was like having a radio on all the time. I went to sleep at night to the sound of his practicing, and he would already be playing when I got up.

***

Q. So that leads to the next question. When and how did you fall in love with the guitar, and at what age did you decide to be a guitarist?

A. Having all this beautiful music in the background, I looked up to my father as if he were some sort of superman. I thought he was the strongest man in the world and could protect us from any and all dangers. He seemed to me incredibly loving and intelligent. Among my other earliest memories are when he would stop playing the guitar in order to rock me to sleep. I would lie on his chest with my head on his neck and my arms around him while we sat outside in a chair that leaned against the wall of the house. And the music changed; instead of my father's playing, I could hear flamenco music coming from the bar next door, called Los Peroles (The Saucepans). This was before Angel was born. Another cherished memory from those early years is of my mother breastfeeding me, until Angel came along. I would be breastfed while my father practiced the guitar, and that is how I fell in love with the guitar! I fell in love with the guitar at the same time that I fell in love with my father and mother and with Celin. In my heart and mind, the guitar and my family were inseparable. Now, the thought of wanting to be a guitarist never entered my mind—because I *was* a guitarist. I never thought "I want to be a guitarist" but rather "I am a guitarist." I don't even remember exactly when I started playing.

***

Q. Do you believe in reincarnation and perhaps you were a guitarist in a previous life?

A. I used to believe very much in reincarnation. I used to believe that I *knew* it was so. But the older I get, the less certain I am about any of my beliefs. What I believe now is that I don't know anything. All I have are thoughts. The unknown is so much greater than the known that all I know is a tiny little piece of the unknown. Perhaps when I die, I will learn the rest. Perhaps I knew the rest when I was born and then forgot it. I had that feeling when I looked at my children and could see the immense knowledge that they had; however, as soon as they started growing up, it left. I believe that whether we are a reincarnated soul of someone else or not, there is a lot of knowledge that we come into this world with, and then we forget it. One of the great powers of music is that it helps us access that forgotten memory as the eternal beings that we are. We come into this world with it, and perhaps when we go, we take it with us. I continue to believe that there are many things pointing to the probability of reincarnation, and one of them is the existence of child prodigies. These are children who play music with a remarkable depth of emotion and understanding, and I can honestly say that I feel no different now than I ever did, as a musician and as a guitarist. At least not as far as I can remember. My repertoire was smaller back then and has grown through the years, but my connection to the guitar has stayed the same. Already as a child, I was connected to my father through the guitar and felt that I was a part of him and the other players that I heard at that time. And now I feel that I am a part of the future with the new guitarists who are coming up, even of the ones I don't know. I hope that when they read this book and when they listen to my recordings, they will catch that flame of love and passion that I feel for the guitar and that they will make it their own. I hope that it will help them as the flame and passion of my father helped me.

***

Q. What was life like in Málaga at that time, in the wake of the Civil War and during the Franco dictatorship? Was there any persecution of the family?

A. One of my father's cousins was a farmer named Juanillo, and he would come to the house to bring us eggs and produce from his land, so that we could eat. On one such visit, though, he arrived completely beaten up, courtesy of the Guardia Civil. Shortly thereafter, I heard from my parents that when the Guardia Civil returned to Juanillo's house to work him over some more, they found that he had hanged himself. So, I recall the tremendous fear that my father, his friends, and relatives all felt. I would listen to them converse about philosophy, literature, art, music, and of course, politics. They all hoped that the Americans would come and get rid of Franco, but that never happened. Thank God I lived long enough to see him disappear, democracy restored, and a new Spain emerge.

***

Q. How would you describe your parents?

A. It is very difficult to describe my father because he was a man of very strong feelings. He could be the nicest, most loving person, and yet he could also become furious and volatile when something lit that side of him. He had a temper, but it had to be provoked in some way. In fact, both my father and mother had tremendously strong personalities, and their tempers were always provoked by jealousy. They were both incredibly possessive and jealous of each other.

All that I have related above is why I felt that my father was such a powerful figure, because he kept all that chaos away from the family. He knew that there were two worlds: outside, where a lot of terrible

EARLY LIFE

things happened, and inside, where there was the warmth of the family, where there was music and talk of books. I learned very early that the way of life in my family was devoted to the imagination. Reality is one thing, but there is another world, the one that we read about in books and poems. That is what I saw in my mother, who shared with us that other reality, which she gleaned from her wide reading. So, I grew up in multiple universes, and perhaps that's why I am crazy and believe that reality is a very subjective thing. Inside the house, it was wonderful. Outside the house, there was fear. That's what I remember: grownups being afraid of and celebrating killing, all at the same time.

***

Q. How did you get along with your siblings? Was there competition? Conflict? Was music a unifying force?

A. Music was always a unifying force, and from early on my father believed that we should play music before we learned to read it. He believed, and I continue to believe very strongly, that playing an instrument has to be taught in the same way that we learn language, and we all learn how to speak before we learn how to read. There has to be a one-to-one connection to the guitar, or to any other instrument, and only then do you learn to decipher the music, so that it can connect you to someone else, as well as to the composer. But it is something you and the guitar do together. It is not that you connect to the paper and then the guitar is there to translate what is written on it.

Thus, the best way to learn technique is to have someone show you directly how it is done; therefore, my father put Celin in charge of teaching me. That way, I learned from both my father and brother, by observing and imitating what they did. One of the earliest pieces I learned was my father's transcription of the "Sicilienne" by Robert Schumann, from his *Album für die Jugend* (Album for the Young), Op. 68, no. 11. He showed me how to play this piece on the guitar just by demonstrating it. Then he had Celin teach me a Minuet in G by Mateo Carcassi (1792–1853), after which my father taught me the Minuet in A of Fernando Sor (1778–1839). And so on and so on. Both of them were teaching me repertoire, but in turn they were teaching me how to play. And we all taught Angel how to play, though he was the rebel. If I was going to show him something, he would protest, "No, no, I already know it!" However, then he would come and ask, "How do you do this?" But it was always on his terms. I was always the least rebellious. I remember having lessons with my father when he was teaching Celin, me, and Angel solfège. But Celin would always start laughing when we sang, so the lessons didn't last very long. I love solfège and really enjoyed singing while my father accompanied me on the guitar, so that I could learn the intervals. I was much more submissive to the discipline of lessons, to the process of learning. My two brothers were much more rebellious.

***

Q. Of course, there was a great love of music, but there was also a love of soccer, which persists to this day. Tell me a bit about that.

A. Soccer is something we have always loved to play as well as watch, but my mother was very afraid that we would get hurt. She would admonish us, "You cannot play with the other boys in the street because you can get run over, you can fall down, you can break a finger." I could play the guitar really well from the time I was a little kid, and every Sunday my mother would take me to a convent in Málaga called El Asilo de los Ángeles, which was a home for elderly people who were poor and homeless. I would play guitar for the old folks, and then we would have lunch. After that, the nuns would invite me to join them in a game of soccer. As long as I was playing soccer with nuns, my mother didn't object.

I was about 5 years old at that time, and I continued to play guitar and soccer at El Asilo until we moved from Málaga to Seville in 1953, when I was 9. Mother loved and admired the nuns, whom she considered to be very good friends. In fact, both my mother and father were grateful to the nuns because they both contracted typhoid before I was born, and some of the nuns took care of them. So, I could play soccer with them, but I also played with my brothers, father, and uncles. It was a family affair!

***

Q. At what age did you start to give concerts?

A. I know that I played in the Teatro Lope de Vega in Seville when I was 7, but I don't have a very strong memory of that because the

EARLY LIFE 9

idea of playing concerts was something that was still a bit foreign to me. I would play for whoever wanted to listen, or if somebody asked me to play, I would play. If friends came to the house, I played for them. If we went to a party with family and friends, I would play. When we went to the convent to visit the homeless old folks, I would play. So, when I got to Seville, I had no idea that that was now a concert because it had been organized in advance, with a stage and an audience. Once again, I was just playing in front of people, and that feeling has accompanied me throughout my entire life. And it's a feeling that I would love to pass along. I would prefer people not focus on the idea of a concert as a formal event, one for which the public has bought tickets so that they can see and listen to me play. When I give a concert, all of that dissipates, and I'm back in the old-folks home, playing because people want to hear the music.

***

Q. What make of guitars did the family play? Were they by one maker or several?

A. Very early in life, I became aware of different makers, but for me one stood out, because he served as the babysitter I didn't want to have. My father would take me to the guitar shop of Francisco Domínguez in Málaga and then leave me there so that he could go visit one of his best friends, Pepe Salas. Before the Civil War, my father had many friends in the arts, and when the Civil War broke out in 1936, some sided with the right and others with the left. Though he himself sided with the left, it was his friends on the right who helped him survive the bloodbath that ensued after Franco won in 1939. Precisely because Salas was a Francoist, he was able to help my father get out of jail and offer him protection. But Salas had tuberculosis, and my father did not want to expose me to it. So, he would drop me off at the workshop of Domínguez before going on to visit Salas, who lived to be an old man. We saw him again in 1971, fourteen years after we had moved to the U.S., and he took us to see Don Juan, the father of the soon-to-be king, Juan Carlos. Pepe Salas was an ardent monarchist.

Returning to the topic of guitar makers, I hated Domínguez's shop because it was so dirty. And all the wood shavings and dust really bothered me, especially because I was used to how really clean my mother kept our house. One time I threw a fit, and Francisco's son, Pepe Domínguez, took me to where my father was, at Salas's house. He was a *marqués* (marquis), and his residence looked to me like a palace. A servant took me up to the bedroom where Salas was lying in bed as my father played the guitar for him. My father got really mad and shouted, "Why did you bring him here. He's not supposed to be here."

But TB was not the health problem I was destined to endure. Instead, very early in life, I had an attack of what the doctors believed was polio. I remember coming back from the fair in Málaga when I was about 4 years old, and all of a sudden I couldn't walk! I couldn't feel my legs. It was as if they were gone. I remember my parents being extremely upset. They cried and cried. I was taken to be examined by doctors using an X-ray machine, where you stand behind a big screen. And they said I had polio. But just as fast as it came on, it departed. Still, I remember my father giving me long massages, moving my legs in all kinds of directions. He reasoned that that would help to restore their mobility. No one had told him to do this, so it was very creative of him. I am convinced that that had a lot to do with healing the affected areas and sped up my recovery. But not so long ago I saw a movie about polio that told the story of an Australian nurse, Elizabeth Kenny, who developed that same treatment while running a polio clinic. She did the same thing my father did, and with great success, though the "experts" disagreed, and she was taken to court by a board of medical examiners. In any case, my father had figured that out years earlier, using nothing more than his intuition.

Not surprisingly, the therapy he applied to my condition included impromptu performances. As I was lying down, he would ask me, "How do you like this? Should I play this on the second string? This in the first position? Listen to the difference and tell me which way you think is best." At that time, he was playing on a Lorca guitar. He asked me, "Do you like this guitar?" But he had also borrowed an Esteso, so he interrogated me about their relative merits: "Which guitar do you like better? The Lorca or the Esteso?" So, though I had once understandably thought that all the guitars in the world were made by Domínguez, now I knew there were also those by Lorca, Esteso, and presumably others. But those were the first guitars and guitar makers of which I was aware.

EARLY LIFE

Now, when I had polio, Celin prayed on my behalf to La Virgen de los Dolores of the Orden de Servitas. My mother was a fervent devotee of this Virgin, whose procession takes places on Holy Thursday during Holy Week in Málaga. It is a very somber event and quite small in contrast to the flamboyant processions of all the other churches. This Virgin has a small throne and is accompanied only by drums. There's no singing. Anyway, while praying to the Virgin, Celin promised her that if I recovered from polio, he would carry me on his shoulders behind the procession for its entire length. The problem is that he still hasn't done it, and I'm still waiting!

***

Q. How did you like Seville compared to Málaga?

A. I loved Seville because it was where I discovered my attractions for women and for flamenco. One day my father said that he had a wonderful present for me: "Paco Ávila is a great flamenco player, and tomorrow he is going to come to teach you flamenco. And you're going to teach him how to play classical." And then Paco came to our apartment, and I loved our exchange of styles. I also felt great affection for him personally, as he was a wonderful human being, musician, and guitar player. One time he brought along his grandfather, who I thought was the oldest man I had ever seen. He was 71 when he came with his grandson, and he also wanted to learn classical. So, I was learning flamenco from Paco and teaching both of them classical. Paco would bring his girlfriend, who was an accomplished *bailaora*, so that he could teach me how to accompany dancing. Above and beyond all that, I just loved the beauty of Seville, and I was now mature enough to appreciate it. I came to appreciate my native Málaga only after I returned there later. Aside from walks on the beach with my mother, I had not experienced much of the city before we moved to Seville, and I was too young to assimilate all that it had to offer. I felt that our family home was in Seville, that beautiful town of orange trees, the Giralda, picturesque streets, the scenic Guadalquivir River, my favorite ice-cream parlor, and—beautiful girls! Seville offered so many magical things.

***

Q. Málaga recently inaugurated an annual festival in your honor. Would you say that you're one of the most renowned cultural celebrities ever to come from Málaga? Who are some others of your stature?

A. Málaga is almost like a city that has specialized in greatness that doesn't get the recognition it deserves. True, Pablo Picasso was born and raised in Málaga, but if I mention the name José Nogales, very few people will know anything about him. But he was one of the great painters of the turn of the century. And in the realm of cinema, the renowned Hollywood film star Antonio Banderas is also a noteworthy son of Málaga. There are many others.

2

EARLY EDUCATION WITH MAMÁ

Q. Your mother was a highly intelligent woman with a passion for the arts, including not only music but also literature. How did she train you?

A. Without my knowing that I was being trained, which was the same way that my father taught me how to play. My mother mostly emphasized reading books, even reading with me. Together we read *El Emilio* by Rousseau, which tells the story of Rousseau's fictional son Emilio. She would read it out loud to me, pausing to discuss it as we went along. She used it to teach me how Rousseau thought a little boy should be raised. It is my understanding that that was a forbidden book in Spain at the time. There was very strong censorship of films, books, art, and other cultural manifestations. But she wanted to convey the psychological implications of the book. And she also read to me writings of the Greek philosophers, asking me what I thought and sharing with me her reactions. And of course, we went through the regular schoolbooks. During the time I was growing up in Spain, children could study at home, go to a private academy, or attend a public school, but everybody used the same textbooks. At the end of the year, all students had to sit for a final exam, and the entire grade depended on that test. The final exam was usually given by teachers who were from a different town or district and had no relationship with the children who had attended local schools. At the time of the exam, the kids who had gone to school and those who had studied at home were all equal, and the grade simply depended on how well you did. So, my mother made sure that I had the necessary textbooks, and because he was almost eight years older than I was, Celin was also one of my "teachers." He was in charge of math and geometry, two challenging subjects I had to study.

In Spain, another subject was religion. Not surprisingly, religion had to be studied from your first year in school until you graduated from university. Religion meant Roman Catholicism. I remember a lot about that subject. I had two uncles, my father's brothers, who had fought for the Republic from Málaga all the way up the coast to Barcelona, only to wind up in a concentration camp in France at the end of the war. They were very rebellious against Roman Catholicism. So, my mother took charge of instructing me in the Spanish Roman Catholicism of the time, on which the educational system placed special emphasis. Indeed, if you failed the religion exam, you had to retake the entire year, whereas if you failed the math exam, all you had to do was retake that exam. Therefore, my mother took studying the complexities of Catholic dogma very seriously. My uncles? Not so much. They entertained themselves by playing chess with me and Celin, interspersing chess moves with instruction in the horrors of the Spanish Inquisition. In fact, Maximino was a communist and taught Celin and me the *Internationale*, the hymn of the international communist movement. From mother I was learning about the good priest Fray Hernando de Talavera, the first confessor of Queen Isabel, who then became the first archbishop of Granada. My uncles balanced this out by teaching me about Cisneros, Torquemada, the Inquisition's use of torture, and the persecution of the Jews and Muslims in Spain. And in truth, Catholic training of that time was very antisemitic. I remember a question on one of the end-of-year religion exams that asked, "Who killed Jesus?" And the correct answer was "the Jews."

And yet, at the same time that she was teaching me about religion, she also exposed me to philosophical works that promoted the equality of men and the value of mutual respect. Now, she was herself Catholic and attended mass, though everyone had to go to mass. She felt devotion in her heart and was sincere in her religious beliefs. Nonetheless, I still found aspects of the faith terrifying. I remember once as a little boy being frightened out of my sleep by a pre-dawn procession of people led by a priest, who were all singing, "El diablo a la oreja te está diciendo 'no vayas a la iglesia sigue durmiendo,'" which is to say in English, "The Devil is whispering in your ear, 'don't go to church, keep sleeping.'" Even as a young child, I noticed that the local nuns were concerned with aiding poor, aged, and sick people. They had taken good care of my parents when they contracted typhoid, from which my father almost died. By contrast, it seemed to me that many of the priests were more devoted to power and control than to charity.

So, in addition to academic subjects, my mother taught me that whatever gifts we have are to be shared with others, including playing the guitar for disadvantaged people in the care of nuns at the convent of El Asilo de los Ángeles every Sunday.

***

Q. Why did she homeschool you instead of sending you to regular school?

A. I believe that, from a very early age, I showed great passion and a wonderful gift for both music and art, and my parents felt I needed unstructured time, so that if I was immersed in painting, I could keep painting all day long. If I was practicing, I could practice all day long. They would give me the training I needed, but only when I was ready to receive it. Poetry was very big in my house. I recall a friend of my father named Luis Ballesteros, who was an actor and *recitador*. He was a master of the art of reciting texts, and he gave me declamation lessons, whereby he taught me to understand the meaning of the poem and put that feeling into the rhythm of the words, the tone of voice, the emphasis, and the dynamics. In that way, the person listening could feel the poem in a way very similar to playing a piece and telling a story without words.

One such recitation we practiced was by the famous Spanish poet José Zorrilla (1817–93): "Corriendo van por la vega, a las puertas de Granada" (Running, they come across the plain to the gates of Granada"). He taught me that when you say, "Corriendo van por la vega," you have to create a sense of expectation in the listeners as to "who is running." And then you give the answer. Create the expectation, the drama, and then offer the resolution. It is the same in a musical performance.

So, I believe that both my mother and father felt that at home I could receive a more complete education and a richer upbringing. I am very grateful for that because they made time for everything, not just study. We would all go on excursions up Mt. Coronado and sing songs along the way. She loved to sing. If we got tired on the

16 PEPE ROMERO

hike, she would urge us on by having us sing marches, which gave us extra oomph to continue walking.

***

Q. You were taught to appreciate the cultural legacy of Spain, especially in Málaga, Seville, Granada. How did they teach you about the cultural riches of where you were growing up in Andalucía?

A. By having it available close to home. My mother wanted to nurture my own artistic talent and regularly took me to the local museum, where we would look at a particular painting for a long time, and then I would have to say something about it. The next week, we would study the same painting again, but I would have to tell her something new about it. And we would visit the studio of a family friend, Luis Molledo, who was a wonderful painter. I carefully watched Luis work and learned a lot about painting. As it turned out, though, he was a great forger, so I was learning about the techniques of the great masters, whose canvases he was trying to imitate.

Of course, flamenco was freely and widely available, and I could hear the sounds of it coming from the bar next door. Upon arriving in Seville, we lived right next to the Pavón school of flamenco. Flamenco was everywhere.

***

Q. What subjects did you like the most or the least when you were being homeschooled?

A. Of course, philosophy was a favorite, but that was not one of the subjects required for the final exams. Among the required subjects, I would say that I liked geometry the most, because I associated it very much with music. The more that I learned about geometry, the more I started thinking that music is all geometric shapes. And I began thinking of geometry as starting from some inner point out of which geometric shapes grow, just the way music does. Studying geometry changed the way I think about making music, i.e., that instead of approaching it as a linear process, it all grows out of one beginning. Just as music is a sort of dance between sound and time, geometry consists of lines and colors. This helped me solidify my

EARLY EDUCATION WITH MAMÁ

experience of music, and the music I play is born in the same way. The genesis of every sound is the same, of every phrase the same, and it develops of itself. Because even though it comes out the same, it assumes different shapes, which intertwine with each other to create incredible "geometric" designs. Then geometry manifested itself to me in the magnificent works of the Alhambra, and I saw the heart, spirit, and beauty that the Muslims left in Spain. So, geometry to me was something that unites the spirit of all of us. It represents music and I loved it. I also loved astronomy.

My least favorite subject was religion. I found that the more I studied it, the more I was erecting barriers in my own thinking; however, my perception of God is without barriers. It is an all-encompassing love that embraces all the wonderful things created by and expressed through the words of all men, in all times, and of all races. Thus, the study of any one religion was to me very limiting. Over time, I became eager to study religious traditions other than Catholicism. I found them really interesting. So, the official religion of the oppressively theocratic Spanish state was my least favorite subject. In particular, there was one religious concept that for a little boy like me was very painful to accept: the notion that certain men and women were predestined for salvation and others were not. That touched my soul in a way I didn't like. Why should anybody be born saved or damned?

***

Q. Were there other subjects that you especially liked?

A. Arithmetic was also very interesting to me, and Celin was my teacher. This was the simple kind of math you get before you are 13 years old. Art was also something that everyone had to take, and my art teacher was Luis Molledo. He would take me to the Museo del Arte de Málaga (now the Bellas Artes), where I went crazy for painters like Francisco de Zurbarán (1598–1664). And I was so taken by the fact that Diego Velázquez (1599–1660) could paint that which we don't see. He was able to make space and air into tangible entities. The other thing that we did in the museum was to discuss the differences between the various painters. Though I loved the great masters of the Baroque period, I also developed a passion for the French Impressionists. And then in Seville, and later whenever the family went to Madrid, I admired the works of Baldomero Romero Ressendi (1922–77), who was one of the truly great masters of the twentieth century. Though in his own lifetime he enjoyed great success, his life was nonetheless difficult. I hope that anyone who reads this book will look him up and study his work. He was a great maestro and the son of a doctor who helped my father avoid combat duty during the Civil War. Baldomero was instrumental in cultivating this love of art that burns inside me.

***

Q. I know that she assigned you to read *Don Quixote*. What did she have you do, and what did you learn from reading that classic?

A. She would make little marks in the text next to phrases that we would think about and discuss. There are marks like that throughout the entire text. We started when I was only 7 years old, and we didn't finish until 1956, in Seville, when I was 12. Every word was read and thought about. This was in essence my mother's way of teaching. And I also learned something that I have practiced in music, which is that when you write something with your own hand, it goes deeper. She would read *Don Quixote* aloud, and I would write down the words as she dictated them. Many years later, when Joaquín Rodrigo (1901–99) sent us his *Concierto andaluz* in 1967 and me his *Concierto para una fiesta* in 1983, the first thing I did was to copy them by hand in order to learn the music. Because when you do that, it goes into your body, into your mind, and then it comes out into the paper, almost as if you had composed it yourself.

***

Q. She was such a good teacher. How was she educated? Did she go to a regular school?

A. No, she was completely self-taught. She was very much helped by the nuns and by friends, but she didn't go to a school. It's a rather mysterious thing that my father's family were all rural peasants, and my mother's father was a blacksmith and carpenter. And yet, my parents became highly educated people. It was their passion for reading, for moving up in the world, that helped them not only to survive but also to thrive during very difficult times and incredibly

EARLY EDUCATION WITH MAMÁ

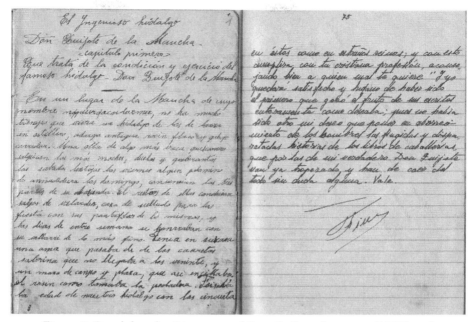

Figure 2. Pepe's handwritten copy of *Don Quijote*, first page (1951) and last page (1956).

difficult situations. They found relief and guidance in the writings and thoughts of great people who had come before them.

***

Q. I know that you got your musical education from Papá and Celin. Still, did Mamá incorporate music into your "curriculum"?

A. That was left up to Papá. In Mamá's mind, I was always going to be a painter. And I remember hearing heated discussions between my parents, with Papá saying, "No, he's a musician," and Mamá saying, "No, he's a painter!"

***

Q. Your lessons took place in your home. Did the family have a library?

Figure 3. Pepe dancing with Mamá, 1998.

A. Mamá always had a large library of books. But in a way, she was our reader, a service she performed even on our tours with the quartet in the U.S., when we spent long hours in the car traveling from one place to the next. While Celin was driving, Mamá would read to us. This was a bit like what José Martí did in Cuba. He designated a reader in all the factories, so that the workers could get an education, not just those who could go to school. She instinctively did the same thing and read out loud to all of us, to my father, my brothers, and to me. She was quite a spectacular woman.

***

Q. What would you say is the most important thing your learned from Mamá in the course of being homeschooled?

A. I learned from my mother to trust in the power of miracles, to share the good things in your life, and not to inflict any pain on other people. I learned from her the power of unconditional love, that once you love, you never take it away. Every single day, she told us that there was nothing we could do that would make her stop loving us. That was the love she gave us. She also asked us to take our dreams seriously, as they are are actually reality before it happens. You follow your dreams and work towards them. She had faith, compassion, and patience. My mother was the reservoir of virtues that it takes a lifetime to try to imitate. She imparted to us the belief that the impossible is always possible.

***

CODA: Pepe holds up his copy of *Don Quixote*, dated 1951–56 (see Figure 2 on p. 19). He then observes that "When Mamá died, this represented so much." When we left Spain, we had to leave everything behind, but she brought this. And when she died, I was going to put this in the coffin with her. You know who stopped me? Celin. I was actually in the process of putting this in with her body, just as the Egyptians did. We buried both my mother and father with different things that were very dear to them. In my father's hands is a facsimile of the six violin partitas and the cello suites of Bach, with a love letter from me thanking him and telling him how I feel about him. Each of us put in something meaningful, and we did the same with my mother. I was going to put *Don Quixote* in her coffin, but Celin stopped me and said, "She didn't bring it for herself, she brought it for you. You keep it." *Mirabile dictu*!

PART II

GUITAR

3

TECHNIQUE

Q. You are renowned for your virtuosic technique. I'm quite certain that if you can't play something, it's unplayable. How do you define or understand the term "technique"?

A. Technique to me is the ability to make the music flow through you. I have always taken great care that a fast note leads as happy a life as a slow note, that it is as beautiful and as sonorous; in other words, you don't lose the essence of the music. To me, every note has a life that is filled with music. Just producing a pitch, a tone, is not enough to please me. And yet, there are many instrumentalists who regard sheer speed as an end unto itself. If I can't play with the kind of tone and subtlety that I want, then even if I can execute the notes at a fast tempo, I will not sacrifice tonal quality merely to achieve velocity. I never play at a tempo that will deprive me of a feeling of satisfaction, of fulfillment.

So, speed for me has been a *byproduct* of looking for substance in my playing. I've always said that if I went deaf, I would continue to play the guitar, because I love the way it feels, the sensory relationship that the strings have with my fingers, the guitar vibrating with my body, and the sensation that when I am holding the guitar, it and my body are like two pieces of a puzzle coming together. When we are together in that embrace, our body becomes the body of the sound itself. I've always felt that one of the most important things to do in developing technique is to avoid the feeling that I am me and the guitar is the guitar and I am playing this instrument and it's doing what I tell it to do. Rather, we jointly experience the body of sound, which means that when I am playing, my body is the tone, and the tone fills the room.

So, I project the sound from inside of me to the limits of the physical space in which I am playing. That has a tremendously powerful impact, both emotionally and spiritually, because the audience is then inside my being as the body of sound. After all, sound is vibration, and everyone who is connected to the sound is vibrating in sympathy with it. This is one of the most powerful things that we can experience. For me, technique has always been a very crucial component that has to be practiced in combination with the music itself, in order to do justice to it.

One of my favorite anecdotes on this subject was shared with me by Paco de Lucía. He told me that he was alone with Sabicas, and they were playing duets. Sabicas said, "Paquito, let's play fast. Let's see how fast we can play." So, they were playing fast scales and tremolos, and then he said, "But now let's play beautifully." And Paco interpreted this to mean that you shouldn't play so fast that you sacrifice the quality of your tone and a sense of beauty.

So, I have been a fanatic about technique from the very beginning. But by telling my story, I want to help the young people who read this to enjoy the practicing of technique as a musical experience, which means that you practice it from the inside out. I've never used the metronome as a means to get faster, though I use and love the metronome. It is my friend, and I enjoy having it in my room, just as a talisman. But I've used it to keep me under control, so that I never play so fast as to lose control, that the production of sound is not in perfect synchronization with the rhythm.

I've always searched for what part of my awareness, or my mind, triggers the finger movements, what makes my brain send a particular message to the nerves and from there to the tendons, muscles, and joints, i.e., to everything that has to move instantly and simultaneously. I was already pondering this subject in my early days as a teacher, when I taught Colonel Antonio Álvarez about the trigger finger and where the movement begins (see Chapter 4, Teaching, for more about this). I realized that for me, there is a master control governing all the senses, and that "master control" is the sound. The senses function as receivers or transmitters. The most crucial thing is that everything is synchronized, and every part of your body knows what it has to do. The visual sense has to be a transmitter, because we can see what's coming up in our mind's eye. When we look with our eyes, we see the space within the guitar.

In regard to the left hand, the fingers dance their ballet on the fingerboard to the tune of the music, but you don't hold on to the image that you see. Your eyes are anticipating where the action is

TECHNIQUE

going to take place on the fingerboard from one moment to the next. And your eyes are also focusing on the strings under your right hand, not on the fingers but rather on the strings. The visual sense of knowing where you're going allows the strings and the guitar to direct the action of the fingers. You're sending signals, but your sense of touch is receiving messages, so the normal sensory process is going in reverse, whereby the result initiates the cause. So, when your hands go to the strings, the sensations they receive determine if the strings are where they should be before releasing the sound. When the fingers feel that the string is happy, the sound is made, the note is produced, and then they release it automatically.

The sense of hearing is the "control room." When you're practicing, you become familiar with the music you're going to play, and you decide which fingerings are best. You visualize the positions of both hands and how they feel, and you think about how the music connects to you best. But then you have to let go of it. It's not you anymore. And at the moment of truth, when it comes time to perform, you have to hear the music inside of your head. So, as you practice this more and more, you learn to listen to music, you think of a piece of music. If you think of a tune, you can hear it in your head. The more you develop it, the longer you can hear it, and the more complete your internal hearing becomes.

I've always had the mystical thought that at the time of a performance, I pretend that I hear the composer communicating to me how the music should go. Therefore, I have to listen very carefully to that inner voice, while at the same time my bodily awareness—my sense of sight, touch, and muscle memory—does the actual playing. And my conscious mind is relieved of all active duty except for listening and being the center of balance between the music I hear in my mind and the music that is emanating from the guitar. Both of them are one and the same. And it all has to happen simultaneously. For instance, when I'm building a phrase, I play the first note, but I am also aware of the last note, which in my mind happens at the same time as the first. I imagine the phrase to be like a bridge that has a column at the end and a column at the beginning. And the phrase is supported by both.

***

Q. How did you develop this approach to technique?

A. Practicing scales is central to my approach, including chromatic, major, and minor scales. Right-hand arpeggios and left-hand gymnastics are also important. All of this I acquired from my father, starting very early in my life. After he died, I found a manila envelope with some music in it, along with a note to me and my brothers that said, "Play this every day." It was the anonymous *Romance* that Richard Long found in an edition from the 1800s, and it's called *Melodía de Sor*. It features an arpeggio pattern that is very much like Sor's Study No. 17 in E Minor, that is, a, i, m, a (anular, index, middle, anular), etc. The envelope also included a Bach Prelude in D Minor, originally in C Minor; the Study No. 19 by Mateo Carcassi; Daniel Fortea's C-major study with a six-note arpeggio pattern, p, i, m, a, m, i (thumb, index, middle, anular, middle, index); the Heitor Villa-Lobos Etude No. 1; and to finish, Francisco Tárrega's *Recuerdos de la Alhambra*. He felt that even if you didn't practice any other arpeggios, by playing these pieces every day, you could keep your arpeggios in good shape.

***

Q. How should one approach pedagogical literature?

A. Whatever studies one practices, I think that the practice of legato, the seamless connection of one note to the next, is very important, as is the practice of staccato, because to play staccato is the equivalent of playing at a very high speed. The more staccato you can play, the faster you will be able to play. In order to move the notes closer together, you are just removing the space in between them. You're not increasing muscular tension, because you play the staccato and immediately you are relaxed.

So, the practice of legato and staccato is very important. I personally think that the mother of all technique is *rasgueado* (strumming), followed by tremolo, then arpeggios, scales, *ligados* (slurs) in the left hand, chord changes, and finally barré. Children should start with pieces that have very few bar chords, and then the teaching of barring needs to be done cautiously. When you're teaching a child, make sure that barring exercises do not exceed the muscular strength of the child's forearm.

TECHNIQUE

***

Q. Of course, you are a big fan of the Carcassi 25 *Melodious and Progressive Studies* and the Giuliani *120 Right Hand Studies*.

A. I am not a fan. I am a fanatic! I am also a fanatical devotee of Tárrega's exercises. I used a version of them in my method book *La Guitarra*, just as Scott Tennant (b. 1962) did in his *Pumping Nylon* method and Julio Sagreras (1879–1942) did in his method. Many teachers have employed them, though I believe that Francisco Tárrega (1852–1909) learned them from Julián Arcas (1832–82) and then passed them on to Daniel Fortea (1878–1953). I am also a fanatic about scales and arpeggios, especially the right-hand studies of Mauro Giuliani (1781–1829). And as I said, for me the mother of all technique is *rasgueado*, for the right hand. *Rasgueado*, along with *apoyando* (rest stroke) and *tirando* (free stroke), is perhaps the most natural technique in the right hand. If you put a guitar into the hands of a child who doesn't know anything about the instrument, they will instinctively strum the strings.

I'm talking particularly about classical players. We spend so much time plucking rather than strumming the strings that we don't build our extensor muscles. To be able to play fast and pluck evenly, to be able to rotate the fingers quickly in chords and tremolos, requires a very fast recovery, which is what the extensors facilitate. We have to develop evenness between the flexors and extensors in order to maintain consistency between moving through the string and returning to it.

And I can tell you that thanks to my belief in that, and to God's miracle, I have been able to recover my technique completely after having been attacked by a virus and suffering the side effect of a medicine. So, I have always been a believer, and now I can say, at 80 years of age, that it works!

***

Q. Do you think you're a natural player? Do you think that there's some element of natural talent that's necessary to be a Pepe Romero, despite all the disciplined training?

A. Yes. I am a completely natural player because I could play like I've always played right from the beginning. I have also seen and

believe that it is possible to become a natural player through training, because a natural player is somebody who has a clear path
between their thoughts and whatever instrument they are playing.
If you have the overwhelming desire and love to do it and you are
methodical, but without obsessive pressure, and if you learn with
the mind of a child, whereby you are content to take things one step
at a time, then it can happen. I have seen it happen.

***

Q. Do you think it is legitimate to use actual repertoire to develop
technique? Or should one tackle concert pieces only when one is
already technically equipped to do so?

A. The way my father started training me was with chromatic scales.
After chromatic scales, the first piece I learned was the Minuet in
G by Mateo Carcassi. My father believed, as do I, that when you are
training a young player or working with students who have a technical problem or an injury to their hands, you do what the flamencos
do: the young students sit with a guitar in front of the teacher, who
then demonstrates on the guitar some piece of music, whether it
be a *falseta* (solo riff) or technical study. And because the student
is learning where to put their fingers, they are watching and then
imitating what the teacher does, without the teacher having to say,
"Do this, no put your hand more like this, more like that. Higher
wrist, lower wrist."

So, my father would sit in front of me and play a couple of notes.
I would then play that couple of notes. The Carcassi Minuet in G
is a very beautiful piece of music, and my father often played it in
his concerts. But it does not require great physical proficiency of
the hands and arms, so it's a perfect piece for teaching a beginner
how everything works together: musical ideas, dynamics, tone, and
learning what to do with your fingers in order to produce a note.
That was then followed by a couple of very easy pieces by Fortea,
studies focused on alternating p and i or arpeggios with p, i, m in
the right hand, and then one for hammer-ons and pull-offs in the
left hand. Then came a lovely "Siciliana" of Schumann. I actually
included three pieces from Schumann's *Album für die Jugend*, Op.
68, on my CD *Songs My Father Taught Me*, including one of my
early favorites, No.10, "The Happy Farmer."

TECHNIQUE

31

***

Q. So, one can use well-chosen repertoire to develop technique, "well-chosen" being the operative modifier.

A. Yes. And my father used repertoire as treats, just like when you get a dog to do a trick or a dolphin to do what you want. He would say, "Okay, you've earned the right to play *Recuerdos de la Alhambra*," which is one of the pieces that I wanted to play for years. But he wouldn't let me learn it until I had mastered the tremolo technique. So, yes, repertoire can be used to develop technique, but at other times, it's a reward for developing technique. You don't try to play a piece until you have the necessary facility.

***

Q. Many players suffer from performance anxiety, even really good players. Do you ever get nervous before you perform? And if so, how does that affect your performance?

A. I think that everybody suffers from performance anxiety. It's impossible not to suffer from it. We all know how easy it is to forget something, how we become nervous about nerves themselves, and then being judged. The way I have thought of nerves for myself is that music to me is like an alternative universe, and we have to transition into that universe. When we play a concert, we enter a different place, which is to say that anxiety is fear, and the antidote for fear is love, becoming aware of how passionately we feel about the music. But the entrance to this state of mind is guarded by demonic-looking figures that try to scare you away from entering. Love is the way to get past those demons. Nothing has helped me more in getting over stage fright than contemplating Mozart's *The Magic Flute*, in which virtue, courage, and love triumph over fear. My daughter Angelina is a magnificent pianist, but she is not able to come to terms with the feeling of being nervous before a concert, and in that respect she is no different from people who are afraid to fly. They may want to be vacationing in the tropics, but that doesn't overcome the fear of flying.

I have felt very much both stage fright and the fear of flying. And I've overcome both by entering that alternative universe for which

I was born, in and out of which I have to navigate and take people with me. I believe in the essence and meaning of *The Magic Flute*. And then you make friends with those little demons that are waiting for you in your dressing room, and when it comes time to perform, rather than being afraid of them, you pet them. They welcome you, and you start looking forward to seeing them. Because you know they're there to guard this Eden of the music. And then you walk out on stage and love the experience. There's nothing more beautiful than the experience of being on the stage, feeling the power of music flowing through you, feeling that what my father called the Great Guitarist is playing the concert through your body.

***

Q. What is your relationship with the audience? Does it matter where you are playing or for how many people?

A. It doesn't matter to me where or for how many. Schedule a concert for me in the smallest village in the most remote country where they have no music critics, and I will prepare exactly the same as if I were going to play in Carnegie Hall. When I'm playing, what I am respectful of more than anything else is the music itself. I feel that the audience is there to do their job, and that is to finish what the composer started. They are a necessary part of this magic circle of music that begins with the voice of the Almighty, which then speaks to the composer, and is then imparted to the interpreter. A lot of people have to work to make it possible for this to happen at a specific moment in a specific theater, where people have come together to experience that connection with the Almighty. And the Almighty is not by definition a god of some sort. It can be anything, for instance, the sort of beautiful tree in the Amazon jungle that inspired Villa-Lobos, those amazing passages in which he makes the guitar sing with the quality of a resonant cello, or those arpeggios in his Preludes that become like a tropical storm. And all of a sudden, the listener is not hearing a guitarist playing arpeggios and moving the left hand fast. They are in the middle of a tropical storm.

So, the audience is there to help the music come to its conclusion. And the people in the audience are my partners. When I come out to play, I feel a great connection with and a great warmth and love for everyone. In front of me are people of many beliefs and nationalities, but they're all going to be vibrating in sympathy with the same sound waves. We're all going to experience that togetherness, that connection, which only music creates, refining and purifying our existence.

4

TEACHING

Q. You started teaching at an early age. How young were you, and who were your first pupils?

A. We left Málaga when I was 9 years old, moving briefly to Valencia and then settling in Seville. There was a military doctor there named Antonio Álvarez who had helped my father get a sort of medical deferment during the Civil War, so that he would not have to serve in combat but could instead work in a military hospital. He remained a close friend of my father and also studied guitar with him even before we moved to Seville. Antonio developed what is called trigger finger, whereby he could not control the movement of his right-hand middle finger. So, he came to my father for help when we were still living in Málaga. But my father chose not to teach Antonio and said, "My son Pepe will fix you. You work with him." Now, I was still just a kid, and I had no idea how to teach. The only thing I knew was the difference between what he did and what I did, that for me, it was easy to play, and for him, it was a struggle. It was easy for my hand to return to a completely relaxed position at a very high speed, but when he would pluck a note, his middle finger would get stuck. He couldn't release it. I found that his forearm would remain very hard after he plucked the strings, so I started working with his forearm. I didn't know anything about tendons, extensors, flexors, or joints, but I just tried to get him to work his right arm the same way that I was working mine.

By solving his problem, I learned lessons that I still apply today, especially in regard to my recent ailment and temporary loss of technical facility. I began feeling that once my hand had played, a relaxed feeling would return to the whole right arm and not just the fingers. And that is a vital element of my teaching. I zero in on what

TEACHING 35

a student is doing differently from the way I do it, if what they are doing is not working. Antonio was my first success as a student, for in the process of teaching him, I also learned valuable lessons.

One day, he called me and addressed me as "maestro," the first person who ever did that. When I was only seven! In looking back now, I must have seemed to him like a weird little creature. But one day he showed up at the house and announced that he had a great present for me. I got very excited wondering what it might be, and then he showed me: he sat down with the guitar, and he was able to move his middle finger in a normal way, without its becoming locked in place. And that *was* a great present. I had helped him to release the tension rather than fight it with yet more tension going in the opposite direction. I could see that there was a conflict, that he would tense his finger going both in and out, rather than flexing and then releasing. And only I could figure it out, not because I knew it, but because I could feel that what I was doing was the opposite of what he was doing.

After we moved to Seville in 1953, there were two American girls who came to study with my father. Now, my mother was always very guarded about my father teaching young women, and she always tried to divert the young women to study with her sons. I don't know if it was because of that, but I ended up teaching these two young girls, who were sisters. They were in Spain and thought it logical to take guitar lessons, though I was only 9 or 10 years old at the time. But I was studying as well as teaching. As mentioned earlier, my father engaged Paco Ávila to teach me flamenco, and by way of exchange, I taught him and later his grandfather classical guitar. But my professional career as a teacher didn't really begin until after we moved to Los Angeles in 1958 and established the Romero School of Guitar in Hollywood the following year. That was located where we lived on Wilton Place, and I painted a sign advertising the Romero School of Guitar. Classical and Flamenco.

As we were putting the sign in the window, a young Mexican fellow named Antonio Frías was walking by, and he immediately signed up for four lessons, which required an advance payment of twenty dollars, at five dollars per lesson. We later moved the school to the intersection of Sunset Boulevard and Gower, where it enjoyed great success. Angel and I painted a gigantic guitar and put it on the rooftop. By this time, my father, Celin, and I were all teaching students. I still have the notebook that I kept starting in 1958, with the students' names and lesson times written in it. It is labelled José Romero, as I was known at the time. (Pepe is the diminutive of José.)

***

Q. Who were some outstanding students during that early period?

A. Every week, I gave one-hour lessons to between forty and fifty students, while at the same time going to Hollywood High School. Among the best of them was Christopher Parkening, who first studied with my dad and then with me. He was a wonderful student. He started from scratch, a rank beginner and all of 9 years old. He had his first lessons with my father, and he soon showed himself to be an incredibly smart and nice little boy. His own father took a very active role in his boy's training, and he was present at every lesson and took careful note of everything that was taught so that he could help young Christopher practice it at home. Before long, he started taking two lessons a week, one with Celedonio and one with me. He was very diligent and made impressive progress. He would get up before going to school every day and practice, under his father's watchful eye. But it got to be a bit much at times, and I once got very angry with his father because of his interference during lessons. He wasn't just observing but also trying to control things. This was not at all the way I had learned, as my father never interfered when Celin was giving me lessons.

So, Christopher's father was very obsessive. He once asked me to give Christopher a four-hour lesson! This would not just be a normal lesson, only much longer, but would also involve practicing with him. So, we practiced scales and arpeggios together. Over time, Christopher became quite the young virtuoso, and I remember him playing Mario Castelnuovo-Tedesco's Concerto No. 1 in D Major, Op. 99, with a youth symphony in Los Angeles, an honor he had won in a competition. But after that he came more and more under the influence of Segovia, and his style changed dramatically. The Romeros had laid the foundation upon which Segovia now built, and Christopher now presented himself as a devotee of Segovia. He went his own way, and that was fine, though our paths would cross again many years later, and under felicitous circumstances. The 2024 Los Angeles Guitar Festival featured a celebration of my eightieth birthday, and Christopher was the first speaker. He gave a beautiful speech about the work we did together when he was a young fellow, and it was very lovely, very nice.

Another name that stands out is Erna Rubinstein, who was a virtuosa violinist but who wanted to learn the guitar. She learned the Carcassi Study No. 1 in a single afternoon! I didn't realize how accomplished she was until she presented me with an LP she had made of violin works. Remember that I was all of 14 or 15 years old at this time. Also appearing in my notebook is the name José Oribe, who went on to become a leading guitar maker, and Thomas Yue, who developed frozen dinners.

***

Q. You seem to have had a natural gift for teaching.

A. By his example, my father showed me how to teach, and I also learned from experience. At that time, we were also very much involved in the activities of the Music Academy of the West, an institution with which I was enchanted, as I had an abiding love of vocal music and opera, which were taught there. I regularly attended as many master classes as I could, of Lotte Lehman, Gabor Rejto, and other outstanding musicians, both vocalists and instrumentalists. In fact, I went to master classes wherever and whenever I could. When in New York, I would go to master classes at the Manhattan School of Music and at Juilliard, not as a participant but just as an auditor. Those teachers dispensed many jewels of wisdom to their students, and by attending the classes, I was also learning about and formulating my own style of teaching.

When I teach, I'm not thinking of myself as a teacher or even the student as a student; rather, I'm thinking about music and the guitar as benefiting from the joint effort that the student and I are making. We are both there to see how the guitar and music can be best served by the person I am trying to help. I want the student to be able to feel the incredible enjoyment that comes from music, from seeing a beautiful melody come out of yourself together with the guitar. I want to facilitate that. And that has been the electricity that energizes me when I'm teaching.

***

Q. You do many kinds of teaching, from private lessons to master classes. Do you prefer one kind over the others?

A. No, I love them all equally. I really enjoy teaching master classes, and I have done a lot of that, especially in my later years. In my earlier years, I gave more private lessons, although I continue to give them as well. For instance, at USC, every semester I give private lessons, and at the end of the semester, I give master classes.

***

Q. We've seen that your earliest teaching was in the form of private lessons. When did you start giving master classes?

A. I gave my first master class at Southern Methodist University in Dallas, Texas, in the early 1970s. The guitar program there had been started by Darryl Saffer, who had studied with my father and me. After that, I taught for many years at the Summer Academy master class in Salzburg, at the Mozarteum, as well as at the Schleswig-Holstein Music Festival. And then, in the early 1970s, I started teaching at the University of Southern California (USC). So,

Figure 4. Pepe explains some fine points of technique to Mark Switzer, 1988.

Figure 5. Pepe conducts a masterclass in Baden, Switzerland, 1983.

I enjoy both. I also enjoy teaching little children, because they're so receptive and innocent. Grownups are thinking of a career or comparing themselves to others. They face too many psychological obstacles. When we lose that childlike innocence and trust, we lose a great tool for connecting to music. Without trust, I wouldn't be able to walk out on the stage. Whom could I trust? I couldn't trust myself because I know that I could make a tremendous mess out of it. Rather, I trust in that mysterious Great Guitarist who is playing through me and connecting me to the "mystery dimension" of life. Children have the innocence and trust to be able to do that.

***

Q. So, you taught at the Romero studio, giving private lessons at $5 an hour. Since then, though, you've taught all over the world. You mentioned Southern Methodist University and USC, as well as leading festivals in Europe. There is also the annual Romero Institute in Oklahoma. How did that come about?

A. That came about when my friends David Palmer and his father, the great conductor Michael Palmer, started the Quartz Mountain

Music Festival in Oklahoma. I appeared at the very first festival, which featured works for guitar and orchestra. And then the following year, there were master classes on all the different orchestral instruments. In addition, Michael Palmer led one on conducting, while I gave a master class on guitar. That arrangement went on for three to four years, but for a variety of reasons, it didn't last. Still, my brother Celin, my nephews Celino and Lito, and I wanted to keep it going, and one of the students at that festival, Matt Denman, had the idea to launch the Celedonio Romero Guitar Institute at Oklahoma City University, where he is professor of guitar studies. That was a big success, and we've continued it to this day. We live together. We practice. We have private lessons, master classes, and rehearsals of chamber music. And then we perform together at the end of the festival.

***

Q. During the 1980s, you taught at the University of California, San Diego (UCSD), which is where I studied with you for my master's degree. However, I think that you've had the longest association with the University of Southern California. Tell us about how that happened.

A. A young guitar virtuoso named Jim Smith was pursuing a master's degree at USC but was studying privately with me. He asked the chairman of the string program, Gabor Rejto, if he could receive course credit for these lessons. Gabor said yes and pulled the necessary strings, so to speak. But soon a couple of other students requested the same accommodation, and Gabor, who was a good friend of mine, concluded that if all of these people wanted to study with me, I should just become a member of the music faculty. So, I became a member of the faculty! However, after I had been at USC for about ten years, the decision was made to move studio guitar (jazz and rock) into our department. I did not like that decision, so when Celin suggested that I join him on the faculty at UCSD, in 1982, I left USC and started teaching at UCSD, which was much closer to my home in Del Mar and would require a lot less driving.

At that same time, Father Nicholas Reveles, the priest in charge of the music department at the University of San Diego, invited us to start a guitar program there as well, though it didn't last long.

TEACHING

Father Reveles left the priesthood, and I don't know what the status of the department is now. I spent a few years at UCSD but eventually returned to USC, because my former students Bill Kanengiser, Scott Tennant, and Brian Head were now on the faculty there, and the situation had greatly improved. So, I went back and have been very, very happy working there.

***

Q. Although it seems unlikely, have you experienced any failures as a teacher?

A. I had one student whose name I shall not mention. I was lying sick in bed with the flu, and he came to audition. He played the Giuliani Concerto No. 2 while I had a fever. I don't know whether I was delusional or not, but I loved the way he played. And I thought that he was potentially a very talented student. So, then his journey with me started. I taught him in San Diego, and he came to master classes in Europe. I taught him for a long time, but with every lesson, he seemed to get worse! I didn't blame him; rather, I assumed that I was leading him down the wrong path. I felt that it was I who was failing. During this same time, he would play for my father, who would give him advice. My father was very impressed with his talent, but my teaching wasn't having the desired effect. Eventually he left, and I didn't hear any more from him. I think he gave up the guitar for a while and worked at various jobs. Then I ran into him at some shopping center, and he said to me, "Oh, Pepe, I would love to come and play for you." And I invited him to do so. He played magnificently, and I said to him, "I don't ever want to hear you play again. You played beautifully. Stay like that." I was afraid that if I got involved again, I would mess him up. He now has a successful career as a composer. That is one of the more unforgettable experiences I have had as a teacher!

***

Q. That was clearly the exception that proves the rule! Which students stand out in your memory, and what do you want to say now to all your many disciples, past and present?

A. Some great students have made careers, while others have not. One of my best students was Tom Gaab. After getting his doctorate in guitar performance (DMA), he decided to become a medical doctor, then a gynecologist, and finally a psychiatrist. He is brilliant and a fabulous guitar player. Vicente Macaluso studied with us and went on to become a wonderful concert and recording artist. We also taught many of the leading studio guitarists, such as Nick Boney, Jack Marshall, Jim Smith, Jonathan Marcus, and the legendary Tommy Tedesco. Robert Mattingly was another wonderful student, and he went on to become an internationally famous guitar maker. Another name that stands out is Vicente Coves. I first met him when he was 14 in the master class I was giving in Granada. Since that time, he has given me many extraordinary opportunities to enjoy his tremendous artistry and musicianship, from attending his performance of the *Concierto de Aranjuez* to sharing two CDs where he and I record the different concertos by Federico Moreno Torroba (1891–1982), with his brother Manuel Coves conducting. He has also become one of my dearest friends, and I will digress a bit here to explain the impact he has had on my life.

Vicente helped Carissa and me find the house that we bought in Granada. We ended up having massive reconstruction done to the house, and Vicente was the captain who navigated this Spanish adventure for the past fourteen years or so. Through him we met Chavalote, a contractor whose tenacity, valor, knowledge, and commitment made it all possible. We met his wife and her Romani family that own a famous cave in Sacromonte, Cueva de la Rocío, which features truly great flamenco artists. I will always remember one enchanted evening at the Cueva, as the moon shone above amidst a multitude of glimmering stars. I played the guitar, and then you, Walter, who had accompanied me on this visit, took the guitar and fulfilled your dream of many years by playing a flamenco number in a Romani cave on the Sacromonte, with the silent Alhambra overlooking the scene. Though you were by this time a musicologist and not a professional performer, I felt that a cycle had been completed, as did you.

Chavalote, whose legal name is Manuel Vargas Larios, has a son named Iván Vargas, who is a legend in the flamenco world. This was the family of the man that was constructing our house. We spent the first couple of summers in the house after we had bought it, but then we wanted to make some changes. For one thing, the bathroom was right next to the kitchen, and they were separated by nothing more than a curtain. So, I would ask Chavalote, "Can you do this? Can you do that?" And he acceded to our requests. But then Celin came to visit us, and he said that we should add a second story to this house. I called Chavalote, and he said that we would need an architect to do that. Fortunately, the architect he was working with was a woman named Josefa López del Valle. Her dreams and designs are magical, and she constructed a magical place that is filled with romance, with the history of the Alhambra and the Sacromonte. The Alhambra and Sacromonte are the two mountains divided by the Darro River, and they gaze upon each other forever. They are realms of mystery and magic.

All that notwithstanding, at first she said, "No, it's impossible to do any work here because of the local building code. The restrictions are severe for any kind of building here." But then she called me a week later and she said, "I've been studying the code, and yes, we can do it." We started meeting, and she designed a house. We loved the drawings she showed us and gave her the go-ahead. It was a real adventure. When we began, Josefa was pregnant with her first child. By the time the house was finished, she was the mother of six. We became close friends with Carlos Sánchez, the senior architect of the firm and Josefa's mentor. He's a remarkable artist and has established a magnificent legacy of preserving and enhancing the architectural treasures of Granada. He has a dynamic personality, one of fire and passion.

During this process we also met Juan Barcelona, a lawyer who guided us through the many legal obstacles that one encounters during reconstruction in a place protected by UNESCO. He displayed gladiatorial fighting skills when it came to the many legal battles, but in his private life he was always gentle and eager to help those in need. These people, their families and their friends, provided Carissa and me with a place where I can pray, study, and recharge my emotional, spiritual, and artistic energies. That is especially important to me at this time in my life. I left Spain when I was 13 years old, and Vicente has played a crucial role in enabling me to return now and enjoy my final years in Granada.

I have derived a lot of satisfaction from the Los Angeles Guitar Quartet, which includes former students of mine and whose performances I have always delighted in attending. Originally, they were the USC Guitar Quartet, created by Bill Kanengiser, Scott Tennant,

John Dearman, and Anisa Angarola, whom I have enjoyed as students, colleagues, and friends. Being on the same faculty at USC with them is a fantastic feeling for me, and I love working with the students of my students, whom I call "grandstudents." Both Bill and Scott have had international careers in the quartet and as soloists. I first met Bill at the juries during his first year at USC, and I became acquainted with Scott when he was in his early teens taking master classes with me in Houston. Anisa also began studying with me at an early age. They all eventually came to my house to take lessons. Bill, Scott, and Anisa would arrive at 11 a.m., and I would have the house full of guitar players for the entire day. I would give a lesson to one, then practice or run errands before giving a lesson to the next student.

They learned the way I did, by being in close proximity to other players and constantly using the guitar as a means to experience life. And I have enjoyed so much seeing those students become internationally acclaimed soloists and performing in quartets, especially the LAGQ. We share a common goal of encouraging composers to write for guitar quartet, which is itself like a single instrument. My father wrote a wonderful poem about his great guitar, with four heads, golden tuning pegs, and twenty-four princesses (strings). That was his "guitar," so to see that my students have carried it forward and made remarkable contributions to its repertoire is very gratifying, just as it is to see that my family and I continue to derive such great enjoyment from our own quartet.

And there have been many other wonderful students, both within and beyond the U.S., though I'm reluctant to start naming them because the list would be so long, and inevitably I would leave out some people by accident. I must not leave out Alex Dunn, who tragically passed away on May 8, 2024.

Alex Dunn was one of my most special students, one of those who stand out. I met Alex after a concert I had played in San Francisco. He asked me if he could audition for UCSD, I said yes, and I remember that he played a piece by Fernando Sor magnificently. So, I accepted him as a graduate student at UCSD without any hesitation. He was a wonderful musician, and I was keen to work with him. He was also an accomplished scholar and introduced me to the works of Johann Kaspar Mertz (1806–56), many of which I subsequently recorded. He also introduced me to another promising young guitarist named Randy Pile. I also accepted him

TEACHING

into the graduate program at UCSD, and both Alex and Randy went on to earn doctorates there. Alex wrote his doctoral document on Baroque guitarist Robert de Visée, while Randy wrote his on the guitar works of Joaquin Rodrigo. Both former students went on to successful careers concertizing and teaching guitar, Alex at the University of Victoria in Canada, and Randy at Saddleback College in Southern California. It was Alex who arranged for me to receive my first honorary doctorate, from the University of Victoria. In his later years, Alex became very involved with the music of Joaquín Turina (1882–1949), and he made some brilliant arrangements for four guitars of Turina's music, arrangements that Randy, Alex, his cousin Bob Ward, and I premiered on a tour of British Columbia. We all miss Alex very much.

I wish to mention another cherished student, and that is Martha Masters, a wonderful musician who is now a professor of guitar at Arizona State University and president of the Guitar Foundation of America. I'm very proud of several students, who are great teachers and are winning competitions: Julia Trintschuk, Martina Schäffer, Helene Widauer, Kenneth Bender, and Alexander Ramirez, professor of guitar at the Robert Schumann Conservatory in Düsseldorf.

Motomi "Pepe" Tashiro and Motomi Kakefu are guitar teachers and performers in Tokyo. Another outstanding student was the late Heike Matthiesen. During her difficult last years fighting cancer, she made remarkable recordings featuring women composers. I take great joy in seeing my students go out into the world of music, giving concerts, making recordings, and winning competitions.

I've had so many wonderful students throughout my life that it is impossible to acknowledge them all here. But I want all my students to know that, regardless of whether they launched successful careers or now play mostly for themselves, if they ever experienced a moment of true inner joy and peace while they were playing the guitar, then they accomplished my mission as a teacher. I feel fulfilled if they found their own path in life and are happy with it. The names Walter Clark and Bill Krause come to mind, fine guitarists who went into musicology! Bill just retired from a brilliant career at Hollins University, and you and he wrote the definitive biography of Torroba.

In the Preface to this book, you recall your first lesson with me and how I advised you to familiarize yourself with Cervantes's novel *Don Quixote* and Mozart's opera *Don Giovanni* in order to understand Spain and Spaniards. But the truth is that you're the only student I've ever said that to. Why? Because I sensed in you a far deeper connection to music than usual. I sensed in you a twin soul about music, and I wanted from the beginning to share with you those things that have always been incredibly important to me.

***

Q. Thank you for that revelation! It is very touching and puts those remarks of almost fifty years ago in a useful context. But to close out this chapter, how would you sum up your philosophy of teaching?

A. My philosophy of teaching is that playing an instrument or singing goes beyond just the physical act of performance. It takes us on an inner journey, as a way to better ourselves emotionally and spiritually. For me, playing music is a type of meditation or prayer, a way to connect myself to the truth, to the best of who I am. I believe that what one strives to achieve through music is to be at peace with oneself. The kind of relaxation we seek is not only at the muscular level when we are playing, i.e., relaxing a shoulder or a little finger sticking out. The music itself is the real teacher, because the closer we get to finding inner peace, the more the body surrenders to it.

My philosophy about teaching music thus embraces the complete journey into one's inner self. That is why whether I play the music of my beloved friends Rodrigo, Torroba, Turina, or of composers whose political leanings or affiliations may have been very different from my own, their music inhabits and takes me to a realm beyond politics. For even as we live in a very mortal moment, music focuses our awareness on the now, and releasing the sound transcends the time-space continuum, thereby connecting us to our immortality. My goal as a teacher has always been to help connect my students to their own center, their own soul. People do so many bad things, and the antidote for that is music, as it awakens love inside of us.

So that's my philosophy of music, and it is what I try to convey in my teaching. It is why I love teaching, because I hope that I will be able to help someone connect to their own goodness through music.

5

GUITARS AND GUITAR MAKERS

Q. What is it about the guitar that you love?

A. There is a mysterious universe that lives inside that box. For me, the guitar is what happens inside the structure. I've always been fascinated by guitar makers and by the process of putting pieces of wood together, taking such delicate care of how every piece of wood is going to vibrate and how all these pieces will function together in harmony, of putting soft woods against hard woods, and then enclosing it all. The most magical moment for most guitar makers is when they close the guitar. That is the time when the makers that I have known, such Rodríguez, Hauser, Blöchinger, and my son, have said that they have a very spiritual feeling, when the guitar is closed. The guitar is not a guitar until the top is connected to the neck. The next thing that happens is that the sides are glued to the top in the grooves that have been carved on the heel block. And then the back goes on top of the sides to create an enclosed space. To me, that space is the guitar.

I think that the whole Romero way of producing sound comes from understanding that it is not what you do with your hands, it is not what the strings do, but rather it is actually what happens to that space inside the box. That sound is the music. And the top becomes like a trampoline, so that when you pull the string you are uniting all the forces that are holding the guitar together, uniting them to create a sort of synergy. And to me, it is still mysterious how you can pull the string, and as you pull the string, you are pulling on the bridge, on the neck, you are squeezing the whole thing together so that the air inside gets compressed, and when you release the string, every single piece of that magical box called a guitar is released to sing, to project your emotions, thereby uniting yourself with every-one who's there—and even those who are not present, as I so often play for people who are no longer here.

Indeed, I have an incredibly beautiful relationship with the dead composers I have never met. I can feel how Sor felt when he played the guitar. I can feel how Giuliani felt, the joy, the happiness, the profundity. They become my dearest friends, and I love them as people who have felt the same magic that I feel. That is what I really love about the guitar.

***

Q. What do you look for in a guitar?

A. The first thing I look for in a guitar is how flexible it is, how it resists and how it gives, how it allows you to push on it. When I'm pushing on the string, I'm actually pushing on the guitar, and what I'm feeling is not really how the string is reacting but rather the whole instrument. That's why it's so important for each guitar to have the right kind of strings and that all the strings have the same tension. That will determine how the guitar pushes back and how it allows me to flex it. That flexibility is probably the first thing that I feel in a guitar. And then I note the quickness with which it releases the energy, because every sound is a burst of energy that you have built up inside. Thus, when you release the string, you create an explosion, and its speed and immediacy are the next things that I look for. But ultimately it all goes back to what kind of sound it has, what kind of voice. I want a guitar with a warm, clear, beautiful voice, one that has all of the emotional content that I feel inside of me. So, I seek the perfect match for the voice I would have if I could sing. The guitar is my voice and the vessel within which I travel to the depths of my being and connect to the unknown that is out there, waiting.

But then I also want it to be comfortable. The neck of the guitar is very important, because I feel the way the neck vibrates and its flexibility. The neck has to be very firm, so that it doesn't bend and instead holds with a gentle power, so that when I pluck the string, I can feel it vibrating against my left-hand fingers. I want to feel the neck vibrate against my thumb, so that my thumb is not just exercising brute force but is feeling the actual tone.

GUITARS AND GUITAR MAKERS

***

Q. How many guitars do you estimate you have owned? How many do you have now?

A. It's hard to say because I've been giving guitars away to my children. But in a way I don't feel that I own any of them. I am simply their keeper. A guitar that is well made, well cared for, and loved can last centuries, and I have some very old guitars. When Antonio de Torres made a guitar for somebody and it was subsequently inherited by that person's children and grandchildren, now somehow it's my guitar. But in a way we belong to the guitars rather than the guitars belonging to us. I definitely have in my possession more than a hundred. And for my entire life, I've been in love with the guitar as a living being with its own distinctive personality. I have quite a few "beings," because I knew how Papá longed for guitars when he was a young fellow. He didn't own a guitar of his own and had to borrow instruments from friends, one of them a Lorca and another an Esteso. He yearned to own a Rodríguez. But after he had established himself on the concert stage in Spain, the guitars he owned were the ones that aficionados gave him. We didn't actually start buying guitars until we came to the U.S. That initiated this incredible quest to try to bring home with me every guitar I fell in love with. There were many, and there continue to be.

***

Q. Who have been your favorite makers? Are there any non-Spanish luthiers that the Romeros have liked?

A. Yes, it is good to know which instruments I have played and in what sorts of circumstances, whether giving a recital, playing a concerto, or making a recording. In fact, I don't have one instrument that I think will be great for recordings, a different one for concertos, another one for J. S. Bach (1685–1750), for Isaac Albéniz (1860–1909), for flamenco, or for classical. It is more a matter of which one best expresses my feelings at a particular moment. I have to say that naming my favorite guitar is like naming my favorite composer. It is very difficult, but the makers whose instruments I have chosen to represent my playing both in concerts and in recording sessions are 1) Santos Hernández, 2) Miguel Rodríguez, and 3)

Hermann Hauser, Jr. Throughout most of my concert career, I have played my father's Santos, several guitars by Rodríguez, my 1969 Hauser, and then "La Wonderful" (1973) by Rodríguez, about which I will say more later.

I first met Edmund (Edi) in 1995 in Munich, when he and Fritz Ober came to my hotel room with Tim Miklaucic to show me a maple guitar with *plantillas* (templates) from Tárrega's Torres. I fell in love with that guitar and bought it on the spot. I remember that the only problem I had is that the neck was a little bit too thin for me. It was uncomfortable for me to play it with such a thin neck. So, Edi took out the fingerboard and replaced it with a thicker one, or he may have added a second layer of ebony, but he made the guitar incredibly comfortable. I have it to this day, and it is wonderful.

That was the first and only guitar by Edi that my father would know and play. My father loved it and would play it often, until the end of his life. Every time, he would comment on its fine qualities. Sadly, Edi and my father would never meet in person. Since that first meeting, Edi's guitars have become my frequent companions in concerts, recordings, and in our home *guitaradas* (guitar sessions), which Celin and I have in the mornings, where we discuss the attributes we love about the guitars we are playing at the moment.

Another of my favorite guitars was also made by Edi, and I named it Mimi, after my wife Carissa's grandmother. It was the last guitar I played for her before she passed away. And I played it for her spirit and her family. During the viewing at the farewell service, I played Bach's Violin Partita No. 2 on it. For that reason, I've named the guitar after one of the dearest people in my life. When Mimi was brand new, I played her in a concert at Dresden Cathedral with the Dresden Philharmonic, conducted by Rafael Frühbeck de Burgos. Fortunately, that performance was broadcast, and there is a wonderful recording of this memorable experience for me. I hope that someday I will put it either on my webpage or release it as a CD and make it available to the public. Anyway, Edi is one of my dearest friends, and Carissa and I are the proud godparents of Luisa Carissa, his first daughter. Celin and Claudia are godparents to his second daughter, Gloria. And Edi was the teacher of Pepe Jr.

A little over twenty years ago, I went to record the concerto by Xavier Montsalvatge (1912–2002), and at that time I was in love with #27 of Pepe Jr., which he had made not for me but for Tim Miklaucic. I borrowed that guitar from Tim to make a live recording

Figure 6. Pepe (*left*) with German master builder Edmund Blöchinger, 2005.

with the Cadaqués Orchestra at the Palau de la Música in Barcelona. Montsalvatge was there, and it would be the last performance he ever heard, as he died a week later. So, it was a very, very important concert for me, and that guitar is the one that I felt that I wanted to take with me. I named it La Timotea. I took that guitar and played it in concert, and then Pepe Jr. made #30 out of an extraordinary piece of wood that Miguel Rodríguez had been saving in order to build a very special guitar. The spruce top looked black just from sitting in his shop for years, and his son Miguel gave it to me, one of the last things he did. After I had played La Timotea, I said, "Okay, Pepe, you are ready to use this piece of wood to make #30," which I then called La Vieja (The Old One). That is still one of my most beloved instruments. Then, when I had #30, I returned La Timotea to Tim. I later bought it back and gave it to Pepe's son, Owen, so that his father would not sell it again.

When it came time to record a new concerto with Neville Marriner, one that Neville and I had commissioned from the Japanese American composer Paul Chihara, I wasn't quite sure which guitar I would choose, La Wonderful or La Vieja. So, I took

Figure 7. (*Right to left*) Miguel Rodríguez I, Angel, Miguel Rodríguez II, Pepe, 1974.

both of them, and just before the recording session, I sat in my room with Chihara and said, "Paul, you wrote this piece. Which guitar do you prefer? Sit, close your eyes, and I'm going to play one and then the other. I'm torn and don't know which one to choose." I then played both guitars, and he chose La Vieja, which is the one I used for the recording.

***

Q. You like to name your guitars. How did La Wonderful get its name?

A. When I met La Wonderful, I fell madly in love, and when I finally acquired it, that was the only guitar that I wanted to play. Rodríguez made it for my father in 1973, but once I played it, I just couldn't let it out of my hands. We Romeros have all loved the instruments of Rodríguez very deeply, and he was going to make a quartet of matching guitars for us. The first of them was La Wonderful, dedicated to my father by Rodríguez and his son. We were in Madrid at a hotel, and Rodríguez sent the guitar to us there. I was alone with my father in the hotel room, and as I opened the case, I thought, "This is the weirdest looking guitar. It is really not that attractive." It had sapwood (the living, outermost portion of a tree's trunk), which later became known as the "church door." There was Brazilian rosewood on the sides and back, but with a lot of sapwood as well. It was not considered ideal at that time, but today it is the preferred wood, and makers charge extra for it. A Rodríguez made from sapwood costs thousands of dollars more than one from any other wood, and it's all because of La Wonderful.

I took it out of the case, tuned it up, played a few notes on it, and then realized, "This is the most beautiful guitar I have seen in my life. This is my dream guitar. This guitar I cannot let go." I started playing, and my father said, "Give it to me so I can try it." But I protested, "No, wait, wait, Papá, I have to have this guitar. Please let me have this one. It's made for you, but let me have this one." He acquiesced, saying, "Okay, but don't tell your brothers." Then I started concertizing on it, and Rodríguez soon began getting letters from people saying, "I heard the wonderful guitar you made for Pepe. I was at his concert, and I would like to have a guitar like the wonderful one you made for Pepe." And Rodríguez, who didn't speak a word of English, asked me, "What is this word 'wonderful' that everyone uses to describe the guitar?" I told him what it meant, and he said, "Okay, let's call it La Wonderful."

Of course, that is not to say that I am not also crazy about Torres, but in 1990, I fell in love with a guitar by Gioachino Giussani, a contemporary Italian maker, and I played it in many concerts, as well as a recording of Rodrigo's *Concierto andaluz*, made in Vienna but of which there is only a tape. Domingo Esteso is also one of my idols, and I have also played instruments by the renowned builder Manuel Contreras. I played one of his guitars for a concert commemorating the centenary of Federico Moreno Torroba's birth, in 1991. This took place in Madrid and was a major cultural event, one featuring my performance of *Diálogos* with Rafael Frühbeck de Burgos and the National Orchestra of Spain, followed by Victoria de los Ángeles and me presenting a group of songs by Torroba. And after that, they did concert versions of the zarzuelas *La Marchenera* and *Luisa Fernanda*. Performing with Victoria was one of the most memorable events of my life.

My 1969 Hermann Hauser is named Astrid, after a young woman I met in Santa Barbara in 1959, when she was an exchange student there from Germany. In January of 1970, on our first European tour, Astrid attended a concert that we gave at the Herkulessaal in Munich. After the concert, Celin, Angel, and I decided that the next day we would go to visit Hermann Hauser, as I had never met him in person before. Astrid kindly offered to drive us to Hermann's house in her little Volkswagen Beetle, so the four of us took off from Munich to Reisbach, where we arrived in the late afternoon. We had a memorable time eating sausages, drinking beer, and talking to Hermann and his family. At that time, Hermann III was just a little boy running around their house. Hauser had a donkey that he would bring inside the house, and it was very sweet.

I played the guitar that evening at Hermann's house for hours, and we went from one guitar to another; in fact, he had recently made three guitars that had not yet been delivered. One was for Michael Lorimer, another was for Segovia, and I think the third one was for Julian Bream. I fell in love with the one for Michael Lorimer. I played it and played it, and I kept begging Hermann to sell it to me instead. "I need to have this guitar, and you can make another one for Michael. Michael is a good friend of mine. I will call him and tell him that I really fell in love with this. I guarantee you Michael

Figure 8. Celin, Hermann Hauser, Jr., Angel, and Pepe, 1970.

GUITARS AND GUITAR MAKERS

will not be upset." But Hermann was adamant: "No, no, no, no, this has to go to Mr. Lorimer." However, when I put the guitar away and we were getting ready to leave, Hermann took the guitar back to his shop, where he inserted a new label that said Gebaut für Pepe Romero (Built for Pepe Romero). He soon came back and gave it to me, and to this day, that's one of my all-time favorite guitars.

Then we drove back to Munich at about 1:30 a.m. It was very stormy and snowing like crazy, and then to make matters worse, our car ran out of fuel. We managed to stop somebody on the autobahn and tied a rope from their car to ours. Angel was now driving, and he managed to make it to a gas station and fill up the tank. All the while, I was holding on to make sure nothing happened to my gorgeous new Hauser. We eventually made it back to the hotel, and I played that Hauser consistently and uninterruptedly until 1973, when Miguel Rodríguez made the fantastic guitar on which I have made most of my Philips recordings: La Wonderful. To this day, Astrid remains one of Carissa's and my dearest friends.

✳✳✳

Q. Your son, Pepe Jr., is now a world-famous builder of guitars and ukuleles. How did that come about?

A. Pepe Jr. and my father were very close. Celedonio was an incredible father and grandfather, and his grandchildren loved him dearly. Pepe Jr. showed great promise as a guitar player, but when he was a little boy, 12 or 13 years old, he wanted us to go to a pavilion at the Del Mar fair, because he had received a blue ribbon for building a cabinet. He had taken woodshop and built this cabinet, which he still has. My father said, "Okay, I want to buy this from you!" I don't know what he paid him, but he bought the cabinet, and that was where he stored whatever music he was playing. From the moment he saw the cabinet, my father became obsessed with the idea of Pepe Jr. becoming a guitar maker. He said, "If you want to build guitars, why don't you just focus on becoming a guitar maker. I will build you a shop in the house here."

My father had a very wide range of beliefs, but in his later years, he became fascinated with the concept of reincarnation. He had strong feelings about certain people having been important persons in his youth and who had then come back. My father was convinced that Pepe Jr. was the reincarnated soul of Santos Hernández. But all Pepe Jr. had built thus far were some little things in woodshop, and he thought he would never become a guitar maker. I don't think I've ever told Pepe Jr. what Papá thought. Then, when my father died, Pepe Jr. began thinking about his future and told me that he wanted to try to make a guitar to honor Papá. And I took him to a San Diego-based guitar builder and repairman, Yuris Zeltins. In my life I've always gone to the workshops of guitar makers, and I used to take Pepe Jr. to Yuris's shop. So, he went there to ask for Yuris's advice about making a guitar to honor my father. Yuris started talking to him in a very philosophical way, pointing out that the first thing he should do is to take a close look at La Wonderful, noticing that there's nothing straight and the top has a dome in it. Yuris wanted Pepe Jr. to tell him what the dimensions of his guitar's dome would be, but he found it too hard to calculate. He went back and reported to Yuris that one couldn't make a perfect sphere, and much to Pepe Jr.'s surprise, Yuris exclaimed, "You have mastered the first lesson!"

Anyway, I took Pepe Jr. with me to Bellingham in Washington state, where he met the superb builder Dake Traphagen, a maker I admire very much. He is a very dear friend, and I have several of his guitars, on which I have performed in many concerts. Dake said, "Come on your vacation, stay with me, and I will show you how to build a guitar." In the event, he spent his summer there and then returned at Christmas. I was coming back from a concert when Pepe Jr. called me and said, "Papá was right. When I finished the guitar and put strings on it, the emotions were so powerful that I knew that this is what I want to do for the rest of my life!" He then went on to study with Rodríguez, but every guitar he makes has a label that features a picture of my father. The image is so faded and because they look so much alike, many people think that it is actually his own picture. But no, it's a picture of my father playing the guitar, and every label says "Dedicada a Celedonio Romero." He really wishes that Papá had played his guitars. I once did an oil painting of my father playing the guitar, and Pepe Jr. has it in his shop, where it symbolizes Papá playing Pepe Jr.'s guitars before he actually makes them.

La Wonderful once met a tragic fate, which left it in pieces. I was practicing while using a traction machine to recover from a car accident that had damaged my neck. I was sitting in front of a bookcase, and then my little daughter Tina came running in to see me and accidentally knocked over the bookcase, which fell on top of me and the guitar, smashing it. I didn't say anything. I just looked at it in shock and disbelief. It was only a year old, during which time I had been touring with and playing on it. I called Miguel Rodríguez to tell him that La Wonderful was completely destroyed. But first he asked, "And you? It's lucky that it was La Wonderful and not you. I can repair it, put on a new top, or make another one like it. So, send it to me." I gathered the pieces, put them in a case, and prepared to mail them to Miguel. But Angel was with me and suggested that first we take them to Yuris, to see what he could do. So, we went with La Wonderful in pieces to his shop, and Angel said to him, "People say you're good. Let's see how good you really are. Can you fix this?" Yuris said that he didn't know for sure. Angel retorted that we all had nothing to lose. "If you send it to Rodríguez, he's not going to fix it, he's just going to make you a new guitar." So, we left it with Yuris, and he worked on it for over a year. But when he was finished, it was better than ever, in full glory. La Wonderful turned 50 years old in January 2023, and she has performed yeoman service. All my Philips recordings are on La Wonderful, and when I performed in Córdoba, Rodríguez himself could not believe how well Yuris had fixed it.

***

Q. Would you play Pepe Jr.'s guitars even if he weren't your son? If so, what is it about them that you like?

A. Absolutely yes. The last thing I would do is show off something my children did that I didn't like. When I play the *Aranjuez* with Frühbeck de Burgos and the Royal Danish Orchestra, I would never play one of his guitars if I didn't believe wholeheartedly in them: their voice, resonance, lyricism, the dramatic sound of the high notes, the depth of every bass note. The extraordinary harmonic structure of each note in Pepe Jr.'s instruments is simply magical. Not even La Wonderful has that quality. To me, Pepe Jr.'s guitars exhibit an incredible mixture of his favorite makers. The reason I have never told him about what Celedonio thought is because I don't want him to think that he has to be the continuation of somebody. But now, after having built about 400 guitars (he just presented me with

Figure 9. Pepe Sr. (*right*) and Pepe Jr. in Pepe Jr.'s workshop, 2024.

#380), he has found his own voice, and it's okay if he knows what his grandfather thought. He loves Santos Hernández, like every guitar maker. But he also loves Rodríguez, as well as Edi Blöchinger, from whom we recall that he learned so much about the building techniques of Torres.

After Dake, Pepe Jr. wanted to study with Rodríguez, who was too sick to teach him and sent him away. Pepe Jr. was devastated, but after Rodríguez looked at his first guitar, he said, "You already know how. Just keep building." Pepe Jr. wanted to go home, so he took the train back to Madrid and headed for the airport. I spoke to him on the phone and convinced him to stay at a hotel in the Puerta del Sol and call me in the morning. That gave me time to call some of my luthier friends in Madrid and ask them if they would teach my son until I could travel to Spain. I spoke to Pablo Contreras, Amalia Ramírez, and Mariano Tezanos Jr., and they all were incredibly gracious and said yes, he could stay and start right away. In the morning, things were looking less gloomy for my young son.

He first went to see Pablo Contreras in Madrid. Pablo was the son of Manuel Contreras, and there was an immediate connection between the two of them. He went every day to take notes and watch guitars being made. Pepe Jr. would fall in love with Madrid, with Pablo and his family. His stay in Madrid was an experience that he will keep in his heart and his memory forever. In addition to being in the Contreras workshop, he enjoyed going to see Real Madrid play soccer. After that, he took lessons with José Luis Romanillos in Córdoba and built his second guitar. By then, Rodríguez had recovered and now gave him some excellent instruction. He handed Pepe Jr. a beloved piece of wood, including a bridge, saying, "I built that bridge, and in it is the secret to the entire guitar. Take it and study everything about the bridge." A while later, there was a guitar-making competition sponsored by Cecilia Rodrigo, daughter of the famous composer, and both Edi Blöchinger and Pepe Jr. presented guitars for consideration, though the winner was an instrument by Pablo Contreras. But a distinct benefit accrued from this occasion in Madrid, as Pepe Jr. bonded with Edi, who invited Pepe Jr. to study with him. That proved to be another formative influence on his building. Edi and my son would become soulmates in the art and love of guitar making. During one of Pepe's first days with Edi in Dorfen, Germany, they built a magnificent guitar, which they call La Papa Frita (The Fried Potato). To this day, I have no idea why they call it that except that its color is golden. I think that we will have to wait until one of them writes his own memoir.

I played a concert at the Marinsky Theater in St. Petersburg, Russia, when La Papa Frita was on its first concert tour. I still remember how beautifully she sounded in this glorious theater. I took quite a chance in trusting Pepe Jr., because I called him before I left and asked him to tell me how good this guitar really is. "Can

I take it on tour?" He said, "Believe me, you can take it on tour. It is really great." That was a guitar that they built together, and that was how Edi passed onto Pepe Jr. so much knowledge about making guitars.

When I was on the airplane from Madrid to St. Petersburg, I was sitting with the conductor who was going to conduct the concert. And he was telling me that he had recently been scheduled to perform with a colleague of mine, who shall remain nameless here. But this guitarist intended to use a microphone to amplify the guitar. The conductor refused to play with him, saying, "I detest amplification, and I will not play with anyone who doesn't play completely acoustically and release the real sound of the instrument."

And there I was, sitting there next to him on the flight with my new guitar that I had never tested on a concert stage. I was going on the word of my son. But I have to admit that I was getting a little bit nervous when he said that, and I thought, "Let's see how this one sounds in the Marinsky Theater. She's going to have her debut in a huge hall with an orchestra performing the *Concierto de Aranjuez*. Let's see how it goes." Of course, I acted completely confident and replied to him, "Oh, yes, I never amplify. I don't like to amplify at all." And when we arrived, I just went on to the stage to rehearse, and I played the opening chords. I was so relieved, so happy, because it sounded so very beautiful

Thus, Pepe Jr. combines the traits of all the greatest makers. His guitars embody everything I love, because he grew up listening to me play the guitars I love and hearing what I love about each one, whether it be a Santos, Rodríguez, or Contreras. And because Pepe Jr. is a very good player and has always loved the guitar, he has a profound understanding of the features that Papá and I love about a guitar, and he puts all of them into his instruments.

***

Q. Your grandson Bernardo is also a fine luthier. Is he still building guitars?

A. Bernardo is a very rare talent. I have played and own the first guitar that Rodríguez built, which he gifted to my father, and then it came to me. I've seen Pepe Jr.'s first guitar. But I've never seen anyone build a first guitar like the one Bernardo built. It's the best

GUITARS AND GUITAR MAKERS

I've seen. I played his second guitar at the Rheingau Festival, a very prestigious music festival, and I played a Bernardo guitar at the Meyerson Center in August 2022. He's an incredible maker, though he will now build guitars on his own terms and time. He doesn't like being under pressure to turn out instruments, so his new day job is as a police officer in the city of Oceanside. Now he can make guitars for the pleasure of it and not because he needs to sell them to support his family. One of the most renowned and expensive guitar makers was Robert Bouchet, and he also supported himself in another profession. He didn't depend on guitar building. For psychological and personal reasons, Bernardo has always wanted to work in law enforcement. We need people like Bernardo.

**

Q. Tell me more about Torres.

A. My father had an incredible love for Antonio de Torres, who made a guitar for the grandfather of guitarist Gil Cobos, a friend of my father. Gil was going to sell my father that guitar, but when Gil's father found out, he said, "No, you cannot sell my grandfather's guitar." So, he made Celedonio give it back. It was as if a piece of his heart had been ripped out. And he heard nothing more about that guitar until one day he got a call from Gil, whose father had died, and now Celedonio could have the 1856 Torres for the same price he had paid many years earlier.

**

Q. Now it's time for some stream-of-consciousness about the builders you clearly love: Torres, Santos Hernández, Domingo Esteso, and early guitars like Lorca, Domínguez, and Ramírez.

A. I have a deep love affair with the guitar as a universe unto itself. The guitar holds the answers to so many secrets that for me it is a temple, a goddess, a friend. And just as I connect with composers and the way they write music, so I am completely fascinated with the way a guitar is put together. It comes from trees the world over, and thus it does spiritually and philosophically what I want for the whole world, which is to come together in harmony and in peace. The guitar maker starts by taking pieces from different forests from all over the world, in Alaska, South America, Africa, India, the Alps, and the *montes* of Málaga. Then the maker puts them together to create this thing we call a guitar. And it can only work when these elements of living things—which have given flowers, fruit, and love, and which have witnessed all that has happened in the world through the centuries—all come together in this little shop.

Hence, I have always been fascinated with the process of creating a guitar and have enjoyed visiting guitar makers' shops. My love and appreciation for the different kinds of makers and instruments started when I had polio as a little boy. As I lay in bed for hours, my father would play different guitars for me. He had a Lorca, an Esteso of cypress, and a Domínguez, and he would play the same piece on each one in turn. I started realizing that you can be the same player but that the guitar itself is an integral part of the end result. The different makers put their own voice into your music, so you are not just connected to the composers but also to the makers.

As I mentioned before, when I was a toddler in Málaga, my father would drop me off at Domínguez's shop. He was a very loving, peaceful man, and when I was left there, he would just continue working. I would sit down, and he would tell me what he was doing: "Now I'm going to carve the neck. See this piece of wood? It will become the neck." I would watch him make a piece with his scrapers, and I was fascinated with that. His son, Pepe, built guitars with him, but mainly he was employed playing the bandurria at night with his friends, so he would sleep until late morning. I really enjoyed being in his shop, except that the dust and wood chips piled up over time and bothered me. I wish he had kept the space cleaner!

And then my father somehow got a Ramírez, though it soon disappeared and didn't return until we were in Seville. I spoke earlier of the 1856 Antonio de Torres that miraculously found its way to Papá and then me. Most guitars are made of spruce or pine, but this one is quite rare because it is made of maple as well as pine from the mountains of Ronda, in the province of Málaga. In Torres's handwriting on the inside of the top it says, "Pino Malagueño 1812." So, although the guitar was made in 1856, it was already a very old piece of wood. And it sounds fantastic. That was Papá's most precious possession, and he played it with incredible love. In fact, that was the last guitar he played during his life. About a week or so before he passed, he was playing Joaquim Malats's *Serenata española*, but he

GUITARS AND GUITAR MAKERS

was so weak that he could only get partway through it before asking, "I don't have any more strength, Pepe, you finish it."

In the early 1970s, we were touring in Colorado, and I had a car accident. I was driving a Pontiac station wagon, with my wife Kristine and our two daughters, Tina and Angelina. We were going over Loveland Pass when the car skidded off a cliff and flew about thirty feet through the air before crashing and rolling another thirty feet, finally stopping by a huge tree. My mother and father were driving in a Chrysler behind us, and when they saw this my father said, "Angelita de mi alma, they have died." However, we were all alive! Kristine had broken her left arm, but that was the extent of the injuries. Behind my parents was a car with a group of young skiers, and they used their ropes to help us out of the ravine. My father rushed out and asked, "Is everybody alive? Are your hands okay? Show them to me!" And then the very next thing he said was, "The Torres is yours." He wanted to celebrate our survival by giving me his most precious possession, and that's how I came to have it.

The car was destroyed, and the young skiers drove us to the nearest hospital, where they fixed Kristine's arm. Then we were driven to a hospital in Denver, where she had surgery the next morning. The car remained at the crash site with all its contents. A couple of days later, the police called to report that they had our car and asking us to please come and collect all the stuff that was in it. Since we were on tour, this "stuff" included suitcases, as well as my 1969 Hermann Hauser. Kristina had been playing and brought with her a José Ramírez that belonged to Celin. When we went to pick up the Ramírez, it was in pieces inside the car because it had hit the tree. It was far beyond anything that Yuris could do to save it. But the perplexing thing was that the Hauser was nowhere to be found. I told one of our rescuers, 18-year-old Tom Cameron, that I thought for sure it had fallen into the creek and would never be seen again, destroyed just like the Ramírez. Papá and the police agreed. The police had checked the area carefully and said there was nothing else there. So that was it.

That night I didn't see Tom, as he had been helping take care of the children so that I could go to the hospital. The following day we were all in the hotel when suddenly there was a knock at the door. It was Tom with my Hauser guitar in its case! He had gone back to look and found it completely covered with snow. That's why the police and I never saw it. I eagerly opened the case and noticed that the guitar had one crack on the top, which Bob Mattingly later fixed; otherwise, it was in perfect shape and even still in tune. I told Tom that he deserved a big reward, but he only wanted to hear what the guitar sounded like. So, I played it for him, and we remained there until Kristine could travel. I asked him if he would like to come with us and help with the children. I wanted to hire him, but, no, all he wanted was guitar lessons, not money. This went on for a month. I never heard from him again, but he became a professional guitarist of some kind.

That guitar was very special to me, but there were others. When we moved from Málaga to Valencia and then Seville in 1953, I took along my little "Berlioz" guitar, a beautiful French or Italian guitar. Soon after moving to Seville, my father bought me a wonderful José Ramírez I of 1909, which he found in the Rastro (flea market) and paid five pesetas for. I really love that guitar. In fact, I still have it in my bedroom as a wonderful memory. However, now that we were settled in Seville, my father did what he always did in a new place, and that is befriend the local guitar makers. Unfortunately, at that time, Seville didn't have many well-established makers, so he made the acquaintance of an amateur maker named Miguel Obando. My father asked him to make him a guitar, something he always did because he had an insatiable thirst for guitars. After all, as a young man and then during the Civil War, he had never had a guitar of his own and had to borrow guitars. Finally, after the war, he went to Seville and was given a guitar by some of his admirers. Obando said, "I'll make you a guitar, but I don't have any wood. Oh, but my mother-in-law has a gorgeous cherry-wood bed. I'll take the headboard of it and make you a guitar." It was beautiful, but that created a problem for Obando because he took the wood without her permission! Makers are in a constant quest for great pieces of wood, and they can find it in surprising places.

When we were still in Málaga, my father got his first Santos Hernández, which he picked up in Madrid on August 6, 1942. In the process, he and Santos became great friends. Before 1942, he had performed in Seville but, not owning one of his own, he played on a flamenco guitar that he borrowed. The aficionados expressed to him their desire to give him a guitar and asked him what make he wanted. Without hesitation, Celedonio said he wanted a Santos Hernández, and they agreed to donate the money to buy it for him.

GUITARS AND GUITAR MAKERS

My father ordered it directly from Santos Hernández, who received the money from the aficionados in Seville and then made him the most exquisite-looking, fanciest of the models that were his trademark—one normally more expensive than what he was paid! And he threw in the case for free. But in an act of incredible generosity, he gave my father half of the money, saying, "For you, I only charge half. You keep the money." He was a wonderful man, though there was something about my father that inspired such kindness. I got to know that guitar very well, because every time Papá and Mamá left the house, I would make sure they were really gone, and then I would play it until they got back.

It was the sound of it that I loved. Sadly, he had to sell that Santos to buy the plane tickets when we moved to California in 1957. And that was not the only guitar he had to sell in order to finance our move. In the early 1950s, he had a patron in Seville who was a general in the Spanish air force. His name was José Rodríguez Díaz de Lecea, and whenever he hosted a gathering of visiting dignitaries, he would ask Celedonio to provide the music. One of the guests offered to get him a guitar and asked what kind he wanted. My father responded, Hermann Hauser. So, he started corresponding with Hermann Hauser, Sr., who accepted the commission and set about building him a fine instrument. But then Papá got a letter from the maker's son, Hermann Hauser, Jr., saying that his father had passed away but that he himself had been working with him for quite a few years and could finish the guitar. My father said fine, finish the guitar. Hermann Jr. appreciated Papá's faith in him, as everyone else had cancelled their order after learning that Hermann, Sr., had died. This made it hard for his son to continue. As a result, we developed a wonderful relationship with him, and he eventually sent Celedonio the 1954 Hauser started by the father and finished by the son. But my father wasn't very happy with it. The neck was too thick, so he took it to a friend, Manuel de la Chica, to have the neck recurved to his liking. That guitar is now in Celin's possession and has survived without incident. Not all of our instruments were so lucky.

In Los Angeles during the early 1960s, Celin had an accident at home that virtually destroyed my father's Esteso, which he had been playing. It would need several repair jobs to fix it. The first attempt was made by Candelario Delgado (Candelas), a Mexican guitar maker in Los Angeles who tried unsuccessfully to put it back together. About this time, Manuel Rodríguez arrived in Los Angeles, so my father took it to him, and he replaced the top. But the guitar didn't sound the same. Then Yuris tried to fix it but got no further than making a perfect replica of an Esteso rosette. The top has since been replaced by Pepe Jr., with a Yuris rosette, and that guitar now sounds better than it ever did. It's phenomenal, and it is once again in Celin's possession.

So, yes, guitars have accidents, and they get destroyed or restored or have a long and peaceful life like my Torres. They represent not only the guitars themselves but the connection to the makers. I mentioned Candelas, who was a very important person to us during our early years in Los Angeles. When you arrive in a city, you need to connect with the local guitar community in order to attract students. Makers play a crucial role in that process. It was Candelas who referred many of his customers to us, such as Vahdah Ollcot-Bickford and Laurindo Almeida. So, we developed a warm friendship with Candelas. When I turned 15, in 1959, I got two guitars, one of them with a spruce back and sides by Candelas and that featured a mother-of-pearl inscription on the back that said Pepe Romero. I still have that. It looks like the suit of a mariachi musician! He put every possible color and design on the purfling of that guitar. And I also got a 1958 Miguel Rodríguez, which I named Henrietta (for reasons I will explain further on). That touched me deeply, and I played that guitar on recordings and on tour. It became a very important guitar to me.

Until we moved to Seville, for me guitar makers were fascinating people, but it was like a piece of history. The only living, working guitar maker I had known personally was Francisco Domínguez in Málaga. In Valencia, I knew no one, and in Seville I met Obando. But I still didn't know the giants I would later meet, like Rodríguez, Contreras, and the Hausers. They entered only later in my life, when I was living in Los Angeles and then returned to Europe. In Seville, I had my own guitar, and by that time my father had traded his Santos to a man named Felipe Alba for a 1932 Santos, one that he liked more than his because it was not so fancy. So, Felipe gave my father his Santos and some money for Papá's Santos, which was the most gorgeous Santos I've ever seen but a very temperamental instrument. It had great days and then days when it didn't sound quite so good, probably because the top was too thin. And I still have that 1932 Santos.

GUITARS AND GUITAR MAKERS

So, Papá had two Santos guitars at that time, as well as an Esteso acquired from Alfonso Bernal, who gave me painting lessons in exchange for guitar lessons. And he had a Flix guitar, made in Barcelona, which is the only one I've seen. That's in Angel's possession because that became Angel's guitar. So, my father would play a Santos, while the Esteso was given to Celin, because he fell in love with it and Papá actually acquired it for Celin. And I had a 1909 José Ramírez, which I loved and played on the radio in Seville. It had a beautiful sound but was rather beat up. And upon leaving for the U.S. in 1957, Papá also sold his Hauser to pay our travel expenses. So, we arrived in Southern California with the Santos he got in exchange from his friend Pepe Cuéllar, Alfonso Bernal's Esteso, my 1909 Ramírez, and the Flix, which was heavy and dead sounding. Now, perhaps I'm not being fair to the instrument from Barcelona, but it was so heavy and so difficult to get sound out of that you had to play really hard. I have played many beautiful instruments from Barcelona, but they have not resonated with my heart like those from Madrid or Andalucía, especially the latter.

It was when we returned to Spain in January 1970, on our first tour of Europe, that I finally met Rodríguez, Contreras, Ramírez, and Bernabé, in addition to Hauser in Germany. It was magical to develop friendships with these great geniuses in the world of guitar making. I got my first Rodríguez when I was 15. I was playing on my father's Santos when we arrived in Santa Barbara in August of 1957, and I had to perform a week after we arrived, for the annual fiesta Old Spanish Days there. I played in the evening at the entrance to the Santa Barbara Mission, and I used my father's Santos. Sometime later, I was practicing on the Santos, to which I almost always made sure to attach a tap plate, because I used it for both classical and flamenco. But this time, I had forgotten the guard, and my father adjured me to put one in place right away. Our family friend Henrietta Kinnell was there, and after that exchange, she immediately asked, "You mean you don't have your own guitar? Well, for your birthday I'm going to give you your own guitar." At that time, we had just begun to play concerts and were doing well in Santa Barbara, and my father had already ordered four guitars from Rodríguez. Henrietta paid for my guitar and gave it to me for my fifteenth birthday, in 1959. And that's how it got that name. I gave that to Pepe Jr. for his fifteenth birthday, and that started the tradition whereby I give guitars to my children and grandchildren when they turn 15 years old. And I give them a concert instrument, a really great guitar!

We met Candelas and his brother Pilo when we moved from Santa Barbara to Los Angeles in 1958, and we started a great relationship with them. Candelas was an artist but never refined his craftsmanship. He was good but more interested in sound than appearances. Then Manuel Rodríguez came to Los Angeles in 1959, and he was a wonderful maker. He came for the same reason we did, i.e., to create a better life for himself and his family, so he opened a shop on Wilshire Ave. and started buying houses. But he missed the bars in Spain, the ease of taking a break at the cantina next door. If he wanted to go anywhere in Los Angeles, he had to drive there. In Spain, you simply go outside and walk to the nearby bar for coffee or beer and to chat with other makers. Though he eventually returned to Spain in 1973, those two makers became a big part of our social life in Los Angeles. We went with Candelas to Mexico for the first time, to Tijuana, Ensenada, to the beach, and rode horses.

Another of my favorite makers was Julius Gido, who came from Yugoslavia to resettle in Los Angeles. His guitars were much better than one would deduce from his relative lack of name recognition. He was a great person, and I used to love to hang out at his shop. Angel felt the same way and actually built a guitar himself in Guido's workshop. I still have one of his instruments.

In addition to these guitar makers, among our widening circle of friends was a sailor who was studying with my father, a Navy guy who was a machinist stationed in San Diego. His name was Robert Mattingly, and he would drive to Los Angeles to take lessons from my father. At the same time, I had a flamenco student named José Oribe. Both of them got married while they were guitar players, went on their honeymoons to Spain, ordered guitars from Rodríguez, fell in love with guitar making, and became great makers. And that's what they're known for. They had very different personalities, but we were good friends of both. However, Oribe was upset from the start that we didn't play his guitars. By contrast, Bob was the greatest fan of Rodríguez, and he completely understood why we preferred his instruments. He also shared my love for the guitars of Hermann Hauser, Jr., and after I got my 1969 Hauser and it broke, he fixed it for me.

Those were two makers who, through our playing Rodríguez, ended up being guitar makers. Then, in 1970, when we went to

GUITARS AND GUITAR MAKERS

Madrid, we started a rewarding relationship with Manuel Contreras. I wound up playing Contreras guitars quite a bit, though I was never "married" to a Contreras guitar. Rodríguez was my guitar, Hauser was my guitar. Nonetheless, I played some of my best concerts all over Europe on Contreras. And he would meet us in different places. When I gave my first solo recital in Rome, he was there to present me with a guitar, which I loved and played right there. I played many times in Madrid, and I bought several Contreras guitars. I think that he was one of the great guitar makers.

The following year, in 1971, we returned to Europe and again toured Germany, during which time Hermann Hauser, Jr., came to deliver a guitar to Angel. Actually, Angel had already received one, but he complained that it was out of tune, and he sent it back and asked Hermann to build him another one. So now Hermann brought Angel the replacement. That guitar became my father's favorite Hauser, and he played it in many concerts. It's now for sale at Guitar Salon. I remember Hauser asking Angel, "What plays out of tune on my guitar?" Angel responded, "When I play the artificial harmonic on the twelfth fret, I cannot put my finger over the fret. I have to move it, and the octave sounds flat." Most Hausers have to have a correction, because when you press down on the twelfth fret, you alter the distance (equidistant from nut and bridge), and it has to be compensated for on the bridge. Rodríguez's guitars all sounded sharp at the octave, and Hausers all sounded flat. Rodríguez didn't compensate, and Hauser overcompensated.

However, after Angel returned that flawed guitar to Hermann, Mrs. Hauser protested, saying, "Mr. Angel, wherever my husband put the harmonic, that's where you put your finger." So, she was very defensive, but Hermann really wanted to learn about the problem. We continued that friendship, and in 1975 I had him build me an instrument. He called me just around my birthday to say it was finished. I said, "Okay, we'll be coming to your house, and I'll pick it up at the end of the tour." But then he had a stroke, and by the time we went to see him, he could not speak, and it was really sad. Hauser wanted to speak because he had many things to say, but he could only mutter. He had a young man, Hasie, who had been adopted and trained by both Hermann Hausers, Sr. and Jr., and he took me to his workbenches and pointed to the inside of two identical guitars. He then used a mirror to look at the label under the tops, one signed by Hauser, and the other, by Hasie. So, there are many Hausers, but you have to look inside under the top with a mirror to see which one built the guitar. They both made Hermann Hauser guitars, and they are all wonderful.

Since Hermann couldn't talk, I had to ask Mrs. Hauser where my guitar was. She said, "There is no guitar for you. My husband didn't make a guitar for you." I said, "Yes he did. I spoke with him a few weeks ago." But she refuted that, as she was furious that I was touring on La Wonderful, though Hermann himself didn't care. She said, "He made that guitar for Mr. Celin." We had a publicity poster at that time in which I was holding La Wonderful and Celin, a Velásquez, which was identical to a Hauser; thus, she thought he was playing a Hauser. So, she was going to sell it to Celin, who really liked it. I was fuming, but she refused to sell it to me, and Celin bought it. He wanted to boil my blood as hot as possible! Hermann was observing this drama but couldn't speak up. I said to Hermann III, "When you have grown up, I will deal with you, but I'm not coming back until you are running this shop." I left infuriated, and Hermann Jr. came running after me, trying to give me a guitar. Of course, I didn't take it because it would have caused too big a problem with his wife. I just left. For the remainder of that tour, Celin taunted me with that guitar, so I bought a Rodríguez, and we exchanged guitars. He admitted that he had just been teasing me, a behavior typical of older brothers. In any event, I also have that guitar.

My friendship with Hermann remained really good, and Hermann Hauser III himself became a fantastic maker. I went back many times, and I made up with Mrs. Hauser. I understood that her feelings were hurt because I had been playing Hauser and then switched to Rodríguez for that tour. She was very protective of her husband. At one point, I was at a restaurant in Vienna and cracked a tooth. She was a dentist, and I went to her. The only thing she could do was insert a gold tooth, which she had made. I kept that tooth for about a year. And Hermann was very sweet. In one of the concerts in Munich, I was playing my 1983 Miguel Rodríguez, which I call "Piano" because it's made from an old piano top. I was doing a TV show with Montserrat Caballé, during which they interviewed us as members of musical families. She would sing and be interviewed, and then I would play and be interviewed. This went back and forth for an hour-long program on Bavarian TV. One of the people running it told me to just keep my guitar on top of the piano, and when

GUITARS AND GUITAR MAKERS

it's time to play, pick it up, and when I finished, put it back on the piano and continue with the interview, because she was going to sing with the piano top closed. Then, out of nowhere came a stage hand who opened the piano lid, causing my guitar to fall on the floor, where it exploded like a bomb, making a horrible sound.

I called Hermann Hauser III, and he came immediately to the station with two guitars, one by his father and the other his own masterpiece, which he had made when he graduated from the school he attended to get his Master Builder certificate. In Europe you have to get a degree in whatever trade you undertake. Your work is judged by master craftsmen, and then you receive your master's diploma. I loved that masterpiece of Hermann Hauser III, and I played it not only on the TV program but continued to use it on our tour and then brought it to the U.S., where I played it in quite a few concerts. I then returned it to Hermann Hauser III, because it's part of his history. We remained really good friends with him. The one that fell off the piano was repaired to perfection by Yuris. It ended up as great as it was before the accident. So, this chapter has a happy ending.

PART III

CONCERTIZING

6

THE SOLOIST AND THE QUARTET MEMBER

Q. You are a very versatile performer, as a solo recitalist and with the Romero Quartet, in addition to playing chamber music and appearing as a concerto soloist with orchestras. Is there one type of playing that you like the most?

A. I like it all equally because there is so much magnificent music for all the different combinations. So, whatever I am playing, I am in love with it, and I'm having a great time. The feeling of connecting to the music by yourself is totally different from being connected not only to the music but also to other performers. Now, it's hard to explain the difference. I think that the major difference for me has been the actual touring itself. And touring with the quartet has been a lot of fun and very lively. There is always drama, comedy, and interchange. It is like a Rossini opera!

However, I also enjoy the peacefulness of touring by myself. I view everything in its totality. I always felt very lucky that I could do all sorts of different things, as meeting, performing, and touring with great artists is very exciting. To fly to Barcelona to play with Jessye Norman, then fly to Brazil to join my friend Rafael Frühbeck de Burgos to tour Brazil and Argentina with him and the Spanish National Orchestra. It has been a real thrill. Yet, the preparation of the music is pretty much the same. When I prepare a piece by myself, I am thinking of it as a complete and self-contained work. When I prepare a concerto, however, I'm not just thinking about the guitar part but rather the entire score. The same is true when I play with the quartet. So, when I'm playing with a group, my body's playing my own part of the music, but my mind and my feeling are playing all the different parts at the same time.

Figure 10. The Romero Guitar Quartet in 2005, after the departure of Angel and the passing of Celedonio: Pepe (*top*), Celin (*center*), Celino (*left*), Lito (*right*).

The rewarding thing about playing chamber music is that it gives me the feeling that I am a great violinist, a great cellist, a great singer, a great pianist. And because I feel all of the music inside my body, it changes the perception of what my body is, i.e., not a physical body contained within my skin but rather a spiritual body that has no

THE SOLOIST AND THE QUARTET MEMBER 77

limits. And when I am playing and traveling with other people as a group, I become the group. Anything that happens to a companion happens to me personally.

***

Q. You have spent most of your life touring. Does it have a special appeal?

A. I actually do not like touring. When I was young, I was fascinated with traveling to new places, but that lasted a very short time. Since then, I haven't really enjoyed traveling, in and out of hotels and airports, dealing with flights that are late. It's all a hassle. I do it because it's a necessary part of playing concerts all over the world. But if it were up to me, I would charge for the traveling and give the concerts for free. Because traveling is the difficult part.

***

Q. So that's the difficult part. You get tired of hotels and airports.

A. Yes, very tired, especially in recent years. Carissa now handles my travel arrangements, and she's very careful to provide me with a cushion of time to get over jetlag before I have to perform. Before, when Columbia Artists was arranging my travel, it was insane. Once, I arrived in London on the same day that I was to give an evening performance of the *Concierto para una fiesta*. I can't and won't do that anymore.

And I remember another anecdote connected with London. There was a Rodrigo festival, with Raymond Calcraft conducting. Once again, I arrived the same day as the evening performance, which was preceded by a rehearsal! Anyway, I got to the hotel only to find out that my room was not ready. So I said, "In that case, I'm going to the restroom to put on my pajamas, and I will take a nap on the sofa in the hall. I have a rehearsal and a concert tonight, and I have to rest." Now, this wasn't just any old hotel. This was the Hilton in London, the one that was later bombed. So, I donned my pajamas and lay down on the sofa. Soon the hotel clerk came over to tell me that my room was ready. They wanted me out of there! So that's what you do. You rest whenever and wherever you can.

***

Q. Where are some of the favorite places you have performed?

A. Well, definitely one of my absolute favorite concert halls is the Palau de la Música Catalana in Barcelona. It's just a gorgeous work of art. And I was so taken by it. The first time that I played there was the celebration of the fiftieth anniversary of the premiere of the *Concierto de Aranjuez* in that historic hall in 1940, with Regino Sainz de la Maza as soloist. This was in 1990, and though I had performed in Barcelona before, I had never appeared at the Palau. I remember the tremendous impression that place made on me, the feeling and mood. It was a very emotional experience for me, especially as I reflected on the significance of the occasion. But it was during the rehearsal that I heard the way the guitar sounded in there. The acoustics of that space bring out all the colors and emotions of the guitar. The guitar is among the most emotionally sympathetic of instruments. It can cry, it can love, it can speak, it can sing, and it can dance.

I fondly recall a trip to Turkey, to perform in the Roman amphitheater at Ephesus. It is such a historic place, and as we did the soundcheck in the open air, I noticed that the acoustics were just amazing. They were perfect for the guitar. I fell in love with that ancient amphitheater. It really impressed me how those people could create such an incredible sound space. I also performed in Greece, where there are similar venues, of course.

***

Q. Were these solo or concerto concerts, or both?

A. I played both solos and concertos. When I played in Ephesus, my first concert was solo, and shortly thereafter, I appeared with an orchestra playing concertos. But going much further back, to one of our earliest appearances in the U.S., I recall the quartet's concert at Boston's Jordan Hall in 1961, which has great acoustics for the guitar, as does New York's Carnegie Hall. Again, the clarity of the sound in such a big place is remarkable. The sound doesn't seem to decay; instead, the soundwaves seem to keep multiplying themselves, so that the people in the back can hear as well as those in the front. The sound fills the entire space. Among modern concert halls, I'm very fond of Meyerson Hall in Dallas.

THE SOLOIST AND THE QUARTET MEMBER   79

And then some of my favorite halls in Germany are in Hamburg and Munich. They are spaces that have a feeling of being sacred, because by the nature of the acoustics of the place, you feel like you're in a protected zone. When I play and hear the way the sound comes back to me, it makes me feel warm, it makes me feel like everything is going to be absolutely fine, as I'm inside this safe space where the music is supposed to happen.

***

Q. So, in a sense, just as the body of the guitar amplifies the sounds you make, the hall becomes an extension of the guitar.

A. Yes, because the guitar actually becomes your own body when you play. My perception of my body is not of internal organs, muscles, and bones contained within the skin of my body but rather within the skin of the sound. And the skin of the sound is the walls of the concert hall. One of the things for which I am very grateful in my career is that I've had the chance to play in many of the great temples of music. I think of them as temples of music because of their architecture and the way that the sound vibrates within them, the way that each note can have a wonderful life. There are places that just seem magical, completely loving to the actual sound. And I have been able to enjoy performing in the great halls for a long time; indeed, I have spent most of my life doing this. As for touring itself, getting from one venue to the next, I don't remember much. One airport runs together with another. But the great halls stand out in my memory.

***

Q. Are there any places you haven't yet performed but would like to?

A. Absolutely. I haven't performed in India or in Africa. There are still some countries in Latin America and East Asia where I have not yet played. I would like to play at least once in each of the countries that I have not yet performed in. Of course, that may prove to be impossible.

***

Q. Is it because they're not interested in classical guitar, because there's no audience for classical guitar?

A. No, I don't think so, though I can't say for sure. I have played many concerts in places where they had never heard the guitar before. I don't think that that's the problem. I think it has more to do with the objectives of managers, concert producers, and concert promoters. They develop a particular relationship, and so you keep going back many times to the same place.

***

Q. So, what are the special challenges of touring? You've already touched on this a little bit, but I'm wondering what you find especially challenging.

A. Being away from my family for such long periods of time, especially from my growing children. It was hard to give that up, to see their sad faces when I left. I always missed them, and a big part of my heart remained with them. When I go to bed at night in a hotel room, I still think back to when my children were little and at home. And that longing, that emptiness was always very present in me and the hardest thing to bear. But I used to console myself by thinking that when I get back, I will be with them twenty-four hours a day. I didn't retreat into a practice studio at home when my children were growing up. Now, of course, they are grown, so I can go upstairs to what used to be my father's studio. I have claimed it as my own, and I can spend hours there practicing in isolation. But when my children were little, I used to practice with them playing all around me, even climbing on top of me! So, I tried to make up for lost time by spending my whole day with them, regardless of whatever else I had to do. And the years that my four children were growing up were the most productive years of my professional life, in terms of the sheer volume of things I produced. Precisely because I was making the most of the time when they were growing up, I was also making at least three recordings every year: one concerto recording, one recording with the quartet or with a chamber ensemble, and one solo recording. And a lot of it was new repertoire.

So, I was going on long tours with the quartet as well as giving many concerts by myself. And when I came home, I had to put in the long hours to select and then learn new repertoire. It's a painstaking process of selection. I had to comb through a lot of music to make the right choices. "I'm going to do this piece. I'm not going to do this one yet, maybe next year." And I did all of that surrounded by them running around, shouting, and even jumping on top of me. I cherish the memory of those wonderful, wonderful times, which presented such an incredible contrast to the loneliness I felt for them when I was gone.

**

Q. In other words, you were able to turn that challenge to your advantage.

A. Yes, and that's how I consoled myself. I thought, "Well, a doctor also has to go to work in the morning. And by the time he comes back, his kids are almost ready to go to bed." So, every working father and mother has to give up a chunk of time, devoting it to those little things that they love so much.

**

Q. But in addition to all those challenges, there are actual dangers in touring. We've talked at other times about car accidents and such, but still, you're not afraid.

A. Yes, of course, though none of the dangers ever play a great part in my thinking. If I cannot do anything about something, then I don't worry. I have always known that my time will come, and when it does, it will be the right time for me. Therefore, I am never afraid of touring. I used to go out for walks in dangerous downtown areas and not think much about it. And yet, I would recommend that other young artists be a little more cautious than I was. I had my guardian angels working overtime.

For instance, during one such evening stroll in Manhattan, I got mugged. I was practicing for a concert, and it was late. I was still on California time, so it seemed earlier to me than it was. I put the guitar away at about 1:30 a.m. or so and then decided to go out in search of some refreshment. I thought that some orange juice would taste good. So, I went across the street, and then, out of the shadows of a building, came some guy with a knife.

I was wearing a short-sleeve shirt and had on a pricey Rolex watch. That was really stupid. I had no business going out for orange juice at that time, and certainly not wearing a Rolex in New York. He asked me for my wallet, which I promptly gave him. Fortunately, it actually had some money in it, maybe $200. He took out the money, threw the wallet on the ground, and ran. My guardian angels saw to it that he didn't ask me for my watch, and he didn't beat me up, much less stab me. And he didn't abscond with my wallet, except for the $200. So, I felt that I had been protected.

But of course, if you want an example of someone who was absolutely fearless, look no further than Federico Moreno Torroba. I hate turbulence when I'm flying, as it makes me very uneasy and triggers a lot of prayers out of me. But he used to love turbulence. He once told me: "Pepe, it is like we are a kite, and turbulence means that there is wind to keep the kite in the air." But he wasn't just fearless in the face of turbulence. Once a couple of thieves broke into his apartment in Madrid while he was alone there, in the middle of the afternoon. They tied him to a chair, and he told them, "Tie me up in such a way that I can take my nap. Then you're welcome to take whatever you want." He did, and they did!

***

Q. You have encountered people in many different countries and cultures. Do you think that music is a universal language?

A. I think that music is the language of God and is absolutely universal. Music takes us to a place where we can find the best of ourselves. It is an inner journey. When we make or listen closely to music and allow it to penetrate deeply into our own being, it takes us to that fundamental place where we are all good. It eliminates the bad in life. We are so constantly bombarded by the evil of man: the lust for power, for aggression and conquest, in order to take that which belongs to others. And even as we write this book, we are living in a very turbulent time, one in which many people are suffering. But music is the voice of God, the healer. Music awakens us to the truth, which is that we are all connected. When one person suffers, we all suffer. And when we hear music, we are suspended by that mysterious phenomenon which is sound. It connects us to each other, in the past and the present. Its peace and beauty produce in us a conscious realization of the now. And we all connect to that now, with the awareness of yesterday and tomorrow, as we vibrate in sympathy with the music. That same vibration is for me the voice of God, of hope, forgiveness, and truth. And the truth is that the material things that we so covet while in this mortal body are insignificant in comparison to our real selves, our immortal bodies. And music is the voice of our immortality coming to save us from the delusion that we are merely mortal beings, busily accumulating things.

7

MANAGERS

Q. Managers are crucial players in any professional musician's career, and they have played a central role in the history of the Romeros. Share the managerial aspect of that history with us.

A. The first manager I met was a neighbor in Seville, even before he was a manager: Jesús Antonio Pulpón, who lived in the apartment beneath ours. We met under rather comical circumstances. When I was 11 or 12 years old, one day my father said, "I'm going to give you an incredible present!" And he introduced me to Paco Ávila, who became my flamenco teacher. We met every single day from that time until our family left for the U.S. in 1957. He would come over and bring his grandfather with him, who was in his 70s, and I would teach him classical guitar. I thought that it was amazing how he could play at such an old age, but look at me now! Paco also used to bring his girlfriend, who was a flamenco dancer, and he would teach me how to accompany her even as he would teach her how to dance to the sounds of a guitar. We usually did this in the evening, and on one occasion, her *zapateado* was so vigorous that it prompted our downstairs neighbor to pay us a visit and complain that his ceiling lamp had fallen off! That was Antonio, who went on to become the most famous flamenco manager in Seville. He managed every great flamenco artist, but he never had anything to do with us, and we never had a manager while we were in Spain.

We came to the U.S. with the assistance of Santa Barbara resident and Hispanophile Farrington Stoddard, who dreamed of managing our careers here. He arranged my father's debut recital at the Lobero Theatre in Santa Barbara in June of 1958. But he was employed as a sailor, maybe by the U.S. government, and suddenly had to go back to sea, so that was the end of him as a manager. Then we became our own managers and presented ourselves in 1961 at the Wilshire

MANAGERS

Ebell Theater in Los Angeles, where we moved to in 1958. Celin had gone into the army reserves and did his basic training at Ft. Ord in Monterey. It was there that he met a fellow soldier named James Lucas, whose ambition was to become a concert manager. And he wanted to manage both Celin and bass-baritone McHenry Boatwright, a great singer who became world famous, particularly in the role of Boris Godunov. His career and ours were launched by Lucas, who was the son of a wealthy Yugoslavian immigrant who had developed a new method of soldering metal. He became very rich and paid for Jim's relocation to New York, where he could start his own agency. His office was in a Manhattan penthouse in Central Park. Celin introduced Jim to the rest of the family with the purpose of creating the Romero Guitar Quartet. That had never been our intention before, but after he heard us play together, it seemed like a very novel and marketable "commodity."

Jim loved music and had money, but he didn't really know how to represent artists; frankly, I don't know how he acquired that knowledge. But in our case, he decided on booking an introductory tour that took us from San Francisco's Masonic Temple to Chicago's Orchestra Hall, Boston's Jordan Hall, and New York's Town Hall. He calculated that we would make a big splash in each locale, so he booked us into the fanciest hotels, had us met at the airport by a limo, hired a publicist to promote not only the concert but also our arrival, and he arranged TV appearances for us. In other words, we got the celebrity treatment, just like the Beatles. They were clearly his models in launching a Spanish "Fab Four"! We would stay for two weeks or longer at this or that fancy hotel, doing engagements on TV and the local news, and it created quite a sensation.

In promoting that first tour of four big cities during the 1961–62 concert season, Jim spent almost $200,000, which in today's money would be millions. But it paid off, and the reviews were amazing. Boston's main critic said that it was the best concert he had seen in three decades. Jim's innate ability to know how to build a concert career was almost magical, insofar as he was only in his early twenties and had never done it before or seen anyone else do it. When we played in New York, he got the idea that we needed to approach a record company, so we got dressed up and rode in a limo to Mercury Records, where his intuition had led him. The day after we gave our Town Hall concert, the reviews were phenomenal, so it was more than likely that Mercury would have heard *of* us. Now they actually needed to *hear* us. As we sat in the waiting room at Mercury, Jim sent a message to Wilma Cozart Fine, producer of the Mercury Living Presence series, and the legendary classical music producer Harold Lawrence. He is remembered as a pioneer in creating a way of recording that has influenced the way that Philips, Decca, and Deutsche Grammophon would record in the future. The message stated that the Royal Family of the Guitar was here and they wanted to record for Mercury. She came out with her assistant,

Figure 11. The original Romero Quartet, in 1963: Angel (*above*), Celedonio (*center*), Celin (*left*), Pepe (*right*).

and we played right then and there, landing a contract on the spot. All of this was engineered by Jim Lucas and his army buddy, Celin.

Jim got to work booking a tour of twenty-one concerts, but before that became a reality, his father died, and he had to go back to California to run the family business with his brother. So, upon Jim's departure, we needed a new manager, and there were two options: Sol Hurok and Columbia Artists. The reviews in the *New York Times* and *Post* were raving about the Romeros, and it was the *Times* review that called us the Royal Family of the Guitar, a name that would follow us through our careers. So, we soon got a letter from Sol Hurok offering to sign us. Columbia also expressed interest, and it was a tough choice. But one of Jim's secretaries, Ann Carson, had gotten a job as secretary to Herbert Fox at Columbia, and because we were familiar with her and wanted to maintain that relationship, we signed up with Columbia, specifically the Fox & Wilford division. Herb was the senior partner and had brought in Ronald Wilford to create that division. We could not have been in better hands.

Jim felt that Columbia was the best choice not only because Ann was there but also because Hurok already had Andrés Segovia and had just signed Julian Bream, whereas Columbia didn't have any guitarists. So, they would be more focused on us, and we would get more work. We definitely had an incredibly devoted manager in the person of Herbert Fox, who was a larger-than-life figure. He had been a football player in college, a big guy, very articulate, could deliver eloquent speeches, and was the kind of person who could sell anyone anything. He was an old-style manager, no computers, no texting, just the phone, and he would contact universities, orchestras, and other organizations in the process not just of booking concerts but also of managing our careers. It was Herb who brought Neville Marriner and me together.

During our partnership with Columbia Artists, Herb collaborated with several managers in New York, and foremost among them were Frederick Christian (Chris) Schang, Audrey Hartmann, Carl Dahlgren, and Steven Gates. They played a very important role in the development of our careers.

Herb was a brilliant man, but he was having marital problems at home, and he fell in love with Ann Carson, who was very attractive. He asked his wife for a divorce, but she said that she would kill herself. He didn't believe her, he left, and she was found dead days later. That generated such a scandal that it became impossible for him to stay in New York. The company could not get rid of him because he owned more stock in Columbia than anyone else, so they decided to create a Columbia Artists on the West Coast, which he would run and be head of. His junior partner, Wilford, went on to become president of Columbia Artists. They had been the best of friends, but now that relationship was finished. Wilford became self-righteous and condemned Fox's actions.

Anyway, Herb married Ann Carson, and they moved to California, where they bought a beautiful apartment overlooking Los Angeles. Herb made a wonderful success of Columbia's West Coast office, as it became more about big touring companies and less about soloists, which is the sort of thing you would imagine in Los Angeles. But he did continue to manage us as a quartet. My father stepped back from having a solo career, and Celin was more focused on the quartet than on being a soloist. He also gave concerts with his wife, Laurie, a gifted singer. So, with the blessing and guidance of Herb, I accepted an offer to be represented by Harold Shaw as a soloist. Shaw was the successor of Sol Hurok, and he put me under the direction of Steven Gates. I had met him in New York because he was then working for Philips Records before becoming a top manager for Shaw. I was with Shaw for only four or five years, when Gates told me that he was considering leaving Shaw.

At that time, I was already missing the personal connection and creative collaboration that I had had with Herb. So, when Herb came to a concert of mine at Lincoln Center Philharmonic Hall, now Avery Fisher Hall, we had dinner and decided to get together again. When I think back over my career, what was really important were the relationships, projects, planning, and discussions that I had with the people involved, more than whether I was playing in New York City or Paris, Texas. I had missed my relationship with Herb and his involvement in my career. Knowing that Gates was going to leave Shaw sealed the deal, and I went back to Herb.

However, by this time, his personal life had become something of a fiasco, because I believe that he himself had never achieved peace about the suicide. He had two daughters with his first wife, and they never blamed him. His first wife was a heavy drinker, and that was the cause of the breakup. But eventually Herb himself started drinking very heavily, and he got an ultimatum from headquarters that if he didn't stop drinking, he had to quit. It was about that time that

Figure 12. Herb Fox (*left*), Mamá, and Pepe when the Romeros received the 1991 Martell Prize.

we were moved to partners of his in New York, Audrey Hartmann and Chris Schang, who was the son of one of the original founders of Columbia and a great manager. Audrey and Chris were a fantastic team, and they also had a secret romantic relationship. So many things in business have to do with romantic involvement!

While both the quartet and I were with Audrey and Chris, I came to realize that as much as I enjoyed working with Shaw and Gates, I didn't like having one manager for myself and another for the quartet. I've never felt that I'm two people, two artists. I always feel that from the core of being a Romero to the end thing of being Pepe Romero, it's all one identity. It is what has given me the strength to endure the heavy work and isolating times of touring. There is so much solitude involved in a successful concert career. But there's a difference between being alone and being lonely. It is from that core of where I come from and who I am that I have learned how to be alone without being lonely. But I couldn't do that with two managers. I wanted one manager who felt the same way I did, who understood my need to be both a member of the quartet and a soloist devoted to that repertoire. I am one person who is serving the guitar in all the facets that I love. I find the solo repertoire to be deeply spiritual and very uplifting, and I want to interpret it to the best of my ability and to the last bit of strength in my body. But I also want to experience, to serve, to produce the sound of the "24-string guitar," which is so rich, so unique.

So, in a very real sense, I feel that I play two guitars, one with six strings and the other with twenty-four. In order to maintain that posture, I needed to work with a manager who understood that I didn't want to separate the two. And I wouldn't let managers influence me to the contrary. Once I was taken by Larry Tucker to a coffee shop in New York on the corner of 57th Street and 7th Avenue. His purpose was to talk me into quitting the quartet. He said, "You should be the absolute top as a soloist. In this business, you cannot be both that and in the quartet." Chris Young had just died of a brain tumor while on a trip to Moscow, so now there was a fight over whether Audrey would head her own division. Herb had by this time sobered up, regained his strength, was back in charge on the West Coast, and we were with him. I played a solo recital in New York, and it was the following morning that Larry took me out for breakfast at the coffee shop to inform me that I had to quit the quartet. "You cannot be an ensemble player and the soloist. The public will not accept it. Think of the Budapest Quartet. They have wonderful chamber players but they don't have a Heifetz. You cannot be Heifetz and concertmaster of the Budapest Quartet." To which I responded, "You know what, Larry, I don't care if the public accepts it or not, whether or not it's possible. I am what I am, and I am Heifetz and I am a member of the Budapest Quartet. I am going to go as far as I can with both without separating one from the other." Larry said, "I'm very sorry that you feel like that, but I'm deeply touched that you do, and I wish you all the best." A few years later, Tim Fox (not related to Herb) became president of Columbia Artists, until it dissolved a couple of years ago. He remains my manager and the quartet's manager. But our history with managers has had many twists and turns.

I gave my first university-level masterclass in the U.S. at Southern Methodist University in Dallas, Texas. It was organized by a student of mine and of my father, Darryl Saffer, who founded both the guitar department at SMU and the Dallas Classic Guitar Society. He also created Fret and Strings, a major guitar store in Dallas. He sold high-end classical guitars, some of them built by a local maker

MANAGERS 91

named David Caron, who went on to become a world-famous violin and cello maker as well. And Frets and Strings was a popular place for guitarists to hang out. So, Darryl was one of the earliest guitar entrepreneurs. He was a wonderful musician, teacher, and performer, and he did a lot for the guitar in Texas in general and Dallas in particular. He introduced me to a gorgeous Italian girl, Susan Carter, whose mother's maiden name was Lamborghini. She was all of 19 years old, and we started having a passionate but short-lived romance, one with an interesting ending. She actually already had a boyfriend, Terry Gaschen, who was a guitar student, but my understanding of their relationship was that it was complicated and perhaps nearly over.

The next thing I know, we are playing in Richmond, Texas, and I get a note saying that a Mrs. Gaschen is in the audience and would love to come backstage and see me. I didn't realize that Terry and Susan had gotten married and that she was now Mrs. Gaschen. They founded the Guitar Gallery in Houston, which was modeled after Frets and Strings, and it became a center for classical guitar, one known all over the state. It was among the most popular dealers of guitars by luthiers such as Hauser, Rodríguez, and Ramírez. And it was the headquarters for the Houston Guitar Society, which promoted concerts by classical guitarists in Houston.

And it was at the Guitar Gallery that I would eventually meet one of Terry's students, a young woman named Carissa. I will have more to say about her later. Susan became a promoter of our concerts, and she was the first to bring Leo Brouwer, Abel Carlevaro, Manuel Barrueco, and Sergio Abreu to Houston. Every year I would go to give master classes. A warm friendship grew between all of us; however, then I received a call saying that they were getting a divorce. Susan wanted to move to Los Angeles and wondered where she might find a job. I called Herb Fox, and after an interview, she became Herb's secretary. She climbed the ladder to become his associate and then a vice president of Columbia Artists. After Herb retired, she took over as manager of the quartet and my solo career. To this very day, she remains one of my closest friends.

We recall that Larry Tucker at Columbia tried to talk me into quitting the quartet, and I gave him the same answer I had always given before. "I don't care how famous I am as a soloist or quartet member. My strength comes from being everything that I am. You cannot tell me that if I had been born somewhere else, I would stand a better chance of being famous. I don't want to change anything. I am so happy that I have been able to do as much as I have as a solo artist and as a quartet member, as a concerto soloist and as a teacher." It has all been an incredible journey, and I wouldn't give up any of it. I never did anything without awareness of the other aspects of my musical life. When I play in the quartet, I give the same energy and drive to my part as I do to Bach's Chaconne or Rodrigo's *Concierto de Aranjuez*.

Herb died in 2000 and was survived by his third wife, Jean. He and Ann had divorced, and then he met this wonderful woman who helped him deal with the drinking problem he had developed after his first wife's suicide. She was a miracle worker in his life, and now he was stronger than ever. He was able to understand himself, forgive the tragedy, and to be at peace. Herb, Jean, and I traveled by car throughout Spain and visited many cities. He was a very romantic person. We went to Córdoba, where I bought the guitar I named Naranjita (Little Orange). And Herb says, "I want to hear you play *Recuerdos* on Naranjita in the Alhambra." So, we went there, and I started played Tárrega's classic work when all of a sudden two dogs appeared and started humping, followed by more dogs who did the same. So, they had a canine orgy while I played *Recuerdos*. It was bizarre, like something out of a surrealist movie. His romantic notion wound up in group sex. After Herb died, we were managed by Susan, who adopted her mother's maiden name, Lamborghini; hence, Susan Carter, then Gaschen, and finally Lamborghini.

***

Q. But you have worked with several other managers around the world, no?

A. Yes, indeed. In 1968, communication started between Herb Fox and Hans Schlote from Konzertdirektion Schlote. Hans was not only the first manager to present David Oistrakh in Germany but also to organize the first appearance of Arthur Rubinstein before German concert audiences. After the war, Rubinstein refused to play in Germany, but he had a soft spot in his heart for his piano professor, who was German, and he loved the great German composers. But he did not want to play in Germany, so Schlote organized a concert for him just outside of Germany, where the Germans could

MANAGERS 93

go to hear him. He was always doing new things, and to bring the Romeros for the first time to Europe was something that interested him very much. He and Herb Fox went to work on the project, and in January 1970, we made our first European tour as a quartet.

However, before starting the tour, we returned to Lisbon, where we had left Europe for the U.S. in 1957. We wanted to spend a few days there to visit my aunt Loli. We also saw my grandfather and cousins, who were all grown up by this time. It was a very moving reunion. While in Lisbon, the wonderful composer Father Francisco de Madina paid us a surprise visit, and he then joined us for the tour, the first concert of which was in London, where we now headed. We were met in London by a young man only 19–20 years old, who promptly introduced himself as Mr. Schlote. And we thought, "You're Mr. Schlote, so young?" In fact, it was his son, Joachim Schlote, and we were his first "job" for his father's agency. He served as our tour manager, and that tour took us to London, Oslo, Frankfurt, Munich, Hamburg, Stuttgart, and Madrid. Outstanding in my memory is also a night that we spent in Alfred Brendel's apartment in Vienna with my friends Gabor and Alice Rejto, who played a Beethoven sonata for cello and piano while we were there. It was all so wonderful! We kept going back to Europe every two years, and soon Joachim started working as a manager himself.

It was not long after that first tour that Hans decided that he wanted to start presenting solo concerts, and he believed that I could have a parallel career as a soloist and as a member of the quartet. So, I ended up touring Europe one year as a solo artist and the next year with the quartet, alternating in that way. That went on for many years, and Joachim and I assisted in launching the American Sinfonietta, an impressive orchestra created by Michael Palmer. I toured with them every year for about fifteen years, performing each of the Rodrigo concertos. The first one we did together was the *Concierto para una fiesta* (1983). The repertoire we have performed together includes concertos mentioned elsewhere in these pages, including those by Giuliani and Torroba, the premiere of Villa-Lobos's *Introduçaõ aos Chôros*, Zearott's *Concerto Mariachi*, my father's *El cortijo de Don Sancho*, and Leisner's *Wayfaring Guitar Concerto*. Our collaboration occupies a deep place in my heart.

Joachim continued to be our manager, and he was always concerned not only with booking concerts, like most managers these days, but also with developing useful connections. He got me

Figure 13. Michael Palmer conducts the American Sinfonietta with Pepe as soloist, 1991.

involved with the Mozart Festival in Salzburg, where I was teaching at the Mozarteum and now playing concerts in and around Salzburg for the Festival. He was also the one to organize my collaboration with the Schleswig-Holstein Music Festival.

Joachim Schlote was really a wonderful manager, very active and creative. After many years, though, his agency became more and more focused on ballets and operas and less on soloists, so the quartet and I decided to move to Hans Werner Funke's Konzertdirektion Goette, thinking that that was a better place for us. To this day, that is the management we have for Germany and most of Europe, except for Spain. We always had a separate manager there, having signed early on with Ricardo de Quesada and Conciertos Daniel. He was the one who worked with Schlote to present the 1970 European premiere of Rodrigo's *Concierto madrigal*. This took place at the Teatro Real in Madrid, and from that moment on, he became my personal manager as a soloist and of the quartet. He was the son of Ernesto de Quesada, who made the careers of, among several others, Segovia and Rubinstein. He was a brilliant person and hatched the idea that each little town in Spain could have a concert series; of course, in order to have places where Rubinstein could play, they needed not only a concert series but also a piano. So, he bought many concert pianos and placed them strategically all over Spain and even in South America. The idea worked incredibly well.

He was a wonderful manager for me personally, and I did many concerts with him until Sonsoles González de Vega became his partner and then my manager in Spain, before her retirement. During that time with Ricardo, I also did a lot of work with Humberto Orán, who was also the manager of Rafael Frühbeck de Burgos. Angel and I gave the world premiere of Rodrigo's *Concierto madrigal* at the Hollywood Bowl in 1970 with Rafael, but I didn't play with him again until the Torroba centenary concert in 1991, during which I accompanied Victoria de los Ángeles and played Torroba's *Diálogos*. It was a fantastic occasion, and from that moment on, the musical relationship between Rafael and myself grew ever deeper, as he and I performed concertos with major orchestras throughout the world. The quartet recorded the *Concierto de Cienfuegos* by Lorenzo Palomo (1938–2024) with him, and I did Lorenzo's *Nocturnos de Andalucía*.

It was a long and fruitful collaboration, and insofar as Humberto was his manager, I also got to work quite a bit with him. But my principal managers remained Sonsoles and Ricardo. Just as I feel that a guitarist and a guitar maker are twin souls working on the same thing, I think that a manager and an artist need to have a particular bond, whereby they are working on a common project, towards a common goal, i.e., promoting the guitar and beautiful music. For that, there has to be a personal connection. And that I really had with Ricardo and later with Sonsoles. Even to this day, long after her retirement, she and her husband, Antonio, Carissa, and I are like brothers and sisters, and they are among the most beloved friends that I have in the world.

After Sonsoles retired, I worked with Humberto, but that coincided with the professional ascent of my guitar student and dear friend Vicente Coves. He is a phenomenal virtuoso but began to shift his focus from playing concerts to organizing them, in particular to creating and managing the International Guitar Festival in Granada and the International European Guitar Foundation. So, as I myself became more and more involved with the Granada Festival, it finally happened that all my work in Spain is now managed by Vicente Coves.

My career has extended to South America, and that was handled by Enrique de Quesada, who had studied with his uncle Ricardo. He revived the Conciertos Daniel that his grandpa started, and most of the concerts I've given in Latin America have been with him as my manager. I have an amusing story to tell about an experience in Ecuador while working for Quesada there. It shows that managers cannot always manage every aspect of a concert!

I was to play in Cuenca with the Orchestra of Guayaquil, and though the conductor was a crazy Russian wild man, the rehearsal

Figure 14. Pepe performs with Vicente Coves at Granada's Auditorio Manuel de Falla, 2003.

MANAGERS

went wonderfully well. That was a magical time in Cuenca, and Carissa and I stayed up in the hills in a gorgeous house with Enrique de Quesada. the grandnephew of Ernesto. I had evening concerts on Friday and Sunday but was free all day on Saturday. The Friday night concert went just fine, and on Saturday we went sightseeing, because Cuenca is a gorgeous colonial city. But then Sunday morning rolled around, and I got an urgent call from Enrique telling me that there was a problem with the orchestra. Apparently, some members wanted to be paid entirely in cash. They had a contract stipulating that they would get half their pay in advance of the concert and the other half by bank transfer within a few days after the concerts were done. But some of them decided they wanted that other half in cash as well. Enrique called me that afternoon to report that everything was settled, so I proceeded to do my usual routine: lunch, siesta, coffee, bath, and perform. But when we arrived at the hall, something looked weird. There was only one bass player, who was practicing on stage.

I like to arrive an hour before a concert and continue my routine. I go to the dressing room to warm up, running scales and then playing some music unrelated to what I'm going to perform. I find that if I practice what I'm going to play, then it gets tight. When I'm performing, I prefer not to think about anything, just to listen and enjoy the performance. I have a sort of out-of-the-body experience whereby I observe myself playing. One has to learn to surrender in that way. The result is not what matters; rather, it is what you are feeling, it is the process by which you give from your heart to the audience when you are playing. You can experience the music flowing through you, not being made *by* you but rather flowing *through* you. Only then can you truly feel the inspiration of the moment, that the moment is special and can't be repeated. It can't be something that you have manufactured ahead of time. For that reason, I like to play unrelated things, so that I can get into this sort of dream state.

So, I'm in the dressing room practicing, and at 7:30 p.m., a half hour before the concert, there's a knock on the door. It's the conductor informing me that "Maestro, I am so sorry for the confusion. It was just a few members of the orchestra who wanted to be paid in cash. See you in a few minutes on stage, good luck." Then, at 7:55, Enrique pops in with some bad news: "Pepe, have you heard what has happened?" "No, what has happened?" "The whole orchestra has walked out. Can you play a recital instead." "Well, yes, just give

Figure 15. Pepe signing autographs with Yoon Kwan Park (*rear, with child*), his first manager in Korea, 1985.

me five minutes so that I can get my head into the pieces I'm going to play." I assumed that the audience had been informed of the situation, but at 8:05 I walked out on stage and immediately noticed that it was still set up for the orchestra. Nothing had been moved. Remaining calm, I sat on the chair where I was going to have played the *Aranjuez* and started performing solos instead, announcing the titles of the pieces as I played them.

Now, this was a beautiful theater, like so many in Latin America, and it was completely sold out. But there were people standing guard at the doors to keep any orchestra or union members from coming in. I assumed that the audience knew the orchestra was not going to appear and that I would be giving a solo recital instead. I played for two hours, and no one said anything to the audience, which seemed quite content and acted as if this was completely normal.

The next day was Carissa's birthday, and I suggested to her that we just stay in the house and have a private birthday party. She liked the idea, though I suggested that she get all dressed up just the same. She was a bit mystified by the request but soon understood why I made it. I had secretly arranged for a whole group of musicians to

MANAGERS 99

come in at night carrying torches and singing for her. She got an old-fashioned serenade with gorgeous songs, and many friends and acquaintances were there to celebrate. Surprise!

Of course, we have performed a lot in Asia. David Lee of South Korea was a wonderful manager, and he became president of the Asian Managers Association. He was brilliant and did business in both Korea and China. I met him through Angel, as he was Angel's manager, and he and I became really good friends. He came to San Diego to meet with the family and then became manager of the Romeros, representing both me and the quartet. Angel invited me to be his soloist doing Papá's *Concierto de Málaga*, which he conducted in Korea, Japan, and China. Then Angel played the *Aranjuez*, conducted by the orchestra's regular director. David continued to represent me for the rest of his life, which was not long. He had a few years left and then died of cancer. He had a secretary, Christina Ma, with whom he was very much in love. After his death, she inherited his management in China, and his nephew took over the business in Korea. She is now my Asian manager and one of Carissa's and my best friends. She visited us at our home in Granada, and we had a wonderful time.

PART IV

REPERTOIRE

8

PREMIERES

Q. Do you have a rough idea how many works you have premiered?

A. The ones that come immediately to mind include *Diálogos* (written for Andrés Segovia), *Concierto ibérico*, *Tonada concertante* (written for Celedonio Romero), and *Concierto en flamenco* by Federico Moreno Torroba; *Concierto andaluz, Concierto madrigal*, and *Concierto para una fiesta* by Joaquín Rodrigo; *Concierto flamenco* by Francisco de Madina (1907–72); *Introduçaõ aos Chôros* by Heitor Villa-Lobos (1887–1959); *Concerto Mariachi* by Michael Zearott (1937–2019); *Troubadour Music* by Morton Gould (1913–96); *Nocturnos de Andalucía* and *Concierto de Cienfuegos* (for guitar quartet) by Lorenzo Palomo; and three concertos by my father: *Concierto de Málaga, Fiesta andaluza*, and *El cortijo de Don Sancho*. It has been a great privilege for me to do so many premieres, including those with the quartet.

***

Q. What initiates the creation of a major new work? Does the composer contact you or do you request a work from the composer?

A. Both ways. Very recently, I premiered a wonderful concerto written by the gifted composer David Leisner (b. 1953), entitled *Wayfaring Guitar Concerto*. I've known David for years, but for most of that time, I only knew him as a guitarist and as a teacher. He teaches at the Manhattan School of Music and has invited me several times to teach master classes there. One day, my friend and collaborator Brian Hays was talking to me and said that he would like to commission a guitar concerto for me. The first one we tried to get was Leo Brouwer, but he was not feeling in the best of health, so he said he couldn't do it right away. Brian knew David Leisner and contacted him about how to go about commissioning a work. David gave him some names and was very helpful, but then at the end of it he said, "Of course, there is always me. I would be very happy to write it!" When I heard that, I asked him to send me some of his music, and I was blown away by how beautiful it is, what a fantastic composer David is. David writes in a modern idiom but with an endearing connection to the past, a bit like Schubert writing in a contemporary style. So, I was very happy to have David write a concerto for me. The work was inspired by a very famous American tune from the Appalachian region called "Wayfaring Stranger." The second movement concludes beautifully with his own version of the song. It is a marvelous composition. I really enjoyed doing the premiere of it, and I'm looking forward to playing it many times.

Then again, there were premieres of wonderful pieces, and now I don't even remember how they came about! Moreover, some of them I played once and never played again. Nonetheless, they're great pieces of music. One such work was a guitar concerto by the Armenian conductor and composer Loris Tjeknavorian (b. 1937). I had earlier performed another concerto with Loris conducting, and he told me about his own work, which had not yet been performed. It was dedicated to his son, Zareh, and thus named after him. It is based on ancient Armenian church music and very beautiful, though it was also a very complex work and therefore quite challenging. Anyway, I was really impressed and eventually premiered it at a concert in Lincoln, Nebraska.

One afternoon I was having lunch with the late Fede Torroba, the son of Federico Moreno Torroba, and he expressed a desire to see the score of the concerto. I gave it to him to examine and soon had an opportunity to appreciate yet again what a terrific musician he was and how well he knew his craft. I said, "Fede, it is so complex and has so many accidentals that I want you to proofread it to make sure I'm playing all the right notes." So Fede checked the piece while I played it, at tempo, and he was like a machine, like a computer, in the way that he processed both the score and my rendering of it. Very few people realize the amazing knowledge that Fede possessed. And that's one of the pieces that I wish I would have convinced Philips to record. I put as much work into preparing that concerto as I put into any of the others that Philips recorded. There have been quite a few key pieces like that: a lot of emotion, a lot of

Figure 16. Pepe consults with composer Loris Tjeknavorian about his guitar concerto, 1990.

love, and a lot of hard work, then that's it. Every new work that I have premiered represents a tremendous effort. For one thing, I am not a super-fast reader.

***

Q. Is that because of your dyslexia? You have said that you have a hard time reading the music, with the notes swimming on the page. How do you learn new music? You couldn't learn it by ear because nobody has yet played it.

A. Most of my work has been done under the burden of severe dyslexia. I look at a piece of music, and the staff dances around. One way to cope with it is to read very slowly, note by note. I could never read an entire musical phrase, like the way you read a group of words. I learn every piece note by note.

***

Q. Actually, you must have been a pretty good reader when you were little and your mom assigned you to read *Don Quixote*. How did you manage that?

A. I had a very strong will to read, and I didn't know that there was anything wrong with the way I saw words on a page. I thought that was the way that everybody saw them. Finally, in about 1983, I went to an eye doctor in San Diego whose specialty was dyslexia. And what he did was to check the light frequencies that I had a problem with. Then he had me put on a pair of peach-colored glasses to block that frequency. The dyslexia went away, and I could read! That changed my life. My daughter Tina and son Pepe also have dyslexia, and he gave them glasses that were some shade of purple. I have some of my music printed on peach-colored paper, and that also helps immensely. But I did a lot of work and a lot of learning on white paper, which even now is very disturbing to my eyes.

So, yes, every premiere or revival where I don't have any sort of memory of the piece and cannot learn it by ear, where I am reading the music for the first time, represents a huge amount of work for me. I like to go back to the written score, even if I have the music perfectly memorized, particularly when I think I really know it. Therefore, I don't agree to premiere a work unless I really like it, which is why I so much regret the fact that Philips refused to record Loris's concerto. But they didn't think that there was a market for it. After all, they are in the business of selling records. But their indifference wasn't confined to obscure composers.

I was asked by Neville Marriner to make my first recording with him. It was right after we had performed Giuliani's Guitar Concerto, Op. 30. And I really wanted Rodrigo's *Concierto madrigal* to go on the other side of the LP. But that was another instance where Philips thought that it would not sell. True, Rodrigo was famous, and people knew his name. But they lacked faith in the *Madrigal*. So, I put my foot down and made it clear that there would be no recording of the Giuliani if they did not include Rodrigo. Eventually Philips capitulated, and that recording proved to be very successful.

Moving on to another concerto premiere, I've always been a great lover of Mexican music, and it was both a pleasure and an honor to premiere the *Concerto Mariachi* by Michael Zearott. Like every other such work in my repertoire, this one had a unique genesis. My dear friend Michael Palmer was the conductor of the American Sinfonietta, and he and I gave hundreds of concerts together in Europe over a period of ten years. And he wanted to give the premiere of Zearott's *Concerto Mariachi*, a work that I requested and was privileged to premiere.

Michael Zearott was a real character, an incredible musician, and a fine conductor. Moreover, he was one of those cases where a great artist leaves whatever they can to the world, and then they're pretty much forgotten. Thus, the world never has a chance to enjoy their greatness during their lifetime. As a conductor, he was the Gold Medal winner of the Dimitri Mitropoulos International Conducting Competition, which resulted in a one-year appointment as music director of the Monte Carlo Symphony. But his renown was short-lived, because orchestras did not like how demanding he was of them. He had one big flaw: he expected people to play better than they could. And when you are a conductor, you cannot require somebody to be better than they are, to play faster or be more accurate than their technique allows. A successful conductor has to have the ability to know how far to push an orchestra without damaging their self-confidence. That was Rafael Frühbeck de Burgos's great strength. He enjoyed a long career, and every orchestra he conducted wanted him to be their music director. Michael used to push people beyond their limits. So, he was rejected and wound up teaching little kids, which was a wonderful opportunity for those children.

Figure 17. (*Left to right*) Miguel Barrón, Pepe, Mayita Barrón, and Michael Zearott, 1992.

PEPE ROMERO

***

Q. But the *Concerto Mariachi* was never recorded, was it?

A. Actually, the premiere was recorded, and it's a beautiful record-ing. I'm working right now with Michael Palmer to get permission to release that recording. The *Concerto Mariachi* is extraordinary in the way it merges mariachi music with Vivaldi. But if you think about it, the exuberant explosion of joy in mariachi music is exactly what we hear in Vivaldi as well. And it is the expression of the undy-ing joy felt by the Mexican people. Whether they're celebrating a wedding or mourning the loss of a loved one, the mariachis keep singing. And that's what this concerto is about, which is why it is one of the pieces I have enjoyed the most, because it combines two of my favorite kinds of music, Vivaldi and mariachi, as improbable as that combination may sound.

And while we're on the subject of Latin American music, my friends Richard Long and John King discovered a piece for guitar and big orchestra by Heitor Villa-Lobos that had never been played. It was located in the basement of the Paris publisher Max Eschig. When they informed me of it, I was immediately taken with the idea of premiering it, which I did. It is entitled *Introduçaõ aos Chôros* (Introduction to the Chôros, 1929 [the choro is a type of Brazilian popular music]), and I am working to make a recording that will include that as well as the *Concerto Mariachi*. In short, sometimes there's a pre-existing piece that wasn't written for you and that you didn't request but that you nevertheless have the opportunity to premiere.

***

Q. The outstanding example of a work written for someone else but that you had the privilege to premiere is the *Concierto madrigal* of Rodrigo, which was composed for Ida Presti and Alexandre Lagoya.

A. Yes, he wrote it for that great duo, but Ida Presti tragically died before they could premiere it, so that honor fell to me and Angel. We premiered it at the Hollywood Bowl in 1970 and subsequently recorded it. The *Madrigal* is a truly great work, but it is very difficult.

PREMIERES 109

Most often premieres result from you requesting a piece or a composer approaching you.

***

Q. What are some instances where you approached someone to compose a concerto for you?

A. I personally became very close to composer Francisco de Madina, who was also a Catholic priest. He was an extraordinary human being and musician, though being Basque, he had not previously been exposed to flamenco; however, by spending time with me and Rodrigo, he acquired a real appreciation of it. I would demonstrate flamenco on the guitar for him as well as play him recordings. He started getting into it, and then I said, "Why don't you write me a guitar concerto," though not suggesting that he write a flamenco-inspired work. I just wanted him to write a solo concerto for me. But he responded without hesitation, "I'm going to write a flamenco concerto." It's a lovely work, and the second movement is especially beautiful. To be sure, though, his *Concierto flamenco* is less about flamenco itself than it is about what Madina felt when he listened to flamenco. So, you will not hear a *soleares* or *bulerías* but rather the spirit of flamenco as it touched Madina.

Shortly after he finished it, I was able to secure a date for the premiere with Robert LaMarchina conducting the Honolulu Symphony. Sadly, the premiere coincided with Madina suffering a stroke. I wanted to help him attend the premiere, but that would not be possible. He had established a residence for Basque priests in the Bronx, and it was named after Thomas à Kempis. As he was thought to be nearing the end of his life, his order preferred him to die on in his birthplace, in Oñati in the Basque Country, not indulging in what they feared was merely vanity by attending the premiere in Hawaii. As it turned out, he cried as he told me that he wanted "to die in the arms of my friends," meaning the arms of his family and fellow musicians, the Romeros. And that was the last exchange that we had. As I was in Hawaii preparing for the premiere, he passed away in Spain.

The second movement is so beautiful, and what I remember most about that performance was that I could hardly see because I was crying, as I already knew that he had died. And yet, I was very, very

Figure 18. Basque priests of the Residencia Kempis in 1969. Back row (*left to right*), Francisco de Madina, Celedonio, and Angelita Romero. Pepe is in the front row lighting a cigar.

lucky to be able to play it quite a few times, with the Los Angeles Philharmonic, the San Francisco Symphony, as well as the New York Philharmonic, with Andre Kostelanetz conducting. There is a rather poor recording of the world premiere, but there is no commercial recording of it. We cannot really blame Philips, because they've recorded more concertos than any other label. What I've been able to do with Philips is extraordinary. Still, I very much want to make a good recording of it.

***

Q. That's a very moving story. There have surely been other works written at your request, no?

A. Yes, and the concerto by Paul Chihara comes to mind. I met him at a party at Neville's house, which wasn't really his house but rather the place where he stayed when he was in Southern California to conduct the Los Angeles Chamber Orchestra. It was actually a

PREMIERES

cottage on the property of Dick Colburn, a very wealthy man who went on to establish the Colburn School of Music in downtown Los Angeles. That's where Neville and I would always go through scores together, to decide the repertoire that we were going to record, to decide on the next LP, or later, CD. And after every concert with the LACO, he had a party in the gardens next to his cottage, and that's where I met Paul Chihara. He is a wonderful man and musician. So, Neville commissioned a guitar concerto, to be premiered by the LACO and me. And it is gorgeous, just beautiful. Neville and I premiered it with the LACO at the old Ambassador Auditorium, and then I played it with other conductors. But then it went out of style, and I didn't play it anymore. But when Neville was getting on in years, he told me, "We need to record the Paul Chihara, because that's how we seal our friendship and our collaboration."

So, then we started looking for possible recording dates and an orchestra with which to make the recording, whether with the Los Angeles Chamber Orchestra or the Academy of St. Martin-in-the-Fields. Because we were both so busy, we could only find dates about two years in advance. And Neville said, "No, who knows what's going to happen? Let's just do it! I'll record the orchestra part in the next recording session, and then you record the guitar part." And that's how we made the recording on the Albany label in 2005, with Neville conducting the London Symphony Orchestra.

But I must say that I never had a more bizarre recording session than that one, because Neville said, "I remember exactly how Pepe played it," but in fact we hadn't played it for over two decades. Anyway, he recorded it, but the producer forgot to make a video. I wanted him to film Neville so that I could be watching him and match the guitar part with his conducting.

This is before recording engineers had perfected the techniques of editing recordings on a computer. So, I just went in and started playing, though I couldn't hear much more than just the introduction. I was wearing headphones, but there was no click track. It just had the orchestra playing. And there were these long, empty spaces where Neville was imagining what I would be doing, and then all of a sudden, the cello comes in. Still, it worked out nearly to perfection, despite the fact that Neville recorded in London and I recorded in Los Angeles. The ensemble is immaculate.

***

Q. And then there are the concertos written by David Chesky for you and Angel. They're really quite modern, quite different.

A. There is the Concerto for Guitar and Orchestra, written for Angel, and then the Concerto for Two Guitars and Orchestra, written for Angel and me. We have never premiered them in concert, only the 2019 recordings. Angel and I recorded our parts in Angel's studio at home, while David recorded the orchestral part. It was a collage collaboration. It is very hard to play because David was obsessed with Rodrigo's *Madrigal*, and he wanted to make this a sort of sequel to it, but in his own, very modernistic style. He was fascinated by fast scales.

***

Q. Do you think that composers make these works difficult in part because they know how good your technique is and they assume you want to be challenged?

A. I don't know if they do that on purpose or if that's just the way that they conceive the music.

I have a feeling that it has more to do with how they envision the work, though there are no doubt instances when they are writing for a specific person and have that performer's style and abilities in mind. Rodrigo's *Concierto para una fiesta*, composed for and premiered by me in 1983, is a case in point. When I was working it with him on it, I asked him, "Why did you make this so hard?" And he said, "Because I wrote it for you!" But he is the only composer who ever admitted that he made a work particularly hard for me.

***

Q. Are there any other premieres we should include?

A. Yes, I recall a very interesting world premiere in Puerto Rico. It was the *Concierto festivo* for guitar and string orchestra by composer and guitarist Ernesto Cordero (b. 1946). He wrote it for and dedicated it to me, and it reflects his fascination with the Giuliani concertos, despite the music itself having a Puerto Rican flavor. I should say that it is a very difficult concerto. Although the *Concierto de Aranjuez* has set the standard for technical difficulty, I actually think that guitarists have more difficulty playing the Giuliani

PREMIERES

concertos than they do playing the *Aranjuez*. And since Ernesto was inspired by the way that Guiliani wrote for the instrument, the guitar part is very challenging. I worked very hard to prepare it, because every time that I'm going to present a world premiere, I feel a great responsibility to do my absolute best. I want a happy birth for the newborn piece!

I later made a video recording in Zagreb with I Solisti di Zagreb, and that recording was nominated for a Latin Grammy in 2012; however, the 2009 premiere was nothing if not chaotic. It was written to celebrate the renovation of the theater of the University of Puerto Rico. It was done under the direction of Guillermo Figueroa, whom I knew very well. He's a fantastic violinist and from a prominent musical family in Puerto Rico. The Figueroas started the Casals Orchestra and are consummate musicians. Guillermo was the principal violinist of the Orpheus Chamber Orchestra, with which I played many concerts, including quite a few times in Carnegie Hall. We toured throughout Europe together, playing in Istanbul in every exotic place you can imagine. He was also conductor of the Puerto Rico Orchestra, as well as the Albuquerque Orchestra.

So, the premiere was to be the opening concert of the newly renovated 100-year-old theater. But the renovation wasn't quite finished, and there were still workers everywhere! The program included not only the premiere of the Cordero concerto but also a Mass by Mozart. June Anderson was the soprano, and just before the final rehearsal, she came to my dressing room and said, "Pepe, may I get ready and wait here? They just painted my dressing room, and I am highly allergic to the smell of new paint. I mustn't let it get into my throat." Of course I said yes, so we shared my dressing room during the final rehearsal, which took place in the morning of the same day as the evening concert. There was to be only one performance, and so many dignitaries and donors wanted to attend that it sold out well in advance. As a result, there was no room for students and their professors! That was clearly unacceptable, so we actually scheduled an extra concert the day before the premiere, which was reserved for students and faculty. The public concert the following day was still the official premiere, but we nonetheless treated this pre-premiere seriously and dressed in concert finery. There were TV crews there to film it, though the official premiere was to be both filmed and broadcast. And everything was going fine.

When it came time to perform the concert, I walked out on stage with Guillermo right behind me. We bowed to the audience and then took our places to begin. But as we started playing, a young man and woman came down the aisle, dancing as they approached the stage. This was not planned and came as quite a surprise. They were accompanied by two other couples, who were holding banners. The dancers positioned themselves at the foot of the stage and danced to the music. The two other couples came on stage with their banners, one next to me and the other next to Guillermo. The signs said, "No a la privatización." They were protesting the possibility that the concert hall might be privatized! Guillermo and I looked at one another and decided to continue the performance, even as they continued their protest. And we played it really well. Once we finished, Ernesto came on stage to take a bow as the public enthusiastically applauded his new work. The protesters were then escorted out of the building, and that was that. The next day was the official world premiere, but that would be yet another occasion on which things did not go as planned.

When it came time to leave the hotel for the concert hall, I went down to where a university car and driver were waiting to take us there. But as soon as we got in the car, the driver said, "Please excuse me, but traffic is very heavy right now, and I'm waiting for instructions when to start." So, we sat there for twenty minutes, which then became thirty and soon forty minutes. Waiting. Concert time was getting closer, and I was getting more and more anxious. I needed to arrive at the hall early enough to warm up. I couldn't just walk out on stage cold. This was getting ridiculous, and I was becoming very agitated. Finally, the manager of the orchestra called and said, "Maestro, don't worry, we'll try to delay the concert a little bit. The governor has been stuck in traffic and his arrival delayed. So please wait. Why don't you go up to your room instead of waiting in the car. I will personally call you when it's time to leave."

So, I returned to my hotel room, while Carissa was doing her best to pacify me. She said, "Baby, sit back and relax. I'll put something on TV for you." At this point, I was burning up, and before long it was past the time when the concert was to begin. So, she turned on the TV, and what do you suppose was being broadcast? The concert! Oh, God. I'm in the hotel room and they're already broadcasting the concert. I think that was probably one of the few times that I've had a real panic attack. I immediately called them to ask what in

PREMIERES

the heck was going on. And he said, "Maestro, please relax. In a few minutes, you're going to see yourself come out and play. We are broadcasting last night's performance." But this wasn't actually the result of heavy traffic. It turns out that the university students were staging a massive protest, and this kept the orchestra out of the hall. The governor and president of the university thought about calling in the police, but that could have resulted in a violent confrontation. So, they decided instead just to cancel the concert.

***

Q. They didn't tell you this at the time?

A. No, they didn't want to. They thought they were saving me from worrying. So that night, June Anderson, Guillermo, the president of the university, Carissa, and I all went out for a fantastic meal. But Ernesto was devastated, and he didn't want to join the party. He was in a deep depression. The official premiere was postponed for a year, and when it finally took place, it was not at the university theater but rather at the Bellas Artes in San Juan. This program featured not only the *Concierto festivo* but also Rodrigo's *Concierto andaluz*, played by the quartet. We had a fantastic time playing there and repeated the concert in Albuquerque. I have since played the *Concierto festivo* many times, including the European premiere with I Solisti di Zagreb in 2011.

***

Q. I'm sure that there have been other notable premieres, though not as chaotic!

A. Yes, indeed. I gave the world premiere of Torroba's *Concierto en flamenco*, even though it was written for Sabicas. Torroba loved flamenco, and he wrote two flamenco concertos, the first one for Sabicas and the second for Mario Escudero. He was inspired by Sabicas's recording called *Flamenco Puro*, which is a classic. Sabicas's compositions on that album are glorious. Torroba wrote the concerto for Sabicas using the guitarist's melodies, but Sabicas could never remember their ordering because Torroba had shuffled them around. He composed very elaborate, intertwining melodies, and the guitarist plays for a little bit, then stops, then goes back and picks it up from somewhere else.

Because Sabicas couldn't read music, he wasn't able to follow the score over a long period of time. He tried very hard to learn it, but he never felt comfortable. Therefore, he kept asking me to do it. I never thought of doing it until they asked me to present it at the Málaga Bienal, a biennial flamenco festival. I had an incredible time performing it with Angel conducting the Málaga Orchestra. That recording is available on YouTube. It was a fantastic experience for me because it brought together the genius of two people, who collaborated separately and at different times. What Torroba does with the melodies of Sabicas, in addition to his original creations, is just gorgeous.

And there is a funny anecdote in connection with this performance, when Angel flew in from the U.S. to rehearse with the orchestra. On that same evening, I played the world premiere of *Concierto en flamenco*, which was recorded a couple of years later in Málaga with the same orchestra, though now conducted by Manuel Coves. (The CD also features Torroba's *Diálogos* for guitar and orchestra, with Manuel's brother Vicente as soloist.) But on the same evening of that premiere, I also played my father's *Concierto de Málaga*, which I had premiered with Neville Marriner. Angel flew into Madrid and rented a car to drive to Málaga. It was summertime and very hot, and the car's air conditioner stopped working. He was with his wife, and they were both suffocating in the heat, which was over 100 degrees! But he arrived just in time to take a much-needed shower and then go to the theater and begin the rehearsal. However, to make matters worse, his luggage hadn't arrived, and he only had the clothes that he was wearing, which were soaked with sweat. So, he asked his wife to hang his clothes out over the veranda so that they could dry in the sun while he took a shower. But then a gust of wind came up and blew the clothes off the veranda and onto the street below, where a poor person apparently thought the shorts and Hawaiian shirt were a gift from heaven and made off with them.

Soon Carissa got a panicked call from Angel asking her to bring over one of my shirts and a pair of pants so that he would have something to wear. Since he was running late, he went straight to the theater with the expectation of having her give him the clothes there. But as a consequence, he arrived clothed in nothing more than a Speedo swimsuit and sandals! We showed up a few minutes later with a pair of shorts and a polo shirt for him to wear, but by then he had made his grand entrance. Can you imagine arriving as a conductor of the orchestra wearing a Speedo? But once he was on the podium, dressed up and being the musician he is, he had the absolute respect of the orchestra. The performance went very well, and I have subsequently performed Torroba's *Concierto en flamenco* many times.

***

Q. Any other anecdotes to share?

A. Of course! At the premiere of the Chihara concerto in Los Angeles, I was also giving the first performance of Giuliani's Concerto, Op. 65, which the composer had originally conceived as a quintet for guitar and string quartet. Neville loved that piece very much and wanted to conduct it with string orchestra, in this case the Los Angeles Chamber Orchestra. It was to be the first such presentation of the Op. 65 since Giuliani's death in 1829. I played the Giuliani in the first half of the concert, and after intermission I would play the Chihara. Opus 65 begins with a theme and four variations on the melody "Nel cor più non mi sento" (Why feels my heart so dormant), which is a duet from Giovanni Paisiello's 1788 opera *L'amor contrastato*, usually known as *La molinara*. This is followed by a delightful Polonaise. I was playing phenomenally well, but then I got to the coda at the very end of the concerto, and things went off the rails. I try not to think in words when I'm performing, but I had the thought that I was really happy I had played this so well. Then it happened: a mental block that made me stop! Neville started the coda again, but when we got to that same place, I stopped again. By that time my mind was fried, so I stopped and we started the coda yet again. Just before we got to the point where I was blanking out, Neville turned around and banged me on the head with his baton. And then I played it really well! But I thought, what is wrong with my mind? What is going to happen with the Chihara? Fortunately, it went flawlessly.

9

REVIVALS

Q. Why revive works? Do you have a philosophy regarding revivals?

A. My philosophy is that revivals are a crucial contribution to our knowledge of the history of the guitar, of Spanish music, and of classical music in general. The guitar is a relatively modern instrument but has an incredibly rich literature. It was a fixture in European salons, on the concert stage, including concertos, and it played a leading role in musical life until the advent of the fortepiano in the 1700s, which caused the guitar to recede somewhat into the background—except in Spain. So for me, reviving music has become a great passion, one that started with two composers: Fernando Sor and Mauro Giuliani. The majority of my revivals have been works by those two giants, especially Giuliani, and I have worked in collaboration with music scholars who specialize in this repertoire, in particular Thomas Heck, Brian Jeffery, Richard Long, and John King.

***

Q. So, do you approach such scholars by asking what new music they have found? Or do they come to you saying, "Look what we found! Do you want to play it?" How does that work?

A. Both ways. Giuliani is a good example. I fell madly in love with the first movement of the Sonata, Op.15, while listening to Celin play it when I was a little boy. During my very early years, that was the only piece by Giuliani that guitarists played; in fact, almost nobody even played the entire Sonata, which is a great piece of music and one I learned and later performed in its entirety. But eventually one guitarist in particular really lit my fire for the music of Giuliani, and that was Julian Bream. He recorded two works that just blew my mind: the *Grand Overture* and the Concerto, Op. 30, which I later recorded with Neville Marriner.

Now, I should digress here slightly to recall that when my brothers and I were growing up, our father did not like us to learn the same repertoire. He was trying to keep us from feeling competitive with each other. He preferred that we love and admire one another's playing. Once one of us chose a work, it was ours. I didn't play the *Sonatina* by Torroba until I was an adult and preparing to record it with Deutsche Grammophon. Even then, I asked Celin for permission, because that had always been "his" piece!

So, at one point, Angel and I flipped a coin to see who was going to get Giuliani's Concerto, Op. 30, or the *Concierto de Aranjuez*. Angel won the *Aranjuez*, and I won the Op. 30, a work that started my relationship with Neville and then Philips. It also initiated my close friendship with Thomas Heck, who was very enthusiastic about the way I played Giuliani's music. He would send me all the neglected or forgotten works that he found during his extensive research, works that no one else knew about or had ever recorded. These included such staples as the *Gran Sonata Eroica*, Op. 150, and the *6 Variations on "I [sic] bin a Kohlbauern Bub,"* Op. 49.

Then I heard Julian play the *Grand Overture*, Op. 61, and I flipped! I called Thomas and told him to send that to me. I continued my exploration of Giuliani by playing his *Variations on a Theme by Handel*, Op. 107. But then lightning really struck when Thomas informed me that there were two more concertos: Opp. 36 and 70. Those were major discoveries, and when he sent them to me, I immediately contacted Neville Marriner and Erik Smith, who was the head of repertoire and a producer at Philips. His specialty was opera, but he presided over the recording that I made of Rodrigo's *Concierto madrigal* and Giuliani's Concerto, Op. 30, with Neville conducting the Academy of St. Martin-in-the-Fields.

All three of Giuliani's guitar concertos are phenomenal; they are so exuberant. They feature gorgeous operatic introductions in the orchestra, followed by an engaging entrance of the soloist. The guitar is like a queen who makes her captivating presence known to the listener. Eric Smith sat next to me with the score of Op. 30 at the recording session. Neville had been telling him about how much he enjoyed playing this piece with me and the Los Angeles Chamber Orchestra. So, Eric was intrigued, and after we finished the first day of recording, he gave me a hug and said, "Pepe, we're giving you an exclusive contract for the next seventeen records," though I don't know how he came up with that number.

Anyway, going back to when I got the phone call from Thomas Heck, he then sent me the other two concertos. As I read through them, I once again fell in love. They were incredible, especially Op. 36, which is very profound. The first concerto is very jovial, loving, and filled with the promise of happiness. Anyone who hears Op. 30 has to feel that life is going to have a wonderful grand finale. The second is more about how we endure that which is painful.

And then comes the third, Op. 70. I had to do quite a bit of thinking about that one because it is written for Terz guitar, and I didn't have one. The range went up to a C, and my guitar didn't have a C. So, I put a capo on the third fret and played the C as an artificial harmonic, though I had to get through it really fast when it was at the end of a scale. I should point out that in the days when I recorded that work, editing was not what it is today, that is to say that now one can make almost any changes one wants to the actual recording. In those days, the process was much more faithful to what you actually played. Anyway, I called Neville and Eric and told them that I needed to record this immediately. And I did!

***

Q. How long did it take you to learn it?

A. Probably three months, something like that. Then I played at a get-together in Los Angeles, where we used to have chamber-music evenings at various people's homes. This one was at the house of Dr. and Nancy Geller (Nancy was a student of Celin). Neville came to the party, as did Michael Zearott, and I played Giuliani's Quintet, Op. 65, for guitar and string quartet. That is followed by a spirited Polonaise. Neville loved the work and noted that the guitar was so prominent that it sounded more like a concerto than a quintet. He wanted to do it with the Academy and record it. So, that was yet another revival. The recording I made with Neville of Op. 65 appeared on the same album as my first recording of Rodrigo's *Fantasía para un gentilhombre*. And I made my recording of the Giuliani Concertos, Opp. 36 and 70, about the same time that I recorded my LP of solo works by Rodrigo.

As I mentioned earlier, the Concerto, Op. 30, appeared on the same album as the *Concierto madrigal*. I used to go to London to record with the Academy in addition to making one or two solo recordings. Every time that I was going to record something by Rodrigo, I would go to visit him in Madrid and sometimes even stay at his home, to practice the music before the recording session. One of Rodrigo's favorite things to do was to improvise on the piano. He loved Giuliani's music so much that he would ask me to play the pieces I was learning so that he could improvise over the music in his own style. Those sessions were some of the most magnificent musical experiences I have ever had, and I wish that they had been recorded.

***

Q. Can you summarize your attraction to Giuliani? What is it about his music that appeals to you so much?

A. Like Fernando Sor, Giuliani was truly a great composer. To me, he is perfection, happiness, and everything that is beautiful in life. Even in the sad moments in his music, there is nothing but beauty. The music of Giuliani is what life would be like in a perfect world, where sadness would result only from the disappearance of something you love in the natural course of things. The departure of a beloved person in old age is sad but nonetheless life as it is. And it is not as sad as when someone dies young or in a tragic fashion. Giuliani's music expresses to me a perfect environment in a perfect world, and it has a dynamic range that explores the guitar to its limits. I believe that he is one of the most difficult composers to play, because one more frequently hears a bad performance of Giuliani than of almost any other composer. But a great performance of Giuliani reveals him to be among the foremost masters, given the range of feeling and the resonance that he's able to achieve on the guitar. Few composers can make the guitar sound as vibrant and as dynamically grand as Giuliani can. One of my favorite pieces is the *Variaciones concertantes* duet, which I recorded with my father but actually performed in concert hundreds of times with Celin. It runs the gamut of expression and effects, from the magical bells of the variation with harmonics to that grand finale, from the first guitar playing those scales to the ostinato bass of the second guitar. It makes the guitar sound like a magnificent, glorious instrument.

***

Q. He must have been a phenomenal guitarist, and I mean Romero-level phenomenal.

A. I believe that Giuliani was the greatest of the virtuosos, and I define virtuosity as being able to play beautifully at any tempo and never losing tonal control. I imagine him playing loud but rich. So many times we hear loud becoming nasal and thin, thus losing a rich and full-bodied tone. I feel a rapport with Giuliani because of the nature of his music, which he must have been able to play wonderfully well. That is borne out by all the contemporary accounts we have of people who heard him play, including Beethoven and Schubert. Like them, I love the way he must have played.

Another guitarist who loved Giuliani was Julian Bream, and he and I were close friends. We shared a lot of ideas and experiences, and once he said to me, "You know what I love about Giuliani? My favorite thing about Giuliani is when I'm done playing it, because it's so difficult!"

But he played that music magnificently. He really had a knack for that style, as well as the courage. You have to be a bit of a daredevil to play Giuliani; that is, you cannot have any fear when you play his music. When you listen to the beginning of any piece by him, for instance, the way that he opens the *Sonata Eroica* or any of the concertos, he makes it clear from the outset: "Here I am, and I am fearless! I am everything but fear." So, Giuliani for me is a passion, and I am so incredibly grateful that I was able to do those revivals. All I have to do is love his music and dedicate myself to being able to play it.

***

Q. So, your philosophy of reviving works has to do with the fact that the guitar has this great repertoire, but there's a lot of it that we still don't know.

A. There is a lot that we don't know. You know what Rodrigo used to call Giuliani? He would tell me, "Come and play some of that *el odioso* Giuliani." He hated Giuliani! I asked him why, because he often asked me to play Giuliani for him. And it turned out that he resented Giuliani because for so much of his life, he thought that he, Rodrigo, had written the first guitar concerto. Then he found out that, no, Giuliani had beaten him to it, and over a hundred years earlier! And he made the guitar sound fantastic. It further aggravated him that I kept showing up with more concertos. "You bring me another one, and then another one after that! That's why he put me in my place." But, in fact, he loved Giuliani's music very much, and we often played it together.

***

Q. Now let's move on to Fernando Sor.

A. Yes, let's talk about Fernando Sor, as well as Brian Jeffery and John King. Thanks to Brian, I was able to get the original manuscripts of the two Grand Sonatas, Opp. 22 and 25, which I then revived. And among my most important revivals was of Sor's posthumous *Fantasy in D*, which was discovered by John King. The manuscript did not appear in any of the catalogues or collections of the complete works of Sor, neither in Brian Jeffery's edition nor in the Chanterelle anthology. It was offered for sale at Sotheby's in New York, and that was the only copy anywhere. He apparently wrote it for a pupil of his, though there is no record that the composer or student ever played it. It was written in Sor's hand without any fingerings, and it's a rather complicated piece of music. But it's just wonderful, and I bought the manuscript, which I still own and am about to make public on my website. Now, I have already published my own edition with Richard Long and Tuscany Publications. And I gave the modern premiere of it in Atlanta, where it was very well received. I then made the first-ever recording of it, though there have been a couple of subsequent recordings by other guitarists. This was a major contribution to the legacy of Sor, one of which I am quite proud.

***

Q. And then there's Luigi Boccherini.

A. I was scheduled to record the three Boccherini guitar quintets that everybody had recorded: including the No. 4 in D Major, with the Fandango, No. 7 in E Minor, and No. 9 in C Major. But about a week before I was going to make the recordings, Richard Long called me and said that there were actually eight quintets, including the three that were already known. Apparently, the Library of Congress had the original guitar version of No. 4. What everybody had recorded until then was a version that Boccherini had transcribed from the guitar to the viola, making it a viola quintet. It was then later transcribed back for the guitar, though not by Boccherini. But the original version is much different and makes much more use of the guitar.

So, thanks to Richard, I got the other five jewels, which are incredible pieces of music. And because I had a contract with Philips for making a lot of recordings, I was able to inform them of my desire to record all of these newly found Boccherini quintets. And they consented. So, I had a lot of new music to learn before jetting off to London and the recording session. In fact, I went on to record the eight quintets in three separate sessions over a period of three consecutive years. In the first year, I did the three that were already known, as originally planned. However, we didn't record them in order, and the last one we did was No. 4, at the very end of the session, by which time it was late and we were tired. However, the cellist had problems with some tricky harmonics in the second movement, and he kept messing it up. By then, Iona Brown, who was the first violinist, was getting on edge, and the situation became very tense. The cellist was actually a wonderful musician but had just developed a mental block, the sort of thing we all experience from time to time. But Iona lost it and started screaming at him, and that triggered me to blow up at her! The session ended up with Iona and me yelling at one another and saying very unkind things to each other. We finally just walked out of the session.

***

Q. So, did you finish the recording?

A. Well, we didn't finish that recording. I was furious and went back to the hotel. I don't know where Iona went. Perhaps to her house. The producer, my dear friend Wilhelm Hellweg, intervened before I left the studio and advised me not to get so upset. He said that we could wait until the following year to finish No. 4, along with the quintets we were slated to record then. The recording wouldn't come

Figure 19. Pepe with producer and pianist Wilhelm Hellweg, 1996.

out this year, but c'est la vie. He invited me to dinner, but I declined because I was too mad and just wanted to return to my hotel.

So, I returned to the hotel, and a little while later, my phone rang. It was Iona, who was calling to apologize: "I'm so sorry. I really don't know what came over me, and I was wrong." I responded by taking responsibility for the argument and expressing remorse for all the things that I said. We had a very friendly make-up session over the phone, and then she suggested that we try to finish the recording the next day, before I flew home. She was certain that we could finish it very quickly. That sounded good to me, so I called Wilhelm to let him know that Iona and I had mended fences and would like to go back to the studio in the morning to finish the recording, so that it could come out this year. He was agreeable to that suggestion, and that's just what we did.

So, the next morning I set off for the recording studio with my guitar. When Iona and I met, we didn't say a word to one another. We just hugged. Unfortunately, the London Symphony was using the studio and running overtime with their recording. We waited and waited, but in the end, we had to resign ourselves to postponing the final session until next year, when the first order of business would be to finish off the second movement of No. 4, with its troublesome harmonics.

But there is more to the story of my contretemps with Iona. It turns out that Wilhelm had engaged an English girl to call me that fateful evening and impersonate Iona. And he had arranged for a Spanish friend of his to call Iona and apologize on my behalf. So this fake apology was all orchestrated by Wilhelm. All Iona and I had to do was hug, forgive, and forget. Only later did Wilhelm disclose his subterfuge.

Iona and I maintained a wonderful friendship after that. We went on many tours together, playing duets for violin and guitar. We enjoyed one another's company and got some great laughs out of recalling our fight and were thankful to Wilhelm for settling our dispute.

***

Q. How about Ferdinando Carulli?

A. Carulli (1770–1841) was another rewarding experience in the realm of revivals. I had never fully appreciated his magnificence as a composer. This was partly due to the fact that much of what I knew of his music was pedagogical in nature, i.e., fairly easy studies to help the guitarist in the early stages of developing technique. They are lovely but not so impressive as concert works. Then Richard Long sent me Carulli's Concerto in E Minor, as well as Francesco Molino's Concerto in E Minor. I had never heard of those works before, and

Figure 20. Pepe performing with Iona Brown, 1981.

REVIVALS

not many other people had either. I premiered and recorded them, and since then they've been recorded by other people as well. That recording also includes Carulli's Concerto in A Major, as well as my transcription of two Mozart Rondos. The Carulli concerto is a musical masterpiece, and the Molino concerto makes the guitar sound fantastic.

***

Q. You seem to have a real affinity for music of the Classical and early-Romantic periods. Is there a reason for that?

A. I love that period of music. It makes me feel very joyous, and it exudes hope, beauty, and romance. It allows your fantasy to open up, and when you hear it, you go to bed and have beautiful dreams, not nightmares. That characterizes the music of all the composers I have been talking about: Boccherini, Sor, Giuliani, and Carulli. And let's not forget Anton Diabelli (1781–1858) and his *Grand Sonate Brillante* for guitar and piano, which I recorded at Philips with Wilhelm Hellweg playing piano. That was another wonderful discovery, that there were pieces for that combination.

I am so grateful to have been able to shed light on aspects of the guitar's illustrious repertoire, aspects of which people were not previously very aware. Historically, the view has prevailed that the guitar was a folk instrument, principally associated with flamenco and performances in *tablaos* (flamenco nightclubs). And then the classical guitar suddenly came to life in the early twentieth century, with the pioneering efforts of Segovia. Of course, that is not true at all. There were major artists besides Segovia, including Miguel Llobet (1878–1938), Emilio Pujol (1886–1980). Josefina Robledo (1897–1992), Agustín Barrios (1885–1944), and Ángel Barrios (1882–1964). And before them, Tárrega and Arcas. And before them, Sor and Giuliani. And before them, Gaspar Sanz (1640–1710). So, the guitar has had an illustrious career, which was of course preceded by the vihuela and the lute, much of whose music we can also play on the modern guitar and is a legitimate part of our repertoire.

I like to reflect on the productive relationships I have had with people like Neville Marriner and Wilhelm Hellweg. I honor them for helping me bring to greater awareness the truth about the magnificent life that the guitar has had over several centuries. That's an incredible pleasure and makes me feel very happy.

10

IMPROVISER, ARRANGER, COMPOSER

Q. You not only recreate the music that others have already composed but you also bring to life new music as an improviser, arranger/transcriber, and composer. So, let's talk about those roles. Which one came first?

A. I think that the first was improvising, because when a guitar is put in your hands, you just start doing whatever comes to you. I have been around many composers and have noted that every composition starts out as an improvisation. And then the composer takes an idea and develops it until it becomes a composition. So, I think improvising came to me first, especially when I fell in love with flamenco, in which one has to improvise a lot. I early on noted that the great flamenco artists immensely valued the art of improvisation. When I was a young fellow and before we left Spain, improvising in flamenco was regarded as living proof that the *duende* (spirit) had descended on you.

Nowadays, flamenco seems much more thought out and rehearsed, less spontaneous. A flamenco piece now seems almost like a composition, though it is not written out because many flamenco guitarists have not been trained to read and write music. But improvisation is still a central component of the art form, no matter how well-thought-out and rehearsed a number may be. But for me, whether one is playing classical or flamenco, there has to be the spontaneous feeling of an improvisation.

***

Q. Is your improvisation connected exclusively with flamenco, or do you improvise in other styles as well? If it is connected mostly with flamenco, which *palos* (types of song and dance) inspire you the most?

A. There are many different varieties of improvisation. One of my favorite varieties, one that has served me very well, is getting out of mistakes when I'm performing a classical work. If I have a memory lapse, I trip up, and the finger hits the wrong note, then I have to find my way back. For instance, on my first tour with the American Sinfonietta, back in 1991, I was performing Rodrigo's *Concierto para una fiesta*. And we all came down with the flu and had raging fevers, even as we continued to travel and perform. During one performance of the *Fiesta*, I struggled with the cadenza in the first movement, which is full of fast scales and is complex, both harmonically and rhythmically. It presents the first theme of the movement, which keeps changing tonalities and is very chordal. And then there's a long scale, and then the theme, another long scale, and then the theme again, and another long scale. Finally, the cadenza ends with a long trill high up on the neck, between the A and B on the seventeenth and nineteenth frets. And then the orchestra comes back in.

Anyway, I had taken some flu medicine and was a little bit out of it. As a result, I lost my way. But I knew the melody and have played so many Rodrigo scales that I was able to improvise my way out of the problem. I think I played scales from every Rodrigo guitar concerto except the *Fiesta*! In that performance, the conductor, Michael Palmer, was suffering from a bad cough, but instead of taking a cough suppressant, he took expectorant, which made matters worse. So, while he was struggling with his cough, he heard me improvise a new cadenza, and it must have sounded pretty good. But it was nothing like what was written, and Michael started flipping pages back and forth in the score to find out where I was. He thought that *he* was the one who was lost! He didn't realize that I was the one who had made a mistake. Finally, I played the long trill and waited for him to catch on, and after that we were back on track. After the concert, Michael apologized for having been so out of it, as a result of his medication. "I completely lost where you were. I couldn't find it. And I couldn't find what you were doing anywhere. Thank goodness Rodrigo ended the cadenza with a trill. When I heard the trill, I came in." I then assured him that he was not the one who got lost, I was. So, learning how to improvise has helped me out of that and other similar predicaments.

Improvising has helped me in other ways as well, for instance, when I get a new piece of music in order to prepare its world premiere. Many such works have been by composers who were not themselves guitar players. Very often, while learning the music, I would practice a passage and then improvise around it in a way that deviated from the score but I thought was worth sharing with the composer. I would present it, they would listen, and sometimes they would agree that it was an improvement. Rodrigo and Torroba often agreed with my revisions and asked me to write them out, though at other times they were not so receptive.

When I am playing classical music, of course, I am completely committed to the written score, though there is a point at which improvisation and ornamentation go very much hand in hand. However, I am probably one of the guitarists who ornaments the least, because it can become a matter of your will against the composer's will. There is a fine line between what is going to ornament a passage and what is going to detract from it, thereby obscuring the composer's intentions. When Bach wanted to ornament something, he did so. I don't need to gild that lily. But oftentimes his notation contains implied harmonies that are much bigger, deeper, and profound than any bass line we may add to it. For example, take the Suites for Unaccompanied Cello. In my transcriptions, I try to find the proper range for that music on the guitar, which has a magnificent low voice. Most of the transcriptions I have heard transpose the music to the higher register of the guitar, necessitating the addition of bass lines. I prefer to keep the music in a lower register, one similar to that of the cello, and not add any bass notes.

In summary, I would say improvising has played an important role in my career as a guitarist. As for which *palos* inspire me the most, I would say the ones that are rhythmically free, such as *malagueñas* and *medias granadinas*. Those are *palos* that inspire me to improvise, though I also like to improvise on *seguidillas*, which has a stricter *compás* (meter). But I like them all!

***

Q. You have arranged many works for the Romero Quartet, and you've also transcribed works for solo guitar and guitar duet. How did you get involved in arranging?

A. It starts with hearing a piece of music and imagining it in the voice of the guitar. Not surprisingly, it has usually been Spanish music with a folkloric connection, especially flamenco, that has called to me. Manuel de Falla (1876–1946) is a case in point, though I have also transcribed many piano pieces by Isaac Albéniz and Enrique Granados (1867–1916). I am very drawn to such works, regardless of medium, insofar as they were originally inspired by the guitar. When I fall in love with a piece of music, I get a tremendous urge to feel it inside my body, to feel it in my heart, in my mind, and to feel it come out of my hands. Examples include dances from Falla's ballets *El amor brujo* and *El sombrero de tres picos*, the zarzuelas *El baile de Luis Alonso* and *La boda de Luis Alonso* by Gerónimo Giménez (1854–1923), as well as the "Jota" from the opera *La Dolores* by Tomas Bretón (1850–1923). These pieces have played a key role in the success of the Romero Quartet. But it always begins with me listening to the original and then thinking that this would sound great for four guitars. The arrangement will give it a different flavor, but the music is not going to suffer.

***

Q. So, you stay as close to the original as you can.

A. As close to the way I think the composer would have written it for the guitar. When I am transcribing or arranging a work, I don't shy away from rendering a passage very differently from the way it appears in the original, as long I adhere to its melody, harmony, and emotion. In fact, a note-for-note transcription from one instrument to another will sometimes betray the composer's intentions, because the music has to remain idiomatic for the particular medium, whatever that is.

My two big teachers of arranging were my father and the arrangements of Tárrega. Llobet's arrangements were also very instructive, though I didn't become familiar with them until I was much older. I studied Tárrega's arrangements already as a kid, and of course I had the example of my father's work as far back as I can remember. He would actually consult me about his transcriptions, asking, "Pepe, which way do you like this better? If I play it this way, or if I play this other way?" He was teaching me not just how to arrange but also how to listen. But he was genuinely interested in my opinion, which he valued.

I have also loved very much transcribing pieces from the Baroque period. My father and Tárrega were my great teachers regarding arranging, but they were drawn to the Romantic period, particularly German and Austrian composers like Beethoven, Schubert, and Schumann, as well as Chopin. I've actually done very little of that. My transcriptions and arrangements have been mostly of Spanish-nationalist composers of the late nineteenth and twentieth centuries, in addition to Baroque music. I find that I can arrange Baroque works for the guitar while remaining very faithful to the feeling of the original. Even orchestral works of, say, Vivaldi, Telemann, or Bach work quite well for a guitar ensemble. The Romantics expressed themselves principally through the piano, for which they wrote in a very idiomatic fashion, and I find that their music is not so convincing in guitar transcription. However, I loved to listen to my father play that music. One of my favorite albums of Angel is called *Bella*, and on that he plays Beethoven very beautifully. I've also had students make arrangements of Wagner's *Lohengrin*. So, it can be done, but it's not what triggers my desire to arrange.

***

Q. What are some of the outstanding Baroque arrangements you have made?

A. If I were to single out one, it would probably be Bach's Violin Partita No. 2, which includes the famous Chaconne. But Angel and I arranged the *Goldberg Variations* for two guitars, and that was a delight. We took turns with the variations. He arranged the first, third, fifth, and so on, while I did the even-numbered variations. Angel played first guitar in the variations he arranged, and I played first in those that I arranged. We performed it in San Francisco, New York, and elsewhere. The most memorable performance, though, took place in La Jolla, at a birthday party we had organized for Herb Fox. That was back in the late 1960s, before I was familiar with the San Diego area. Of course, we have lived in Del Mar, north of San Diego, for about fifty-five years. At the party, we played the *Goldberg Variations* for him as a birthday present. But this time we played them along with harpsichordist Rosalyn Tureck. As you know, each variation is repeated, so she played the first statement of each variation, and we played the repeats. Herb was delighted, as were we.

IMPROVISER, ARRANGER, COMPOSER

***

Q. Are there any more recent transcriptions that you would like to mention?

A. There was a project that has been gestating for a long time. David Lee, my manager and the quartet's manager in China and Korea, started telling me that I should play some Chinese works. And I said, "Okay, find me one that would be good." And he replied that there was one that everybody in China loves. It's the biggest hit there. So, I said I would arrange it for guitar and play it in China. The name of the work is *Butterfly Lovers*, a beautiful piece based on an ancient love story, a sort of Chinese version of *Romeo and Juliet*. I had never heard it before and thought that it was some kind of song. So, I agreed to do it. In any case, it is a lengthy and very virtuosic violin concerto, written in 1959 by two Chinese composers, He Zhanhao and Chen Gang. I wound up doing a TV interview along with Chen Gang, and during that interview, he kept talking about how happy he was that I was going make a transcription of his violin concerto. I was now committed, and despite my reservations, I did it. Right there on TV, we agreed to get together in his studio and work on the transcription. He had a gorgeous studio out in the country, and I went there to go through the score with him.

I love the music, and I love the composer. He's a wonderful man. He was at both premieres, in Shanghai and Beijing. But it has not yet been recorded. The music is very romantic and makes lovely use of traditional Chinese scales, especially pentatonic. But it is also very Western.

***

Q. Of course, there are some things that can be done on a violin but that can't be done on a guitar. Still, you have managed to find equivalent ways to express the music.

A. I have had a lot of experience doing that. My first transcription of violin music was the Bach Partita No. 2, followed by the Vivaldi Concerto for Four Violins, followed by two Mozart Rondos for violin. And then came *Butterfly Lovers*. So, I've tackled some violin concertos, and I'm not done yet. On my bucket list is a transcription of the Beethoven Violin Concerto. In fact, I'm already working on it, but there is still some work to do before it's ready. I have a bet with a dear friend that I will finish it before I am 85, which gives me five years. It's actually not so hard to do because Beethoven originally conceived the concerto for the piano. So, the chords make sense. I will rely on the original piano score and find a way between the versions for piano and for violin.

***

Q. The last thing we want to cover has to do with your composing. Of course, you've already pointed out that improvisation is a form of composing and that composing starts out as improvisation.

A. Yes, I do consider improvising to be a kind of composing, and I've known some great improvisers. In jazz, Joe Pass comes to mind, and in flamenco, Niño Ricardo, Sabicas, and Manolo Sanlúcar. Though we were good friends and liked to hang out together, I never actually witnessed Paco de Lucía in the act of improvising.

The most impressive improviser, however, was Rodrigo at the piano, because he was a magnificent pianist. Everyone who plays his music should listen to his recording of *Joaquín Rodrigo Plays Rodrigo*, which is available on Spotify. That provides a vivid example of how to play his music, how it is connected. It is easy to play it a little bit disconnected because of the technical difficulties, but he was a great master and could connect it without losing the improvisatory feeling that is so necessary in playing all music. It has to sound as if you're getting it directly from the source, and he had that ability because he was such an incredible improviser. He used to love to improvise spontaneously. It wasn't just a matter of giving him a theme and then having him build a piece around it. He liked for me to play a piece for him that he had never heard before, and then he would sit at the piano and make up something that meshed beautifully with the music. Those were remarkable sessions.

***

Q. But I want to talk now about your own compositions. What are some works that you've composed, and what inspired them?

A. They're usually inspired by flamenco and my love for the Spanish-nationalist composers. And most of what I have composed for solo guitar have been improvisations that keep coming back to

Figure 21. Pepe plays for Joaquín Rodrigo, 1983.

me. My written compositions have been more for the quartet, and I haven't really done that many, because I think that I can serve music more as an interpreter.

I love composing, but I'm not that sure of myself as a composer. I have probably discarded more compositions than I have kept, though I have enjoyed very much playing my own compositions with the quartet. These have included tributes to Sabicas, to my father, and sometimes to a friend who has passed on.

However, there are a couple of pieces of mine that I really like. Many years ago, Carissa and I were in Sankt Johann in Tirol, Austria. After the concert, we were treated to dinner in a beautiful cabin up in the mountains. And the people from the town who were there with us having dinner after the concert started singing yodels for me, and I loved them. I went crazy about them. And I told the organist of the church to send me one of the yodels, because I wanted to write a set of variations on it. So, he sent me one, and when I went back the next year, I had written a set of variations, as a kind of tribute to Giuliani. I actually enjoyed that piece so much that I decided to digitize and publish it on my website.

The other one is the last thing I have written, which is a piece for tenor and guitar. A couple of years ago, we were staying with Sonsoles González de Vega, who was my Spanish manager for many years. Her husband and my dear friend, Antonio Alix, is now retired, but he was a lung surgeon in Madrid and himself the son of a very famous lung surgeon, José Alix, a man of many talents. He studied at a school of fine arts along with Salvador Dalí, and he became a very good artist. We have a beautiful drawing of a dancer and a guitar that he made quite a few years ago. He was also a poet, so on the wedding of his son, Antonio, to Sonsoles, he wrote a poem for them. We happened to be at their home on their fifty-eighth wedding anniversary, and Antonio read the poem aloud to us. I was very touched and moved by it, so I told them that I would use that poem as the lyrics for a song I would compose as an anniversary present. *Entrelazados* (Intertwined) for voice and guitar is dedicated to Antonio and Sonsoles on the occasion of their fifty-eighth wedding anniversary. My grandson Jacob Romero Kressin and I premiered it live in the beautiful Laeiszhalle in Hamburg. Indeed, it has been a joy to see Jacob become an accomplished musician and beautiful tenor, and our concerts together have been some of the most exciting and loving highlights of my life.

I will digress a bit here to relate another occasion on which I participated in a recital of music for voice and guitar, an experience that was both fun and stressful. Just after I had returned from a concert in Europe, Celin informed me that the next day I was going to give a concert at UCSD with his wife, Laurie, a very fine singer. He and Laurie had had a fight, and he no longer wanted to play the concert with her. Not one to turn down such a challenge, I said yes. The repertoire consisted of some German songs by Giuliani and a song cycle by the American composer Dominick Argento (1927–2019), *Letters from Composers.* It was a fabulous piece of music but long and difficult. The next morning, I was already busy learning the music and then rehearsing it with Laurie. That evening, I had a fantastic time performing it, even though it was a little bit stressful. But that's how life is: all of a sudden, unforeseen circumstances introduce you to new music that you absolutely love. And that experience was wonderful. The concert was recorded, but it has never been released professionally. Maybe someday we will go through our family archive of recordings and sort these things out.

However, returning to the subject of my own creations, I also enjoyed composing a piece entitled *Malagueñas de Jotrón*, for guitar quartet, guitar orchestra, and voice. During the COVID pandemic, I was asked to participate in a work that my good friend Sergio Assad had written for the Virtual Guitar Orchestra, so that was my introduction to the ensemble. After my performance, I was invited to write this piece, which I did in celebration of the sixtieth anniversary of the Romero Quartet in 2021. Jotrón is a village in the mountains north of Málaga, and it is where my paternal grandmother came from. My father was actually born in Cuba in 1913, but the family returned to Spain when he was 6 years old, and that is where they settled. My grandfather actually stayed on in Cuba for a while after the family departed, but upon his return, the family moved to Málaga, which is where my father taught himself how to play the guitar. So, the distinctive music and dance from that region are called the *verdiales*, a kind of *fandango*. *Malagueñas de Jotrón* first evokes a characteristic song in slow, free rhythm, and then it transitions into a very rhythmical *fandango*. I actually enjoy that piece quite a bit. Anyway, I think that in the future I will compose more songs, because I'm very excited about working with my grandson Jacob. I have quite a few ideas for songs that we can perform together.

I have to pay homage to the incredible work done by my publishers, specifically Tuscany Publications with Richard and Mary Long, and my collaboration with Brian Hays.

Richard Long not only became a tremendously important friend and adviser in my life with his work as a musicologist, but he is also my partner in bringing to the world gorgeous publications of many of my transcriptions in his magnificent editions with Tuscany Publications, which he did together with his soulmate, Mary. They crafted each of their publications as true works of art, and I treasure the memories of our work together and the fruits of our efforts.

Brian Hays is a guitar disciple whom I share with my brother Celin, who is his "father teacher," while I am his "uncle teacher." Brian and I have worked together for many years, and he has given me much joy with his guitar playing. I will always remember a particular performance by him of Albéniz's "Cataluña," from the

Suite española no. 1. Our guitar relations evolved even more as we became a real team in collecting, organizing, editing, and finally publishing many of my arrangements and original compositions, which without Brian would still be in their manuscript form, residing in various drawers of my desk. I am so grateful to Brian, proud of what we have accomplished together, and excited to see what is still to come.

***

Q. Can you name a few works you've written for the Romero Quartet?

A. Yes. *En el Sacromonte,* which is dedicated to Carissa; *Fiesta en Cádiz,* which is an *alegrías*; and *De Cádiz a La Habana,* which is a *colombianas.* There is a recording from 1962 that includes many pieces that I wrote, but I didn't attach my name to them because I didn't consider them real compositions. I was just improvising on a *rumba gitana* or some such, and it was listed as Traditional Flamenco, not a work by Pepe Romero.

***

Q. Can you name somebody who passed away and in whose honor you wrote a piece?

A. The mother of my good friend Gabriel Garzo. I wrote a piece for solo guitar entitled *Elvita,* as we called her Doña Elvita. I actually like that work very much, and if it had been written by someone else, I would say that it was very nice. But I have played so many fantastic compositions that I cannot call myself a composer.

V

CONNECTIONS

11

CELEBRITIES IN POLITICS, RELIGION, SCIENCE, ARTS, ATHLETICS

Q. You yourself are famous. How do you feel about fame?

A. I am not aware of being famous. I have never really been interested in my own fame or anyone else's in my life. Fame is something that I've never thought about. Every single president I've met is famous, but what matters to me is how I feel about the person, what he or she has done, what they have contributed. And I ask myself that same question: What have I contributed? Take President Jimmy Carter, for instance. We met him way before he became president. He started coming to concerts before he became governor. He loved the guitar and music, and I early on became aware that he was a beautiful person, a really nice guy, one who vibrated in sympathy with and got emotional about music. He would come anytime we played in Atlanta, before and during his governorship. Then, when he became president, he invited us to perform at the White House.

One experience with him stands out in my memory of that occasion. I couldn't make it to the rehearsal the day prior to the concert because my daughter Angelina was having eye surgery that very day. Her mother, Kristine, was doing needlepoint, and the needle accidently went through her eye, doing major damage. She was only 8 years old and couldn't take care of herself. So, I went with her to the surgery and then caught a flight the day of the performance. The dressing room that Carter gave us was the private bedroom he shared with Rosalynn. I remember telling him I was sorry I couldn't make it to rehearsal because of my daughter, and he was so empathetic: "Let me check with my doctors. I have access to the best doctors. Who is taking care of her?" I told him that her doctor was Perry Binder, and the next morning he reported to me, "You know, I have checked, and he is one of the greatest eye doctors in the world. There is no one better." The day before, he had even offered to send a plane to fly her to wherever would be best. He was and is a very nice man. I ran into him on a plane a few years ago, flying to a concert in New York City. An FBI agent came through the cabin telling everyone to please stay seated because Jimmy Carter was on this flight and wanted to greet everybody. He quickly recognized me and gave me a big hug. So, for me it wasn't just that he was president but that he was such a nice person.

And we became acquainted with another very famous politician, who had a completely different personality and set of beliefs. Richard Nixon also invited us to play at the White House, twice! Again, when he was with us, he was not Richard Nixon the president, he was Richard Nixon the music lover. He was very interested in the guitar and its music, and on both occasions he introduced us and talked about the works we were going to play, all from memory, without any notes. As always, it is the person that matters most to me. Of course, I'm perfectly aware that these two important world leaders represented different segments of the population, with their conflicting beliefs and ideals. But then there is music, and it brings them together. Through music, you cut away all the pretense that comes with fame. For me, fame is actually something that sets people apart from other people. It puts them on a pedestal and surrounds them with an energy that makes them unapproachable, almost like a statue. Fame erects barriers between people, and those who stand out in my memory and heart are the ones who step out of their own fame and become authentic, who are attuned to the music that connects them with other people.

No one was more famous than Pope John Paul II, who invited us to perform for him at the Vatican. We played on a stage before a huge crowd in the piazza, but because there were so many people, John Paul II came out in his "popemobile" to greet us before we performed. Afterwards, we had a wonderful talk with him about the power and spirituality of music, how it is the voice of God. He told me that the one big regret he had about having been shot is that it injured one of his hands and he could no longer play the guitar. He lovingly held each of our hands, and there again, not only was

CELEBRITIES

Figure 22. Pepe (*right*) and his family with Pope John Paul II at St. Peter's, 1982.

he a pope but the Catholic Church later made him a saint. He had the most incredible aura, but his charisma was both very powerful and very gentle. He emanated love and peace, which I personally pray for every day for the world. There is nothing I want more than peace and brotherhood for everyone, along with the end of suffering. That's when I think about the power of music and the famous people we have come into contact with through the guitar. What I gained from John Paul II was a tremendous experience of love, of empathy, of an incredibly tender yet large spirit. And for me to hear his feelings about music was very important.

I met another pope, though before he became pope, which is why I always say that I've met a pope and a half. Cardinal Joseph Ratzinger, later Pope Benedict XVI, was a great lover of music. I met him in Salzburg at a banquet given by Polygram, Philips, DGG, and Decca, which he attended along with Jessye Norman, Claudio Arrau, Bernard Haitink, and Claudio Abbado, among others.

Virtually everyone who has recorded with those companies was there, and many of us performed. Now, these two men practiced the same religion, but they had very different personalities. Yet, they were completely open to music.

And there was another famous religious figure I met, though one representing a completely different group of believers: the Dalai Lama. Some years ago, I was invited by my dear friend Rodney Scully to perform in Mexico for President Vicente Fox. He had just completed his six-year term as president, and he was going to be hosting some dignitaries at a party. He wanted me to perform a concert for them, so off I went. Vicente Fox and I hit it off very well in a personal way, and we ended up sharing not only a love of music but also of fine cigars and espresso. He had a very luxurious "man cave," and we retired there to savor some excellent *puros* (cigars). Later, I received a phone call inviting me to spend a weekend with him at his hacienda, along with the Dalai Lama. He wanted to go to Mexico, but the current president could not receive him, as it would anger China. So Fox, now a private citizen, would host him instead. Carissa and I ended up in the bedroom next to the Dalai Lama. What an amazing person he is! And what a great love of music he has, including Western classical music.

Perhaps more than any other instrument, the guitar has a special way of penetrating faster and deeper into the spirit of the person. I love all the instruments, and each has its particular strength, but the guitar has an intimacy that immediately opens the listener's heart. Friendship, connection, and oneness spread in a concert situation. I saw it happen when Arthur Rubenstein played Chopin. It is a very common experience with the guitar as well.

In 2021, Ardem Patapoutian, an Armenian scientist living in and doing his research in San Diego, won the Nobel Prize in Physiology or Medicine. He had discovered where in the brain the sensory receptors are located that detect pressure, menthol, and temperature, which was hugely important for many purposes, especially brain surgery. He was 50 years old, and because of COVID, they cancelled the ceremony. Instead, they told him to arrange a place to receive the award, and they would fly it in. Once the pandemic had subsided and they were able to resume holding the ceremonies, he would be invited to participate. But in 2021, he could do what he wanted in the way of a ceremony, and he said, "I want a concert of the Romeros!" We accepted and performed in San Diego

CELEBRITIES 145

at the Scripps Institute, where he had his laboratory. He chose the repertoire he wanted to hear and loved the concert. He and I soon became and have remained good friends.

Just two weeks ago, he was here smoking cigars with Celin and me. And he told me, "Pepe, you are a famous person, and you seem unaffected by it. I want to be like that. I want to have the Nobel Prize and then go on with my life." He himself is one of the most humble and sweet people you can imagine. I said, "Ardem it's very simple. Don't think that *you* got the Nobel Prize. Your *achievement* got the Nobel Prize, but it is done and belongs to history. Now you can feel happy that you got to do that, feel grateful that what you did was recognized. You achieved the ultimate. You love science, so carry on, and you will be unaffected."

All of us, musicians, presidents, popes, and scientists, do what we do because we get enjoyment out of it. Even plumbers enjoy fixing whatever is causing a problem. When they stop a leak from flooding the house, they get great satisfaction. Imagine if there was a leak flooding your house and they sent you a Nobel scientist or a guitarist to fix it! Or imagine if you had cataracts and they sent you a king to operate on them. It wouldn't do any good at all. We are all a part of one big thing.

Among the famous people I have known are members of royal families and the nobility. Foremost are the former King and Queen of Spain, especially Sofía, who often came to our concerts and would then stop by backstage to chat. And I felt a deep friendship with José Peris (1924–2017), whom she appointed *maestro de capilla* (chapelmaster) of the royal house. He was a truly great musician but is not as renowned as other giants of Spanish music, because most of his life he was dedicated to the royal house and selecting the music for all the events, including baptisms, parties, and masses. The last thing he was working on, but didn't finish, was a concerto for me. I have the manuscript and plan to finish it for him. He also made a remarkable arrangement for string quartet and soprano of Haydn's *Seven Last Words of Christ* (1787), which was originally composed on a commission from the city of Cádiz in southwestern Spain. Queen Sofía's love for music is immense, and King Juan Carlos also very much enjoyed José Peris's rendition of this classic work.

As for other royalty I have known, I value my relationship with Prince Rainier III of Monaco and his son, now Prince Albert II. They held wonderful concerts in the castle courtyard, and I played the

Concierto de Aranjuez with Raphael Frühbeck de Burgos on two occasions there. Then the quartet performed the *Concierto andaluz*, with Jesús López Cobos conducting. Not surprisingly, the former Prince Charles, now King Charles III, stands out in my memory. We met him in Austin, Texas, where he was being honored as a visiting dignitary by the Austin Symphony. We performed in that concert, as did Willie Nelson! Austin wanted to present Prince Charles with a diverse array of musicians who lived and made their careers in the U.S. After the performance, we four Spaniards conversed about music with the Englishman Charles and the American Willie. We were definitely a diverse group! And I should add that I have played several times for Queen Beatrix of the Netherlands.

***

Q. You yourself are an accomplished painter. What famous artists have you known?

A. Artists with whom I became acquainted included Luis Molledo, the great forger after whom I am named because he went with my father to register me on March 11, 1944, as José Luis. I was actually born on the 8th, but my parents waited to see if I would survive before registering me, which they did three days later. Molledo was also my inspiration for wanting to paint, and he gave me my first watercolors. But I got so mad at him because he gave me this big case of watercolors but took all of them away except for blue, yellow, and red, saying, "When you can paint anything with these three colors, I'll give you the other ones back." Then there was Baldomero Romero Resendi, legendary in Spain in his own time as a phenomenal painter.

From the mid-1970s until his death in 1993, Carissa and I enjoyed the friendship of an extraordinary artist, Lajos Markos of Hungary. I loved him and his Italian wife, Maria, a brilliant soprano. I miss the long sessions where I played and he painted, while praising art, music, friendship, and great artists. What an exceptional artist and beautiful person he was.

And there was another marvelous artist whom I came to admire and befriend, though my path to him was rather indirect. In 1958, we met Jean Cook (no relation to Joan Cook in Chapter 15), an incredibly talented young soprano studying with William Eddy,

Figure 23. Lajos Markos painting a portrait of Pepe playing the guitar, 1981.

Kristine's father and eventually my father-in-law. Jean would go on to sing major roles in all the leading opera houses. A few years later, when the family was in New York, Celin and I asked out Jean and her then-roommate Janet Millard. Janet was a brilliant flutist who later played with the New York Philharmonic, among other great orchestras. We went for a walk in Central Park, Celin with Jean and I with Janet. However, very soon into the walk, Celin and I found that we were not communicating so well with our companions. So, we decided to trade places, Celin walking instead with Janet and I with Jean. The spark was ignited, and Celin and Janet would actually have a very passionate romance. Jean and I had a long-lasting and beautiful friendship, and she married a great artist, David Kreitzer. Once, after giving a quartet concert in the Bay Area, we went to their house, where I was mesmerized by David's paintings. Being an incredibly generous person, he presented me and my family with several of his canvases. Carissa and I remain best friends with David, who remarried after Jean passed away after a long fight with cancer. His new wife, Jacalyn, is also a singer, a mezzo-soprano with an international career in opera.

***

Q. You have an abiding passion for literature. What famous writers have you known?

A. When we moved to San Diego in 1969, we soon became connected with the local Spanish community, through which we met a fantastic painter, Sebastián Capella (1927–2013) from Valencia, who painted Angel, my father, and me. Then, through him, we met novelist, essayist, and journalist Ramón Sender (1901–82), who was among the greatest figures in modern Spanish literature, one whose many books I strongly recommend. He escaped Franco's Spain and was subsequently going to be joined by his wife, but she got caught and was beaten to death for refusing to disclose where her husband was. He never remarried. I loved listening to him talk about a wide variety of subjects. He was so eloquent, so pro-freedom, so anti-fascism, of course.

But getting back to your original question about celebrity, it occurs to me that many persons have achieved greatness without achieving fame. One of the greatest musicians I ever knew was Michael Zearott, who wrote the *Concerto Mariachi* for me. At the outset of his career, it looked as if he would be the next Herbert von Karajan. He had the talent, knowledge, spirit, and the music inside of him to do it. But fame is fickle, and becoming famous is something that either happens or doesn't, often for reasons that defy explanation. Sadly, he died in obscurity and poverty in Washington state, giving private lessons to little kids and collecting welfare. And yet it bears repetition that he was one of the most talented and versatile musicians I have ever known. Fate and fame can be unjust.

***

Q. Famous actors, dancers, and media personalities?

A. I became acquainted with Johnny Carson, Merv Griffin, and Barbara Walters, but more in a professional capacity, not so much on a personal level. Now, we've been watching movies lately, and that has gotten me to thinking about my experiences with dancers, because one of the most famous dancers became a superstar: Rita Hayworth. She was the daughter of a well-known dancer, Eduardo Cansino, who was from Seville and taught dance in Los Angeles.

CELEBRITIES   149

He used to come over to the house, became a good friend of my parents, and was one of the dancers I used to practice with. A lot of dancers and singers sought me out once they discovered that I could play flamenco and was a good accompanist.

So, Eduardo used to come over to go through some of his choreography, and he would talk all the time about his daughter Margarita, i.e., Rita Hayworth: Margarita—Marga = Rita. However, he talked about her more as a dancer than an actress. During those early days in Los Angeles, I was spending four hours nearly every evening with either Eduardo or María Rosa, who became a celebrity in Spain with her ballet. For years, she and her mother would come to the house for dinner, starting in 1958 at our home on Wilton Place.

The experience with Eduardo and María Rosa helped me polish my skills as an accompanist. That culminated in the first *World of Flamenco* LP (1967), featuring the quartet, dancer Raul Martín, and María Victoria Barbeyto, formerly a pop singer in Spain who moved to Los Angeles, where she met our family and collaborated with us. In fact, there was an active flamenco scene in Los Angeles at that time. Sabicas was playing at the Troubadour, and Carmen Amaya was dancing at the Purple Onion Café, accompanied by the guitarist Marote.

Our little school on Wilton Place was a meeting place for a wide variety of people, and later we would meet at our next house, on Maplewood, which Celin still owns. It became a real melting pot of classical and flamenco musicians, as well as dancers. There is no school that I could've gone to anywhere to get the kind of training I got accompanying dancers. As a result, you can pair me with any radical conductor, he can do whatever he wants, and I'll be right there with him. And I am so thankful for the opportunity to accompany not only flamenco dancers but also singers. There is a harmonic pattern that the singer often but does not always follow, and you have to listen closely to change chords correctly even as you match the dancer's rhythm. Where I have really used these skills is in playing concertos and chamber music.

***

Q. Famous athletes? The Romeros are big fans of soccer.

A. I have not known that many, but I enjoyed very much meeting Muhammad Ali. I was at a camera store looking at different lenses, and all of a sudden I looked to my left and saw this big guy: Muhammad Ali! I recognized him immediately, and we started talking. He was so nice, gentle, and friendly, and I told him how I used to take my nephew Lito to see every fight of his that we could get to because Lito was totally into it. Of course, he was more than just a boxer, he was a global celebrity. Then he said, "Well, do something. Hit me. Punch me." I responded in disbelief, "Are you kidding? Your reflexes will be activated, and I'll be dead in a second." But he insisted: "No, hit me, and then you can say that you're one of the few people who have ever landed a punch on my face." So, I hit him, though not as hard as I could! Another idol of mine was the Brazilian soccer star Pele. I once met him quite by coincidence in an elevator in Seoul. We were both going to the lobby to have a beer and smoke a cigar, which we wound up doing together. Both of these athletes were completely knowledgeable about the guitar and the work I had done, and both loved music.

12

CONDUCTORS, ORCHESTRAL MUSICIANS, SINGERS, PIANISTS

Q. You have collaborated and become friends with a small army of musicians. We'll begin with conductors.

A. There have been so many, but among the ones who have really touched my heart, let's start with Neville Marriner, whom I met just by chance. I was hired in 1972 to play the Giuliani Concerto, Op. 30. I was going to play it with conductor Henri Tamianka, the first violin of the Paganini String Quartet who had started a chamber orchestra in Los Angeles and hired me to play it in UCLA's Royce Hall. I was overjoyed at the thought of performing with Henry, as I had collaborated with him many times. We first met him when we moved to Los Angeles in 1958. There were many chamber-music evenings, as every single weekend there was a party at the home of cellist Gabor Rejto or Al Davis or Phil Goldberg, who was a fantastic viola player and contractor for Hollywood orchestras. He and I became like high-school buddies, though he was in his late 40s. We tried out duets, trios, and quintets for guitar, flute, cello, and violin by Boccherini, Paganini, Haydn, and Castelnuovo-Tedesco, among others. I was hungry for repertoire, and these get-togethers were very satisfying. Among the musicians I really enjoyed playing with was Susan Greenberg, a wonderful flutist. She and I played chamber music during one of the soirées at Phil's house, and Phil was so taken with her artistry that he gave her all her first breaks to play with orchestras in Los Angeles.

We played many times with Henri Tamianka, who now invited me to perform the Giuliani Concerto, Op. 30. But then, for whatever reason, he cancelled my appearance and offered the gig to another friend of ours, one who had sent us many students and helped us survive in Los Angeles. That guitarist was the Brazilian virtuoso Laurindo Almeida (1917–95). I was very disappointed, because I was looking forward to doing it in Royce Hall with Henry.

A couple of weeks later, I get a phone call from our manager, Herb Fox, and he said, "Pepe, we're very lucky. I just got a call from Neville Marriner. He recently founded the Los Angeles Chamber Orchestra, and he wants you to play the Op. 30 with them, two weeks after you would have played it at Royce Hall. You could not have done this if you had played it with Henry. You are on to play it with Neville." We are nothing but balls on the billiard table. Then there was a program called Luncheon at the Music Center. It was an hourlong radio program featuring people who were to perform there. They interviewed Neville and me in the restaurant upstairs, asking about the upcoming concert. There was a wonderful chemistry between the two of us, even before we played a single note. It was very special, almost like mental telepathy, whereby two minds could think the same thing at the same time. Soon after the interview, we were on stage rehearsing. I had already played with many great conductors, but with Neville, it was a very special thing, the way that we could grow and have real "conversations" with the Op. 30. We both loved the experience. We had a couple of rehearsals and then gave the concert. Backstage was my father, along with Laurindo and Vicente Gómez. Once the concert was over, no one could have been sweeter or more complimentary than Laurindo and Vicente. I knew I had experienced something magical.

After every concert, Neville hosted a party, and he now took me to his studio to place a call to Eric Smith at Philips, the person who decided who would record what. Neville and he were longtime friends, and he said, "Eric, I want my next record to be the Giuliani concerto that I just played with Pepe. You will not believe it. I'm not asking you, I'm telling you. This is the next record." I was very touched, but so many things are often said after a concert, and some come to fruition, and some don't. However, a few weeks later, I got a phone call from Herb Fox, who reported that the date was fixed to go to London to record the Op. 30 with Neville and the Academy of St. Martin-in-the-Fields. But they needed a second piece for the flip side of the LP. I said definitely I wanted to record Joaquín Rodrigo's *Concierto madrigal* for two guitars and orchestra, which would include Angel. But Philips rejected the idea. They wanted something with only one guitar, not two, and they weren't familiar with

CONDUCTORS, ORCHESTRAL MUSICIANS

the *Concierto madrigal* and had no idea how well it would sell. So, I adopted a prima donna stance, something I rarely do, and insisted that I would not make the LP unless it included the *Madrigal*. It took a lot of negotiation, but Eric finally consented, and it became one of their all-time best-selling recordings.

The recording of the *Madrigal* is one of the highlights of my career. Angel and I recorded it first, and then I stayed on to record Giuliani. Eric sat in on the session with the score, and that same magic with Neville continued. The recording was done mainly in single takes, because with Neville, I never had to discuss anything in detail. We talked a little about the mood of the piece, a little about tempos. That's it. Then we just went on. It was like an improvised conversation. What touches me about the work I did with Neville is that we could pass the phrase from one to the other in a way that was inspired by what the other one had just done. I would take what Neville had done and continue it wherever my feelings led me. Then he would pick it up. I feel so fortunate, because not that many artists have been able to record as many concertos with one great conductor, one great orchestra. We played many times together, manifesting that friendship, that gift of surrendering to the moment and to what music was doing to both of us. You can hear that incredible connection in the recordings. He was one of my dearest friends, and I'm very grateful to the cosmos for bringing us together. And he was so receptive to my ideas for recordings that I would go to his cottage at the Colburn house and say, "Okay, let's have lunch and decide on the next recording!" Of course, other people were crucial to our creative collaboration. Guitar scholar Thomas Heck recovered the second and third guitar concertos of Giuliani, and that enabled me to make the premiere recordings of them with Neville.

Another great conductor who played an important role in my life was Rafael Frühbeck de Burgos. The first time I met him was at the Hollywood Bowl, where Angel and I were slated to give the world premiere of the *Madrigal* in 1970. I had been practicing it on my 1969 Hauser, but the concert would be the first time I used my Rodríguez guitar named "La Wonderful." When we arrived, Rodrigo and his wife, Vicky, were already there. Rafael got hung up in rehearsing *El amor brujo* again and again and again, and the *Madrigal* hardly got any attention. We finally rehearsed all but the last movement of the *Madrigal*, and Rodrigo was furious. Rafael had not timed it right, and we ended up premiering it without ever having run through the last movement, which is the *caccia a la española,* a type of Spanish fugue, and very long and difficult. But Rafael always had such mastery, such absolute perfection of technique, and the last movement was impeccable. The whole premiere was impeccable. Halfway through the performance, though, the amplification cut off. Rodrigo was nonetheless happy with the premiere, though it took him a little while to get over the fact that Rafael hadn't given it enough time for rehearsal. After that, they did so many things together that there were no hard feelings.

My reconnection with Rafael took place at the 1991 concert celebrating the centenary of Moreno Torroba's birth. During the first half, I played *Diálogos* and a set of songs with Victoria de los Ángeles.

After the intermission, the orchestra presented concert versions of his zarzuelas *La Marchenera* and *Luisa Fernanda.* In that concert, the musical spark between him and me was intense, and after that, I played hundreds of concerts with him in Latin America, the U.S., Europe, and Japan, including many performances of the *Concierto*

Figure 24. Pepe (*left*) with Rafael Frühbeck de Burgos speaking with Queen Sofía of Spain, 1991.

Figure 25. Pepe performs with Victoria de los Ángeles at a concert honoring the centenary of Federico Moreno Torroba's birth, 1991

de Aranjuez and *Diálogos*. Then, he became music director of the Deutsche Oper, where Lorenzo Palomo was pianist, and that is when Lorenzo composed the *Nocturnos de Andalucía*. We gave the premiere in Berlin and then took it all over the world. Rafael recorded Palomo's *Nocturnos* with me, and *Concierto de Cienfuegos* with the Romeros. The last concert we were supposed to do together was in Hamburg, featuring the premiere of a Palomo concerto for guitar, violin, and orchestra entitled *Fulgores*, a work commissioned by Rafael. But Rafael got very ill, and while a magnificent substitute conductor, Leopold Hager, violinist Ye Eun Choi, and I were performing *Fulgores*, Rafael passed away.

In Rafael, we have another great conductor who touched my life very deeply, both musically and personally. He and Neville had very different personalities and energies, different ways of feeling music. But I was one with each of them. I still really enjoy watching a 2014 video of my last performance with Rafael of the *Aranjuez*, as well as the 1992 documentary film about Rodrigo, *Shadows and Light*, in which I play the *Aranjuez* with Neville.

Figure 26. Pepe (*left*) with Lorenzo Palomo in Berlin before the premiere of *Nocturnos de Andalucía*, 1996.

Figure 27. Filming of the documentary *Shadows and Light*, with Neville Marriner conducting, 1991.

CONDUCTORS, ORCHESTRAL MUSICIANS 157

And on YouTube I can be seen playing it with Rafael and the Royal Danish Orchestra, possibly a month before his passing. I was with him backstage before that performance, and he was lying down with a high fever. But then it was time to go on stage, and it was incredible to see what the music could do to a body that was nearly finished. He became completely alive and energized, and you can see that in this recording. But you can also see the difference between him and Neville as conductors, as interpreters. I'm so happy I got to make that music with each of them: the same piece, the same soloist, but with different conductors and orchestras. Still, both were absolutely genuine and made music from the heart. To see how music can manifest in different but wonderful ways through two people is amazing.

After one of my recitals at the Auditorio Nacional in Madrid, Cecilia Rodrigo, the composer's daughter, came backstage and brought along a friend—Charles Dutoit, the great conductor. He was very enthusiastic and told me that he had had a very bad experience with a guitarist as a soloist and had decided never to play with another guitarist. But he would love to invite me to play with him conducting! We had a wonderful collaboration and gave concerts around the world, including such famous venues as the Place des Arts in Montreal and Carnegie Hall in New York. I'm very grateful for the opportunities to make music with such a great artist.

Once, the quartet was slated to appear with Charles at Carnegie Hall, in a program featuring the *Concierto andaluz* in the first half and a concert version of Falla's *La vida breve* in the second. Charles invited me to play the guitar part in *La vida breve*, and I enthusiastically accepted his invitation, as it is one of my favorite operas. At the high point of the drama, the Romani girl Salud learns that her beloved has betrayed her and married someone of his own class. Indignant, she, her grandmother, and granduncle go to the wedding party to confront him, and as they enter, a flamenco singer is intoning praises to the young married couple. So, this opera, with its grandly orchestrated score and choir, reaches a musical climax with one flamenco singer and one guitar. I loved the experience of playing it, though that was the only time I had the opportunity to do so.

But the experience was not without some controversy. Just before the concert, the mezzo-soprano who played the part of the grandmother was in the dressing room next to us, though I won't say her name. The quartet was there, and I was practicing scales like a fiend, getting ready to go out in five minutes. We were about to play the *Concierto andaluz*, which is not an easy concerto. None of the Rodrigo pieces are easy. But as I was warming up, the mezzo knocks on the door and angrily says, "Can't you wait to practice later? I'm trying to get into the role. I cannot think with you playing so many notes." And I replied that "No, I cannot wait, because I'm going to be playing a concerto in five minutes." She immediately backed off, saying, "Oh, I'm so sorry. I apologize. I thought that you were only going to play in *La vida breve*."

Life has been so wonderful to me, and I'm a very, very lucky man. One day, Celin and I were watching a young Spanish conductor accompany many great singers in a concert broadcast from Vienna. It was one of those evenings where they are singing arias and featuring great stars. We were totally taken by the tremendous talent of the young maestro, Miguel Ángel Gómez Martínez. Destiny saw to it that I would perform with him many times and experience firsthand his genius. We enjoyed a beautiful friendship.

On the 100th anniversary of Andrés Segovia's birth, in 1993, I was invited to perform Torroba's *Diálogos* in Linares, Segovia's birthplace. The conductor was Odón Alonso.

Figure 28. Conductor Miguel Ángel Gómez Martínez with Pepe, 1983.

Figure 29. Pepe performing in Linares, Spain, to honor the centenary of Segovia's birth, with Odón Alonso conducting, 1993.

This concert marks a very significant event in my life, because it began a wonderful collaboration with a great maestro in many performances together, including his farewell concert in Málaga, in which I performed the *Concierto de Aranjuez* and my family and I played the *Concierto andaluz*. At that concert, a wonderful music lover and gentleman, Vicente Coves Castellano, was joined by his young son, Vicente Coves. That was the first guitar concert that the young boy attended, and he was so taken with the music that he decided then and there to give up the piano and instead study the guitar. He took lessons with me from the time he was 13 or 14 years old, and he has become one of the leading guitarists of our time.

Manuel Coves, Vicente's brother, is one of the finest conductors I've worked with. Our first collaboration was the world-premiere recording of *Concierto en flamenco* by Torroba. I immediately recognized Manuel as a major talent. And I enjoyed recording two other Torroba concertos with him: *Tonada concertante* and *Homenaje a la seguidilla*. Again, this was the felicitous consequence of that little boy going with his father to a guitar concert.

Another conductor I have had the pleasure to work with is Enrique Diemecke. My family and I performed with him in Mexico City, and on that concert he also conducted *La noche de los mayas*, a 1939 film score by Silvestre Revueltas. It was just gorgeous, and that was a musical experience I will never forget. Enrique later invited my nephew Celino to play Manuel Ponce's *Concierto del Sur* on a concert he was to conduct in Long Beach; however, Celino got ill and couldn't perform, so I substituted for him, playing instead the *Fantasía para un gentilhombre* by Rodrigo. The following year, Enrique once again invited a fully recovered Celino to play the Ponce concerto, and in that concert, Enrique also premiered one of his own compositions, which I loved. So, I asked him to write me a guitar concerto, and he accepted my invitation. The following season, we premiered his *Concerto a Celedonio*, dedicated to my father, and it is a fabulous contribution to the concerto repertoire for guitar. I have performed it many times.

The first time that we were to appear together at the Teatro Colón in Buenos Aires, the orchestra went on strike. I had flown all the way to Argentina just to stand backstage and listen to a union member speaking to the musicians for the entire rehearsal—two days in a row! Regulations required the musicians to sit and listen to a union representative, and I had to stay there because I didn't know if at any minute he was going to stop. But he didn't stop before the rehearsal was to end, and the boycott of the concert was effective. So, Enrique and I just enjoyed a fine dinner together, and then I flew home. We returned to Buenos Aires the following year, and this time the concert took place. The historic Teatro Colón is one of my favorite concert halls in the world. We performed the *Concierto de Aranjuez*, and it was a big success. I feel very grateful to have had so many wonderful memories of rehearsing and performing with Enrique.

Yet another conductor who has played a very important role in my life is none other than my very own brother Angel. He is a sublime musician, and his performances as both guitarist and conductor have moved me to tears many times. I remember listening to him play the *Fantasía para un gentilhombre* in Seattle and how deeply touched I was by his performance. When I listen to his recording of Rodrigo's *Elogio para la guitarra*, it seems to me to be sheer perfection. But I have also been deeply touched by his interpretations of

CONDUCTORS, ORCHESTRAL MUSICIANS   161

the orchestral repertoire, particularly of Beethoven's symphonies. And he is also a wonderful conductor of operas.

In fact, he always had a very strong desire to be a conductor, and it was under his direction that I first performed the *Fantasía para un gentilhombre*. I thought that I was going to play it with Jorge Mester conducting the Louisville Orchestra, but at the rehearsal, Jorge surprised me by passing the baton to Angel, who conducted not only the rehearsal but also the performance. This was one of his first stints on the podium. I should mention that the quartet performed the *Concierto andaluz* with Jorge, and we enjoyed our collaborations with him. As I mentioned earlier, Angel and I once drew straws to see who would play the Giuliani Concerto, Op. 30, and who would play the *Aranjuez*. Angel won the *Aranjuez*, so for many years, I didn't play it. Eventually, Philips wanted me to record it, so I first played it with Angel conducting and then performed it with Neville Marriner in Los Angeles two weeks later. Neville and I finally recorded it in London in 1978, with the Academy of St. Martin-in-the-Fields. I have enjoyed very much being Angel's soloist many times. Together we gave the world premiere of Torroba's *Concierto en flamenco*, and a video of this performance can be seen on YouTube. He is an excellent accompanist and is very sensitive to the interpretive inclinations of the soloist.

A very important conductor in our life was the great Jesús López Cobos, with whom the quartet and I as soloist played many concerts. These appearances stand out in my memory and in my heart as what Arthur Rubinstein called "moments of eternity." We first met Jesús during the Hollywood Bowl premiere of Torroba's *Concierto ibérico* for guitar quartet and orchestra, a work composed for us. We immediately became close friends, and I later collaborated with him on the U.S. premiere of Lorenzo Palomo's *Nocturnos de Andalucía* for guitar and orchestra and *Concierto de Cienfuegos* for guitar quartet and orchestra. He was also a fabulous opera conductor, and I was fortunate to attend many of his performances as music director of the Deutsche Oper and the Madrid Opera. Whenever I played with Jesús, the music took on a very noble, loving feeling, filled with tenderness and dignity but lacking none of the sunshine and fireworks of Spain. One evening, I believe it was in 2017, Jesús called me to ask if I would be the soloist in the *Aranjuez* for his son, François López-Ferrer, as this would be his first time conducting a major orchestra in a subscription series. This was to be his grand debut, and it would take place in Santiago, Chile. I had known François since he was born, so I was very happy to accept this invitation. And I grew even happier during the first rehearsal. He had all of his father's wonderful qualities, but with his own personality. During the second half of the concert, I had my phone on video, and I was sharing it with Jesús, who was in Japan conducting *Aida*. He was extremely proud. Sadly, this was the last time that he and I spoke, as he died shortly thereafter.

One of the most unforgettable experiences I have had working with any conductor was during my trip to St. Petersburg, Russia, performing the *Concierto de Aranjuez* with the Spanish maestro Juanjo Mena in the magnificent Marinsky Theater. Juanjo and I developed an immediate rapport, even before we played a single note together. At the first rehearsal, I was taken with the gorgeous voice he has when he sings to the orchestra the way he wants a phrase to be rendered, because he's a marvelous countertenor. My family and I also had the privilege and pleasure of performing the *Concierto Andaluz* with him in Granada. To me, Juanjo is one of the most inspiring musicians to work with, and he belongs in the line of the great conductors.

Other conductors with whom I felt a deep connection included Eugene Ormandy. When I was a young man, Ormandy fell in love with Rodrigo's *Concierto andaluz*, and the quartet played it many times with the Philadelphia Orchestra. Andre Kostalanetz is known more for his renditions of popular music, but he was a deeply serious conductor, and we shared unforgettable experiences. We did two performances of the *Andaluz*, one with the Los Angeles Philharmonic and the other with the New York Philharmonic. And we performed Francisco de Madina's *Concierto flamenco*. Arthur Fiedler, another serious conductor but one known more for his "pops," conducted the premiere of Madina's *Concierto vasco*. Another great conductor, as well as one of my favorite composers, was Morton Gould. I enjoyed so much performing with him the work that he wrote for the Romeros, *Troubadour Music*, a truly inspired American masterpiece of the twentieth century. And speaking of American musicians, Michael Zearott was another major figure in my musical life.

So, I have worked with famous and not-so-famous conductors, but all of them were great. In fact, there are so many names, and I

Figure 30. Pepe (*left*) with Morton Gould at Carnegie Hall, 1992.

truly apologize to any conductor who has touched my heart but is not mentioned here. It's not because I didn't love working with them!

***

Q. Other famous musicians?

A. I was only 13 years old when we Romeros arrived in Santa Barbara after leaving Spain, and at some point, I went with my family to the Music Academy of the West there. That was where I met William Eddy, the professor of singing and my future father-in-law. We participated in chamber-music evenings at his house on weekends, and I met a lot of Academy students who would go on to have successful careers in music. And I also met the legendary Lotte Lehmann, a girlfriend of Richard Strauss for whom he wrote the opera *Der Rosenkavalier*. She sang in the premiere of that work and was now in charge of the vocal department at the Academy. I was born with a passion for opera, so I didn't miss a single masterclass with her during our first year in Santa Barbara. Knowing my love of opera, she asked me if I would play for her class, which I gladly did. She loved the guitar and my performance.

I also met a very nice, young English girl visiting the U.S., and she was there when I performed. I met her again many years later.

Her name was Molly, and by the time our paths crossed once more, she had become Mrs. Neville Marriner. She often accompanied Neville to California when he conducted. She is a wonderful person and an incredible partner to Neville. When he went back to tell her about the experience he had with me, she said, "I heard him at Lotte Lehmann's class many years ago." So, through the Academy and those chamber-music evenings, first in Santa Barbara and later in Los Angeles, I got to befriend and play with phenomenal people. One of my dear friends in Los Angeles was Mischa Elman, a legendary violinist in his mid-to-late 70s. He used to invite me to go to his rehearsals and concerts, and we became good friends. And it was through Mischa that I met violist Phil Goldberg, the main contractor for all the movie studios. He assembled all the musicians for the chamber orchestra that Henri Tamianka conducted and for the orchestra directed by Neville.

Once Mischa was getting ready to perform a concerto, and the rehearsals were at the Local 47 Musicians Union Hall in Hollywood, of which I've been a member since the age of 14. My father and I went to the rehearsal at Mischa's request because the conductor was a famous Spaniard named José Iturbi. He was a fantastic pianist but also somewhat infamous for having quite a temper. I later found out that it resulted from being nervous, and thus he had a phobia about anyone watching a rehearsal. When he noticed us sitting in the hall, he said, "I cannot have anybody in the audience. The hall must be empty!" And he kicked us out. Mischa quickly intervened, explaining to him that we were there at his invitation, that we had recently arrived from Spain, and that we played the guitar. Mischa was nice, but José was unpleasant. So, we went home, but as soon as we arrived in our little apartment on Wilton Place, the phone rang, and it was José offering an apology. "Please, you have no idea how bad I feel. I didn't realize you were musicians invited by Mischa. Please accept my apologies and come to dinner this evening at my house. I will make a paella for you."

He was a great cook and lived by himself with a housekeeper. Amparo was his sister, and he said that she was a better pianist than he. In fact, he had had quite a troubled life. The housekeeper was also his domestic partner, but that was completely secret, and nobody knew. They had to be very discreet. Shortly before we met him, his daughter had committed suicide. She was very jealous of Amparo's daughter, Amparito. Later we got to know her well

CONDUCTORS, ORCHESTRAL MUSICIANS   165

because she was a flamenco dancer. She would come to our studio, and I would accompany her and other dancers. Anyway, he lived in a mansion and kept a big Baldwin piano in the living room, along with two Steinways in his bedroom; however, because he was a Baldwin artist, he kept that a secret.

He was not only a major pianist and conductor but had also starred in Hollywood movies. And he was an avid collector of art. He had paintings by artists of the caliber of Diego Velázquez and Francisco de Goya. Most of all, he just loved to sit at the piano and play for us. He would render an excerpt from Albéniz's *Sevilla* and then wondered aloud why Segovia played it a certain way and inquired how we thought it should be played. This went on for hours! I was fascinated with his way of playing, his comments, though he admitted that "I get so nervous before I play that many times I wish the theater would catch on fire or there would be an earthquake." To overcome his nerves, he projected excessive pride to the public, making him seem as if he had an incredible ego. But that was simply how he dealt with his insecurity.

Some of the best lessons I have learned have come from seeing "giants" forget, have mental lapses, drop notes. It happens, and it does not affect them at all. Mischa invited me to a concert at Carnegie Hall featuring him as the soloist and with José conducting. I believe that it was his farewell concert in New York, and he played magnificently. And yet, at the end of the concerto, he had a mental lapse and had to repeat several measures a few times. I got to hear twenty unforgettable versions of the same passage! But he was nonetheless a very important person, as was the great Hungarian cellist Gabor Rejto, who taught at the University of Southern California and invited me to join him on the faculty there when I was in my early twenties.

It was at USC that I also got to know Jascha Heifetz and had the opportunity to sit and watch him practice. On those occasions when I could only hear and not actually see what was going on in his studio, I could always tell if it was him or one of his students playing. Because his students would be playing the way you imagine that Paganini did, going all over the violin, while Jascha would play at less than half the tempo, no vibrato, working on the purity of the sound, intonation, and hitting the note perfectly. He had a very precise way of practicing, which I always did too, but observing him really reinforced a way of practicing that I have maintained to this day. His left-hand exercises were amazing, and he was a big guitar enthusiast. In fact, I adapted those exercises to the guitar. It's a way of executing left-hand slurs and *ligados* with a muted sound and with having the fingers all on one string, isolating the movement of each finger. It is all about precision.

Of course, as time went on, my family and I met and collaborated with many other great musicians. I got to know soprano Elly Ameling by listening to Franz Schubert's *The Shepherd on the Rock*, D. 65, for soprano, clarinet, and piano. When I heard it, I fell in love with the music and her voice. What a musician, what purity! Schubert is one of my idols, the composer who connects me to my own sense of spirituality, the deepest part of me—simplicity, beauty, that sense of wonder that children have and that leads them to understand things in a way that we adults do not. Schubert connects me to such a beautiful place, and when I heard Elly sing that music, she became Schubert. She took the listener inside his heart and his mind so that one could hear the music as he heard it before he wrote it.

I finally met her at a party thrown by Philips, the label for which we were both making recordings. She was the most loving, humble, beautiful person, and to my great joy we hit it off and played many concerts together. She invited me to perform with her at the Concertgebouw for her farewell concert. That was an amazing experience, as was playing with soprano Jessye Norman. I met her at a dinner after having gone to hear her at the Metropolitan Opera. This was in the 1980s, when one of my dearest friends, Nancy Zannini, was the head of Philips North America. She and I went to many operas together, and after one such excursion to the Metropolitan Opera, we went to a dinner afterward and met Jessye Norman, who had starred in the production. The famous minimalist Philip Glass was also at that dinner, but Jessye and I connected in a personal way, and we decided right then and there that we would do something together. And we did: the *Siete canciones populares españolas* by Manuel de Falla, which we performed all over the world. Even though she didn't speak Spanish, she nonetheless had phenomenal Spanish diction. She had such a passionate and lyrical style, and surprisingly enough, her huge and powerful voice matched the guitar to perfection.

And then Jessye and I decided to do a recording for Philips and set about choosing the repertoire. Sadly, the project never reached fruition because she got sick at recording time, and then that was

CONDUCTORS, ORCHESTRAL MUSICIANS   167

getting close to the end of Philips. She finally recovered, but by then Philips had stopped recording. It was a great misfortune, because we were also going to do a lot of Rodrigo's songs. In fact, it was for that recording that Rodrigo wrote *Aranjuez con tu amor*, with lyrics by his wife, Victoria, and music based on the second movement of the concerto. The poetic lyrics tell the story of how she and Joaquín fell in love at Aranjuez and how that love had faded. But Rodrigo protested, "No, I still love you." I still wish that we had made that recording, but I did perform with her in many venues.

Torroba's centenary was where I got to know and work with Victoria de los Ángeles. Her beautiful voice and interpretations touched me deeply and helped to formulate my sense of what it means to be not just a musician but also an artist. Besides my father, it has been the great musicians with whom I have collaborated, especially singers, who have made a deep impression on me. Victoria and I met the day before the concert in Madrid in her hotel room to rehearse. We got into an animated discussion, and she said, "You know that I love all your recordings, and I particularly like the way you play Giuliani. My studies at the Liceu in Barcelona were not as a singer. I was originally going to be a guitar player!" That helped to explain why she spoke so knowledgeably about the guitar. We kept talking and didn't spend much time actually rehearsing our program of Torroba's songs.

So, through my love of singing, I've gotten to work with diverse singers. I remember what a tremendous experience it was playing with the great Mexican tenor Francisco Araiza, who is one of my favorite Mozart tenors.

I always feel that Don Octavio doesn't really challenge or rival the power of Don Giovanni, but Francisco Araiza did. He was an amazing singer who brought tremendous character and strength to Mozart's tenor roles. I got to do the *Siete canciones* with him at the Salzburg Festival, as well as with another singer, who was to become one of my dearest friends: Thomas Quasthoff, a remarkable bass-baritone who recorded with Herbert von Karajan.

My manager in Europe was Konzertdirektion Schlote, and Schlote had a special gift for finding talented musicians who would go on to become legends. He had been the manager of Erich Leinsdorf and David Oistrakh. Among the singers that he represented was Quasthoff, and he had the idea of bringing the two of us together. We met at a restaurant in Salzburg to get acquainted, and we got

Figure 31. Pepe performing with Mexican tenor Francisco Araiza, 1988.

along very well, subsequently giving many concerts with a repertoire that included Dowland, Schubert, Rodrigo, Falla, and García Lorca. We would always finish with the serenade "Deh, vieni alla finestra" from *Don Giovanni* by Mozart.

It was an enriching experience, though one not without complications. I had just finished the arrangements of these songs, especially those by Schubert, when I decided to take a few days off to visit my sister-in-law Elisa, who had recently been divorced. I wanted to offer her my support. I went to check in at the ticket counter in the Houston airport and set my briefcase and guitar down. Once I had the boarding pass, I reached down for the briefcase, and it was gone! It contained all the Schubert arrangements I had made, and now they were gone. Carissa and a friend of ours called CNN, which announced the disappearance, asking anyone who had mistakenly taken my briefcase to please call me and return it. But I never heard anything.

The only thing that brings me a little bit of comfort is knowing that whoever stole it was expecting to get something more than a whole bunch of handwritten transcriptions for guitar of Schubert

Figure 32. Pepe performing with German bass-baritone Thomas Quasthoff, 1994.

songs, along with a book of German poetry. I now had only a couple of weeks in which to redo all that work, though my daughter Angelina was a big help. I also had the assistance of a guitar student of mine, the late Heike Matthiesen, who did the arrangement of the *Don Giovanni* serenade. All such travails aside, I treasure the memories of those concerts. And my friendship with Thomas Quasthoff is enduring. He's a phenomenal artist, singer, musician, and exceptional human being.

Montserrat Caballé met Lorenzo Palomo when he was a pianist with the Deutsche Oper, and he wrote a set of songs for her. However, after giving them to her, he got no further response for almost six years. Then, while in San Diego, he got a letter from her telling him that she was premiering his songs at Carnegie Hall. They became good friends, and he wrote *Mi jardín solitario* (My Solitary Garden) for her and me. Sadly, it was never performed by her because on the very day he gave her the music, she had been diagnosed with a brain tumor. So, we met often but never worked together. The closest we came was in Munich, where we were interviewed for a special TV show about musicians from musical families. Still, I got to enjoy

Figure 33. Philippe Entremont conducting the Munich Symphony Orchestra in a performance of Rodrigo's *Concierto de Aranjuez* with Pepe as soloist, 2015.

her as a friend and admired her immensely as an artist. *Mi jardín solitario* led me to work with another fantastic Spanish soprano, María Bayo. We recorded it in Germany on the Naxos label.

One of my favorite musicians is Philippe Entremont. In 1959, when my brother Celin started to buy recordings, he introduced me to the LPs of a young French pianist named Philippe Entremont. I loved his musicality, his tone, his phrasing, his ethereal virtuosity, his sense of style. Imagine how excited I was when, years later, I was invited to play at the Concertgebouw in Amsterdam with Philippe conducting! From the beginning of the first rehearsal, the experience was more wonderful than I had even imagined. Philippe is an extraordinary human being, and I can truly say that his music is a reflection of his soul. He invited me and my family on a later occasion to his festival in Santo Domingo, and not only were the concerts unforgettable, but so was smoking cigars together!

13

GUITARISTS

Q. It goes without saying that you have known many guitarists during your lifetime. Let's explore those connections.

A. Outside of my family, the list is enormous, but perhaps the first one that I became aware of was Rogelio Molina, a student of Tárrega, who used to come to our house in Málaga every weekend and sit for an entire day talking with my father about how Tárrega did this and that. When I was still a little boy, there were many times when Narciso Yepes performed in Málaga, and he would come over to the house to get ready for the concert. He was such a wonderful gentleman, and what impressed me was that he and my father were like brothers, despite the fact that aficionados might like to imagine or create a rivalry between famous musicians. I never heard either one say anything bad about the other. Once, while Angel and I were talking with Narciso about various guitarists, he said that before we mention Celedonio, we should observe a moment of silence and clear our minds in order to talk about the greatest guitarist ever. The admiration and brotherhood that they felt were remarkable, and they were both very proud of us. He told me about a time when Narciso listened to Celin play Torroba's *Sonatina* and Albéniz's *Rumores de La Caleta*. Narciso praised Celin's playing, and when I was a little older, we also became very good friends and enjoyed talking about the concertos we were recording. Narciso was recording for Deutsche Grammophon when he started touring with the ten-string guitar.

Venezuelan virtuoso Alirio Díaz became an close friend of my father, as did Regino Sainz de la Maza. I didn't know Alirio Díaz that well personally, because he was not around very much when I was growing up. But he was very close to my father when they were quite young, and as a matter of fact, they were roommates for a while in

Madrid. He was studying with Segovia, but what I remember is his tremendously effusive admiration for my father. He always used to say to me, "Your father is the greatest guitarist in the world." He felt a great deal of love and admiration for my father, which my father reciprocated. I had a much closer relationship with Narciso Yepes, who would visit the house just to hang out and have dinner. And we went to one another's concerts. We had a real friendship.

Regino Sainz de la Maza attended the premiere of Torroba's *Concierto ibérico* for guitar quartet and orchestra, and that night after the concert, we had dinner at his house, playing his guitars. I loved a maple Santos he had, and though both Regino and my father also tried out guitars, I did most of the playing, with my father choosing the pieces. At one point, Regino said to Celedonio, "You have surpassed me by far, and you didn't have to play a note. You did it with your penis!" He then started dedicating some of his own compositions to my father. And just as a side note, in those days, we didn't talk about politics. Regino was reliably right-wing, whereas the Romeros were leftists.

I must mention the legendary flamenco guitarist Sabicas. We first met him and Carmen Amaya in Santa Barbara, and later, after we moved to Los Angeles, we enjoyed daily visits from him during the year that he was in residence there, giving concerts. He was one of the great instrumentalists of his era, as a performer and as a musical creator. Torroba wrote a magnificent *Concierto en flamenco* for Sabicas, which I actually premiered in Málaga, with Angel conducting the orchestra there. Another flamenco guitarist who has played an important role in my career is Serranito. I met him in the early 1970s, when he was a featured artist at the Café de Chinitas in Madrid, and I was simply blown away by his artistry, virtuosity, and the dynamic range of his playing. I returned very often to hear him. It was during one of these performances that I met Enrique Morente, the famed flamenco singer, and the three of us developed a lifelong friendship. I was delighted that at the Pepe Romero Festival in Málaga in 2023, we gave Serranito a well-deserved Lifetime Achievement Award.

Returning to the realm of classical guitar, one of my dearest guitarist friends is Manuel Barrueco, as we have known each other since we were very young. We met in Houston at the Guitar Gallery, which is where I also met Carissa. I spent a lot of time there, as it was one of the early guitar centers in the U.S. After Manuel won second prize at the 1978 Toronto competition, he performed in Houston. That brings me back to Cervantes and *Don Quixote*, in which he talks a little bit about his own participation in a competition and dismissing first prize because second prize was the real one! I don't like competitions because they separate people by pitting them against one another, whereas the purpose of music is to search for the oneness in all of us. That is the magic and the power of music. So, competitions mean nothing to me. But winning second prize when everyone present knew he deserved to win first prize gave a major boost to Manuel's career. I met him in Houston, and we have remained close friends to this day. We have shared many deep feelings about music, about being a musician, about the challenges we face as musicians. That has been a relationship I have enjoyed immensely.

And as a result of attending many music festivals over the years, I have also developed a wonderful relationship with Scottish virtuoso David Russell. Oscar Ghiglia was a very close friend when he was active as a concert artist. He would come over to our house to try out both guitars and pasta! In Germany, I developed a sense of camaraderie with both Siegfried Behrend and Karl Scheit. One thing I dislike about mentioning particular guitarists, however, is that we cannot include every single one who is dear to me. That would require a separate book! There are so many colleagues who have touched my soul and are dear friends of mine. So, for those who are not mentioned on these pages, I want them to know that I love them just as much.

I went to a concert of the Abreu brothers many years ago, and they were fantastic. After the concert, I went backstage to say hello, and Sergio was very happy to meet me, showing me his guitar by Hermann Hauser, Sr. But his brother, Eduardo, was completely reserved, and I learned later that he was autistic. On stage he was magnificent, but face to face, there was no interaction. He did not respond at all when I reached out to shake his hand and compliment him. But when I started trying Sergio's guitar, then we bonded. From that moment on, we were friends, because now he trusted me. Once, while they were on tour, and just before a concert, Eduardo said to Sergio, "I'm not going to play this concert and I'm not playing anymore. I'm done." He quit cold turkey, like Forrest Gump deciding not to run or play ping pong anymore. Sergio continued for a couple more years as soloist and then gave that up and became a guitar maker. But we remained close friends. I played quite a few times in Brazil, and he made me a guitar in the early 1990s. Gioachino Giussani had made me a guitar that I fell in love with in 1990, and I was playing that guitar in Brazil. Then Sergio came to show me the guitar he had made for me, but after playing my Giussani, he changed his mind and said, "I cannot show it to you because it does not compare to this." He was very humble, but I have seen truly great instruments by him. His guitars were influenced by the Hermann Hauser and Santos Hernández instruments that Eduardo played. After giving up concertizing, Eduardo went on to teach mathematics; sadly, Sergio died on January 19, 2023.

The first time I played the Giuliani Concerto, Op. 30, with Neville, my father, Laurindo Almeida, and Vicente Gómez were all rejoicing backstage over the success I had just had. I have enjoyed a very rewarding reciprocity of admiration and respect with my colleagues. Moreover, I have never been aware of jealousy, envy, or ill feelings from any colleague. I have certainly felt none towards them.

My relationship with Julian Bream was more brief but very intense. He was extremely charming, and his praise of me bordered on the hyperbolic at times. But I felt the same way about his playing, as he was one of the guitarists whose concerts I most enjoyed attending. Bream was fearless, and he allowed himself to do whatever the music told him to do at the moment. Though he had some reservations about his own technique, he could do anything, and he played magnificently. Still, he sometimes doubted himself and would share with me the misgivings he had about his own method, about how he had taught himself to play. But then would come the moment of truth on stage, and he abandoned those reservations and played the music as he felt it in the moment. It was terrific, and I found him to be a very inspiring person.

He once invited me to spend a weekend with him in his village, but I didn't think it would be possible because I was making a recording in London and didn't have the time. But he insisted, saying that we wouldn't play and not even to bring my guitar. We would just relax and have a good time. I remember that we talked a lot about Rodrigo's *Concierto de Aranjuez*. Though he was British, he's one of the players whose interpretations of Spanish music I most enjoy. He does a beautiful job with Albéniz's *Córdoba, Mallorca, Granada*, and *Cádiz*, as well as the *Serenata española* by Malats. He had a great feeling for that music.

GUITARISTS

I met John Williams many years ago in London, when Angel and I were recording the *Madrigal* there. John gave a concert, and Angel and I attended and then went backstage to meet him. After that, we appeared on many festival programs together. Once, we spent quite a few days together in Belgrade, where I had a weird experience during a press conference with me, John, and the other participants. One of the journalists asked about our teachers, noting that I had studied with my father, and John, with Segovia. And John looks at me and says, "You go first." So, I talked about what it was like to study with my idol. It was a privilege, an honor, everything positive. Then John's turn came, and the first words out of his mouth were that he learned nothing from Segovia and that his style was not anything like Segovia's! And I agree. Though I admire both of them, they don't play anything like one another. One of my father's students for a short time was John's father, Len Williams. So, John plays more like us than Segovia.

Celin, Celino, Lito, and I once spent a week in Cuba with John. We were in the same hotel, and none of us practiced! All we did was drink rum, smoke cigars, and sit on the veranda listening to Cuban musicians. And there was this young guitar player, Fabián, accompanying a singer named Luz Ángela Jiménez. He was such a natural talent, and he could play a tremolo with the little finger of his right hand, as if it were a pick. He played chords, melodies, and other things most classical players don't attempt because we "know" it's impossible. But he didn't know it's impossible. John turned to me and said, "This guy has more talent in one finger than I have in my entire body!" John is a very humble, wonderful gentleman, and he deserves every bit of fame he has achieved. I've enjoyed not only his music but his personal friendship. So, I'll always remember that week in Cuba. I should add that my good friend Eduardo Fernández was there, as was Leo Brouwer, of course. I also recall meeting Jesús Ortega, another wonderful guitar player from Cuba.

Once, in New York City, Angel and I did a TV interview, and the station had also invited another young player to be interviewed, one with whom I immediately bonded: Jorge Morel, the legendary Argentine composer and guitarist who wrote a piece dedicated to my father, *Al maestro* (To the Maestro), which I have also premiered in concert and then recorded. It was composed in 1996 in memory of Celedonio, who had recently passed away. That became a very important friendship and connection in our lives. He was like a member of the Romero family and is one of the guitarists, composers, and arrangers I most enjoy and respect. His guitar arrangement of the suite from *West Side Story* is remarkable. He lived in New York but came to California and stayed at our house, and we benefited from the kind of sharing that occurs between artists who are very creative but also very different. He was always busy making new arrangements, of Gershwin or whatever. We became close to his entire family and went through the death of his wife, who suffered a ruptured pregnancy right in front of his eyes. And yet, he turned that horrific experience into some of the most beautiful music. When his brother died, he wrote one of my favorite tangos, *Otro tango Buenos Aires*. It is dedicated to the memory of his brother.

Another legend who impacted our lives a lot was a young flamenco guitarist about to make his debut in Madrid playing at the Café Chinitas, a *tablao* that was a launching pad for some of the greatest flamenco players. His name was Manolo Sanlúcar, and he was performing for the first time the night before Angel and I premiered the *Madrigal* in Madrid. So, we went to see him perform, and then I got talked into going to a party after he played. But I was furious with myself because I got back to the hotel about 6 in the morning, had a rehearsal at 9:30 a.m., and then the performance that night. How could I do that and not have stayed at the hotel and gotten a good night's sleep? Fortunately, youth was in my favor, and the concert was a great success. But that was the night that Manolo and the Romeros met, resulting in a friendship that lasted to the end of his life and resulted in many wonderful experiences.

One such experience stands out in my memory. A few years later, I recall Celin waking me up in Madrid one morning, saying, "I'm really sick Pepe and have to go to the doctor. I have a terrible pain on my face and I'm sure I have a tumor." He was very upset, so I called Rodrigo to get a referral to a doctor who could see him right away. Rodrigo suggested taking him right away to the emergency room at the hospital, but before doing that, I decided to call someone else who might possibly have connections: Manolo, who by this time was a huge star in the world of flamenco. Manolo said he would send a car to take Celin to his doctor, and a few minutes later, the car arrived and the doctor was able to see Celin immediately. Meanwhile, Manolo was in his pajamas in the waiting room! He was a very emotional, hot-blooded, effusive person who took every experience very seriously, so as we were waiting there, he was

Figure 34. (*Left to right*) Pepe, Angel, and Celin Romero enjoy their beloved *puros* in 2000.

extremely upset, even more than me. Finally, the doctor came out and announced that Celin was fine and just had an inflamed facial nerve. There was nothing else wrong with him.

We celebrated this benign diagnosis by going with Manolo to a new restaurant, La Dorada. When we walked in, he was like a rock star, and everybody knew him. It was during our meal together that evening that he was inspired with the main theme of what would become his ballet *Medea*, which I played recently but he unfortunately didn't hear. I was going to play it in 2019, but then COVID caused the performance to be postponed. By the time I finally played it, in 2022, he had recently passed away. But when I called him and told him I was going to play it, he was exuberant. When he played it, of course, it sounded very flamenco; however, he actually wanted it to be played more in the classical style of Albéniz or Rodrigo. I love playing it, and as a matter of fact, I recently performed it for my eightieth birthday in Milan. And I am going to record it.

Manolo wasn't the only flamenco maestro to whom I was close. I was on an airplane from Madrid to Hamburg, where Philips used to have many meetings with all the directors of their different centers around the world. They had their own representatives who took care of promoting and distributing recordings, as there were a lot of record stores in the golden days of recording. I was going there to present my Giuliani LP. As I was going through passport control, however, there was a young fellow in front of me having problems with the police, who said that his name on the papers of invitation that he had received did not match his name on his passport. I asked the policeman if he could speak English, so that I could provide translation and help solve the problem. It turned out that the invitation letter was for one Paco de Lucía, but his passport said Francisco Sánchez; of course, Paco de Lucía was his stage name. I quickly informed the police that they were going to have the same problem with me because my invitation said Pepe Romero but my passport gave my name as José Luis. I patiently explained that, in Spanish, Pepe is the diminutive of José! That cleared the way for us both. Now, neither Paco nor I recognized one another, but we immediately hugged each other and became longtime friends. He was headed to the Philips meeting to present one of his recordings, because he was under contract with Philips just like me.

One of the great things about this job of concertizing and traveling around is the people you meet, the connections you make. It is fascinating to meet someone who is from somewhere else in the world but doing exactly the same thing you are, though from a different angle. In the summer of 2022, I had a wonderful time meeting José Luis Merlin, another outstanding player and composer. This was about the same time that I met the legendary troubadour Amancio Prada. Both remain very close and valued friends of mine. It's a wonderful experience to see how many of us are doing our best to bring the joy of music into the world, to connect with people who use the guitar as a means of transporting our own spirit to connect with other spirits. It doesn't matter who plays faster or who plays more pieces. All that matters is what we feel while we are doing it and what people who listen to what we leave behind will feel. It should help all of us to look inside and find the better part of ourselves.

One of our managers, Susan Lamborghini, had the idea of creating the Guitar Summit, which was one of the most memorable tours for me because it involved presenting the guitar in all its aspects: flamenco with Paco Peña, American fingerstyle with Leo Kottke, jazz with Joe Pass, and classical with me. We all appeared on the

GUITARISTS

Figure 35. Jazz guitarist Joe Pass (*left*) with Pepe, 1994.

same program, each of us playing about twenty-five minutes, and at the end, everyone would improvise together, except for me. I played *Recuerdos, Asturias,* and Bach, while the others improvised around those pieces in their own style.

Leo Kottke's fingerpicking style draws on blues, jazz, and folk music, a genre I had no idea of. He and I remain very good friends, and we share very similar political ideas of freedom. And meeting Joe Pass on that tour really enriched my life because I had not yet been much exposed to jazz either; however, after hearing him, I fell in love with it. I really bonded with Joe, not only as an artist but as a human being. On this tour we traveled in a bus, and we would get in the bus after the concert and eat a wonderful dinner served to us there. The bus was equipped with individual small bedrooms, and I would sit in Joe's as told me his entire life story: about his problem with drugs, the four years he spent in a Texas penitentiary, and his establishment of a chain of eighteen recovery houses for addicts. It was very inspiring to see the power of music in helping a person to find what is best within them and to express that outwardly, after having fallen to the bottom. He was a not only a great artist but also a great person, in the way he was able to use his problems to alleviate other peoples' problems. His father was Italian and deeply involved in the Mafia. So, Joe left home at an early age and soon had to overcome many difficulties.

Instead of warming up before our concerts, Joe would just listen to me practice backstage. As I have mentioned before, I like to just let loose and play whatever pieces come to mind, so that I get in tune with the moment. Joe would listen and say, "Fatso [his nickname for me], you really fuck my mind. After I hear you play, it's hard for me to play." He loved classical guitar. Our penultimate concert was at the Ambassador Auditorium in Pasadena, but he did not perform. Sadly, he died from cancer during the second half of the Summit, in 1994. He was very brave, receiving treatments before the concerts, and we would accompany him to the hospital. He and I loved to smoke cigars and talk. "Fatso, when I die and you and I are alone, I want you to play Sor's Op. 9 for me. And then I want you to smoke a cigar and blow the smoke and close the coffin so the smoke is locked in there with me." I did as he requested, but I wasn't alone. Susan Lamborghini was there with me. After the viewing, I spoke to the funeral home, and they allowed me to play Sor's *Variations on a Theme of Mozart*, Op. 9, smoke a cigar, and blow smoke into his coffin. Rest in peace, my friend.

PART VI

LOVES

14

LOVE OF GREAT COMPOSERS

Q. In this chapter, we want to explore your abiding love of certain genres of music and the composers who wrote masterworks for them. Of course, this includes the guitar and other instrumental pieces, but it also embraces musical theater, i.e., both opera and *zarzuela* (operetta). Who are some of your favorite opera composers?

A. We could go on and on and on, but over the years, I have had a tremendous love for Italian opera. I am especially fond of Mozart's Italian operas, *The Marriage of Figaro* and *Don Giovanni*, though I also adore *The Magic Flute*. I never tire of listening to those works, and I have returned to them over and over during my life. I also love the operas of Verdi and Puccini. I'm overwhelmed with their dramatic gift, their ability to tell a story, and how masterfully they merge words and music. They delve into the deepest part of the listener's spirit, so that you don't just listen with your ears and with your mind; indeed, their operas tap into the deepest emotions.

So, listening to opera is for me a way to work through some deep emotions. It's like having the Ultimate Therapist, because you work through your unhappiness, your anger, your depression, through everything. And at the end, there is beauty in all of it. The music of those three composers, Mozart, Verdi, and Puccini, speaks to me about life.

***

Q. Among Verdi's operas, I think you have mentioned *Rigoletto* as a favorite, no?

A. Yes, *Rigoletto*, as well as *Un ballo in maschera*, *La Traviata*, and *Otello*. *Nabucco* is especially moving for people who feel very

Figure 36. Pepe standing next to the theater door through which Mozart passed at the 1787 premiere of *Don Giovanni* in Prague, 2000.

connected to tragedy, especially the tragedy personified by the journey of the Jewish people, their yearning for freedom. The Roma (Gypsies) are a similarly persecuted culture. So, when you listen to *Nabucco*, you find great comfort in it.

Music is the light at the end of the tunnel not just because it is beautiful but also because of what it teaches us about life. Ideally, it puts us in perfect harmony with our deepest troubles and joys. Verdi certainly knew the tragic dimension of human life. He had problems with his own father, and then his wife and children died when they were young. Not surprisingly, therefore, almost all of his operas are tragedies. And yet, he was able to convert all of that sorrow into sublime music dramas. By connecting with the emotions of the composer, we explore the depths of our own emotional life.

***

Q. And among Puccini's operas, I believe that *La Bohème* and *Tosca* are favorites.

LOVE OF GREAT COMPOSERS 185

A. Yes, though if I were stranded on an island and could only have one of Puccini's operas to listen to, I would choose *La Bohème*, for all the reasons I mentioned in connection with Verdi.

***

Q. The *zarzuela* is a Spanish variety of operetta alternating spoken dialogue with musical numbers, including dances, arias, duets, and choruses. You feel a very close bond with the zarzuela, no?

A. I have a great love for the zarzuela as well as for Spanish operas by Albéniz, Bretón, Granados, Falla, and others. Spanish opera combines my love of Italian opera with the musical nationalism of Spain in a wonderful way. *Pepita Jiménez* by Albéniz, *La Dolores* by Bretón, *Goyescas* by Granados, and *La vida breve* by Falla are all great favorites of mine. I have transcribed for the quartet many numbers from both zarzuelas and operas, and they figure prominently in our repertoire, especially the famous "Jota" from *La Dolores*. That's always a big hit, because it is one of the most compelling and memorable versions of a traditional *jota*, a type of music and dance associated with Aragón, though there are several regional variants of it elsewhere in Spain. I made that arrangement when I was only about 17 years old. I know the date I finished it because I always date my scores. I should say that I am good friends with Antoni Ros-Marbà, the Catalonian conductor, and his interpretation of *La Dolores* is just superb. It is available on YouTube, and everyone who wants to understand Spanish music should watch it, along with his other splendid renditions of Spanish classics. He and I once performed together on a tour through France, and I treasure that memory.

In fact, the Spanish repertoire is both wide and deep. When we think of Tomás Bretón, for example, we associate him principally with his zarzuela *La Verbena de la Paloma*. *La Dolores* is less well known, especially outside of Spain, though it reveals a great debt to Wagner and is a masterpiece in its own right. It is very dramatic and lyrical, with a wide range of dynamics and emotions. And the way that he introduces the *jota* is marvelous. It is really quite authentic, using the traditional plucked-string instruments like bandurrias and mandolins. That's why it works so well for guitar quartet, something I recognized already as a teenager. So, my love for Spanish opera is very much alive. Of course, for me, zarzuela is the heart and soul of Spanish musical theater. We perform many pieces from that repertoire, for example, the Preludio to *La Revoltosa* by Ruperto Chapí (1851–1909), an arrangement made by Lorenzo Palomo.

***

Q. Obviously, two of your favorite zarzuela composers are Bretón and Chapí. Of course, you also love Torroba, who wrote some exquisite works for the guitar but whose legacy rests mainly on his zarzuelas, especially *Luisa Fernanda*. What can you tell us about him?

A. If I were going to be stranded on that island with the music of only one composer, that composer might well be Torroba. He sums up the whole tradition of Spanish music in general and zarzuela in particular.

***

Q. I think I understand why. He was so inspired by Federico Romero and Guillermo Fernández Shaw's libretto of *Luisa Fernanda* that he wrote the entire work in just three weeks. He was a genius.

A. I got to witness both Torroba and Rodrigo in the creative act, when inspiration struck them like lightning and they were completely under a spell. I watched both of them do that. I also saw Francisco de Madina under that spell. To watch that happen as a performer of their music means that, when I walk out on stage, my job is to recreate that moment in which the spell was cast upon the composer. I have to take that same lightning and strike the audience with it, scoring a bullseye in their heads and hearts at the same time. My purpose has never been to show off how I play but rather to feel the composer's inspiration and pass it on to those who are listening. I am the archer and the audience is the target. The music is the arrow.

Once, while on tour with Torroba, we were in a pancake house eating breakfast, drinking coffee, and talking about everyday matters. Then, all of a sudden, some musical idea hit him with a bang, and he had to have a piece of music paper immediately. And there he sat, in a trance in front of his pancakes (which he didn't like), writing down whatever the inner spirit was dictating to him. And he had a very angelic expression on his face as he wrote. I have observed that trance many times in the great composers I have known. Some

LOVE OF GREAT COMPOSERS

187

emotionally charged idea possesses them, and they have to write it down right away. They become a bit like a translator, but instead of translating Spanish into English, they are translating lightning bolts into musical notes. The music then penetrates the listener's consciousness and takes them back to its source, thus completing a magic circle. I am only one segment in that circle.

When Rodrigo's muse called to him, he became totally silent, and only his fingers would move, as if he were playing an invisible piano. You could talk to him, but he wouldn't respond. Nothing. He was gone. And he had to write his ideas down right then and there, so that he could remember them. It was amazing to witness his process, and I imagine that it was basically the same way that Mozart worked. It was just effortless. The music flowed like wine from a cask. Both Torroba and Rodrigo had music coming out of them throughout the day, and that's why they were so prolific. I have a piece of paper on which Torroba wrote two themes, and on the back of that page, he wrote how he was going to turn that into a guitar concerto.

***

Q. And one assumes that it was the same with composers like Giuliani.

A. Yes, he had that same spontaneous quality. Sor was more like Rodrigo, i.e., more deliberate, more thought out.

***

Q. Well, while we're on that subject, who are some composers of purely instrumental works that you feel passionate about?

A. J. S. Bach and his Suites for Unaccompanied Cello, the Partitas for Solo Violin, and several other works. Now, I do have to include a kind of instrumental music that I have been drawn to my entire life and that provides food for my soul: sixteenth-century music for vihuela. And one name that stands out in my mind is that of Luys de Narváez (1526–47), though that takes nothing away from Luis de Milán (d. 1561), Alonso Mudarra (1510–80), Diego Pisador (1509–57), and several other performer/composers of the Spanish Renaissance.

Regarding the Baroque guitar, I believe that Gaspar Sanz is not just the father of the guitar but also laid the groundwork for what we understand to be Spanish music in general, including flamenco: the chord progressions, the use of both *punteo* (plucking) and *rasgueo* (strumming), and the ornamentation. It's all there. He paved the way for Sor and Giuliani several decades later, who then took the guitar to the highest musical levels. I feel very grateful to Johann Kaspar Mertz (1806–56), who was a bridge uniting the guitar to the music of all the other instruments. He was, in a way, our Franz Liszt. Of course, there is a lineage from Dionisio Aguado (1784–1849) to Sor, Arcas, and Tárrega. Indeed, we must not forget Arcas, who was an important transitional figure between Sor and Tárrega. I have always felt a great affinity for him because he was a phenomenal artist and equally adept at both classical and flamenco styles, which was and remains unusual.

***

Q. Yes, he did both—as do you!

A. He did both, as do I. To Arcas, the Spanish guitar was one, and he moved smoothly and convincingly among the various styles. Tárrega was fundamentally a classical guitarist and felt a deep connection to the German Romantics. And all of his students followed that path. Arcas's legacy is continued on the one hand by Tárrega and on the other by such people as Paco de Lucena, the man who taught both Andrés Segovia (classical) and Ramón Montoya (flamenco). So, I have always felt very close to Arcas, because although I consider myself a classical guitarist, I love flamenco music. But the class structure in Spain placed the Roma and their flamenco art at the bottom, and that is why, in my opinion, Segovia chose to conceal that aspect of his past and not perform flamenco. He denied it because of class prejudice.

And he wasn't alone in navigating the implications of prejudice. During our rehearsal for a planned (but unrealized) performance of the *Siete canciones populares españolas* of Manuel de Falla, Victoria de Los Ángeles and I talked about accents and diction, how to deliver a story through a song. She said that she wished she could have used an Andalusian Roma accent in her recording of the *Siete canciones*, which would have been more germane to the character of

LOVE OF GREAT COMPOSERS

the music. And though she was Catalan, she had some Andalusian ancestry. But in the days when she had previously recorded them, it was not proper to use an Andalusian accent because that was considered lower class; therefore, she felt compelled to Castilianize the accent. In other words, she had to conform to the tastes of "polite society," just as Segovia had done. However, she was quite capable of changing her diction, and I think I persuaded her to do so.

***

Q. Speaking of art song, you have mentioned that when you were growing up, your father was a huge lover of Schubert in particular and German Romanticism in general. So, already as a kid, you acquired his passion for that repertoire, correct?

A. Yes, but his passion for German music didn't come out of nowhere. The love for that repertoire was instilled in the minds and hearts of Tárrega's followers by Tárrega himself, who transcribed many such works for the guitar. Among his chief disciples was Daniel Fortea, whom my father knew well. However, I must say that one of my most beloved composers is Chopin. I have flown across the Atlantic many times listening to his music for the entire trip!

***

Q. Any pieces in particular that you like?

A. I love the Nocturnes. Traveling long distances is not my favorite thing to do, but I've done it many times with the help of Chopin's music, especially the Nocturnes. Before the invention of Walkmans, I would read through the score and listen to the music in my head. But I much prefer being able to listen to an actual recording. His sublime music brings peace to your entire body through your heart. In general, if I am in a stressful situation, I love to listen to music played on instruments other than the guitar, because if I hear guitar music, I can't help but thinking about how it feels to play it. It's a little too personal and doesn't provide the mental and emotional relief that I need.

***

Q. Okay, Chopin does the trick. Any other composers?

A. I love Schubert's Sonatas and Impromptus. I have told my daughter Angelina that when I depart this world, I want her to play the Impromptu No. 3. in G-flat. It has a very lyrical melody in the right hand, supported by a powerful bass line in the left. He keeps repeating it, and with every repetition, it's as if he's removing layers of different dimensions until you are face to face with God. That is how I imagine it must be like to die, as we take a journey from this reality to that of the Creator. But to do so, we have to break through many layers of self-identification and attachment to this reality, layers that we have been making since we were born. We return to the supernatural dimension from which we came by removing various obstacles. Schubert takes us on a perfect journey from this world to life everlasting. That's why I asked her that, when I die, I want her to play that Impromptu, just by herself. And not just to play it because it is beautiful music but also in order to remember how deeply I have loved her and will always love her.

At my funeral, I want a recording of the final movement of Morton Gould's *Troubadour Music* to be played, because I think of my life as that of a troubadour who comes into people's lives to play for them, to bring them some joy and happiness, and then who simply walks away. On my final journey, I want my body to dissolve into the sound of music. For there are moments in music that express the very deep feelings and thoughts that have accompanied me my entire life. The finale of Falla's *El amor brujo* is like looking into the future, to the time for which I pray and hope: the awakening of the consciousness of humankind, when we all are enlightened by the truth and the oneness in all of us. That's the resurrection predicted by Falla at the end of *El amor brujo*, a spiritual resurrection of human consciousness through music.

***

Q. So, we have established that you love the piano music of Chopin and Schubert. Are there any symphonic works that resonate with you in the same way?

A. The first work that comes to mind is the *Symphonie espagnole* of Édouard Lalo. I've been talking about deeply spiritual music, but there is much to be said for the sort of lighthearted virtuosity one hears in that work. It conveys the sounds, light, and joy of Spain and

LOVE OF GREAT COMPOSERS

is very entertaining. And there is beauty in entertainment. I also love Fritz Kreisler's music, especially *Liebeslied*.

***

Q. Of course, there is another side of your musical personality, and that is flamenco. Tell us about the *palos* (genres) that you especially like?

A. The first *palo* that comes to mind is *colombianas*, as sung by Niña de la Puebla and played on the guitar by Melchor de Marchena. If one wants to talk about a cultural explosion, one need look no further than the trade between Spain and the New World, which gave rise to a continuous exchange of traditions in music and dance. This is called *ida y vuelta*, or departure and return, referring to the Spanish songs and dances that sailed across the Atlantic to the Americas, were transformed by exposure to Native and African styles, and then returned to Spain. The *colombianas* is one such example, and according to my father, the man who established it was the guitarist and composer Esteban de Sanlúcar (1912–89). He was no relation to Manolo Sanlúcar, whose real surname was Muñoz. They were both born in the town of Sanlúcar de Barrameda, and Manolo later changed his surname to Sanlúcar.

But returning to the piano, I have a special fondness for the *Valses poéticos* by Granados. Of course, Granados was a great interpreter of the music of Chopin and Schumann, and their influence shows up in his music. But the *Valses poéticos* are pure Granados and not imitations of anyone else's music. That work sings not of a country but rather of the most beautiful human heart, Granados's heart, which was so big that it was connected to everything. It has been transcribed for the guitar and played gorgeously by my friend Julian Bream.

***

Q. As a listener, you seem to have a real attraction to the Romantic repertoire. It speaks to you.

A. When I am playing, I experience within very romantic feelings, because that is my motivation. I feel that love is the wellspring from which music comes; thus, for me, playing the guitar is a romantic experience. Before I come out on stage, I consciously connect to my source of love. And I perceive romanticism not only in the nineteenth-century repertoire but also in Narváez, Milán, and Bach! However, lately I've been going through a difficult time with my technique, because of COVID and various medications. I have had to cancel a few appearances, and I have sometimes wondered if I'm getting to the end of my career. With every concert now, I have to ask myself if I can get the musical point across, if I can convey how deeply I feel about the music. If yes, I perform. If not, I don't. It's all about the music, not me.

15

LOVE RELATIONSHIPS

Q. You are a person who exudes a passionate love of life, music, art, family, and everything beautiful. But aside from your parents and brothers, it is probably safe to say that your greatest human loves have been and continue to be your life companions and offspring. Where should we start?

A. I will say that my great loves began in my own fantasy when I was just a child and reading books, especially the love stories of *Don Quijote*. And I was moved by the great love affairs in Spanish poetry. Not surprisingly, I had my own imaginary woman, or girl. I cannot really say, because in my fantasy she was ageless. While playing music, I have always felt love, a physical love. And very often it was inspired by an imaginary love partner.

***

Q. All right, so love starts in your imagination.

A. Yes, and then as a result of wonderful circumstances. When I was little, I fantasized about different women or young girls, first envisioning and then finally meeting them. There was a young girl who lived near us in Seville; once, when I got sick with a high fever, she would come over to take care of me. On one occasion I was alone in the house, and her ministrations developed into a very romantic affair. At that time, we were living on a little farm on the outskirts of Seville, but then we had to move, and I was very sad to leave my first girlfriend behind. I was only 9 years old, and she was 15. I always went for older women, but then again, I was a very weird 9-year-old kid. I was deeply moved by the love letters of composers, how they expressed their love in words to the people they were in love with, and how they simultaneously conveyed those same sentiments in music. That was the main reason I played the guitar, so that I could have a more eloquent voice in expressing my feelings of love.

But then I fell in love with flamenco, which to me was just like a lover, though in sound and not in the flesh. And it was more than music. It was also poetry and dance, even a way of life. Flamenco is a goddess, and she possessed me like a secret lover. I may have been married to classical music, but flamenco became something extraordinarily physical and tangible to me. But in the realm of love, there are some things flamenco can't do. On one occasion during our time in Seville, I was privately exploring the pleasures of my own body, and quite by accident, a woman suddenly entered the room where I was relaxing. Her name was Luisa, and she was a professor of philosophy at the nearby university. Naturally, I was mortified, but she sympathetically gave me permission to continue. She told me that everybody does it, including herself. And she provided a demonstration. That was an extraordinary encounter, though it led to nothing else.

I continued to make love to the guitar and flamenco, but before long, we moved again, this time to settle in the U.S., a land of opportunity that beckoned to our musical family. We arrived in New York on August 13, 1957, and were met by one Admiral Fullan, who gave us our green cards. Then his wife gave us a tour of the city, which was very impressive. I had my first-ever encounter with an escalator, and I thought that it was the most amazing thing I had ever seen: stairs that moved! New York was such a big, dynamic place, with so many different cultures and kinds of food. In Spain, I had been used to getting milk from a milkman who came by with three cows and then milked them right in front of our house. But in New York, I was able to get a glass of milk from the refrigerator, and that seemed incredible to me.

But our final destination was California, not New York, and we soon flew to Los Angeles, where we were picked up at the airport by Theodore Norman. He was the guitar professor at UCLA for many years and had been a student of my father in Málaga. He picked us up at the airport and took us to Santa Barbara, where we would live. A few days later was the annual Spanish-themed Fiesta in Santa Barbara, and I gave an evening performance at the door of the Santa Barbara Mission. That appearance was actually recorded and is available on YouTube.

LOVE RELATIONSHIPS

195

School began shortly after that, and I was enrolled in the eighth grade at Santa Barbara Junior High. On my first day there, I met another eighth grader, a girl by the name of Joan Cook. She saw that I was sitting by myself during lunch, and she sat next to me and struck up a conversation. The problem was that I could not speak a word of English, nor she a word of Spanish. But somehow, we communicated. She didn't know that I was a guitarist, and I didn't know that she was a violinist. In those days, the junior highs and high schools usually had an orchestra, and she played in ours. She kindly offered to show me around and help me get oriented during those first days in school, and that started an incredibly beautiful friendship. She helped me acquire English, and we became best friends.

In June of 1958, at the end of my eighth-grade experience, my father gave his debut concert in Santa Barbara, at the historic Lobero Theatre. In came a young girl to ask him for his autograph, and that was Kristine Meigs Eddy, whom I would later marry. Only a few days earlier, she had started taking guitar lessons with Celin, who had enrolled in Santa Barbara Junior College. Celin sang in the choir there, and the person who directed that choir was Margrete Eddy, who would become my mother-in-law. Kristine's parents brought her to the concert, and that is how we first met. But shortly thereafter, our family moved to Hollywood, which offered much greater opportunities for professional growth. So, that relationship was put on hold.

Nonetheless, I remained very close friends with Joan, though we were not romantically involved. I would go visit her, and she would come visit me. However, on the day before she left for New York to attend the Manhattan School of Music, we had a party at the beach, and all of a sudden, the magic happened: we suddenly realized that we were very attracted to each other. But nothing else happened. She left for New York, and I didn't see her again until 1962, when the quartet performed at Town Hall and signed a contract with Mercury Records. I also signed a contract with Contemporary Records for a solo flamenco album. The night before I made that recording, Joan and I lost our virginity, together. Everything before that had just been playing around. This was the real deal. So, that provided extra inspiration for the recording session the following morning. I was now 18 years old. Joan and I fell deeply in love, and fortunately, I was able to go quite often to New York and spend time with her. Like me, she loved opera, and we used to go as often as possible to the Metropolitan Opera, where we bought standing-room tickets and listened together. Sadly, she died suddenly of a heart attack when she was only 20. She was my first love, but life goes on, and there would be other loves.

I had such an incredibly fulfilling time in New York with Joan, going to hear so many wonderful concerts and operas, and then going back to her little one-bedroom apartment or to my hotel to spend the night together with somebody whom I loved and with whom I shared such an incredible passion for music. But I found that when it came time to return to touring with my family, performing in front of enthusiastic audiences, attending parties, and enjoying incredible success, still, I felt very lonely. We spent long days driving across the Great Plains, across Oklahoma and Texas, and at night I would see homes with the lights on, and I would get envious of the people who were inside. There I was in the car, driving endlessly through the night to find the hotel where we would stay, finally arriving there in a state of exhaustion.

We tap into our emotions when we are exposed to music, whether we are listening to it, studying, playing, or performing it. The profound need to share your passion with someone else is an amazing force, and when that certain someone is not there, it makes you feel really lonely. And I felt very lonely, which is probably a big reason why I got married so young. I fell very much in love with Kristine, and when my first daughter, Tina, was born, and then with every one of my children, I finally felt that my soul would never be lonely again. I had wonderful times with the family, and I adore all of them, not only because they fill that space but because I had a good reason to be really emotional. I understood better now how my father and my mother felt about me, as well as my feeling of brotherhood with my siblings. There is nothing like the feeling you have when you see this new life form, to which you remain committed for the rest of your own life. That sort of love is unconditional and begins with the first breath they take, which is an amazing thing in itself.

Just before I became involved with Kristine, though, I was briefly enamored of the daughter of a friend of ours, who was an editor at the Santa Barbara Press. His name was Larry Pidgeon, and his daughter was Charlene. I was very taken with her, and I thought that this relationship was going to go somewhere. Once, she and I were attending a concert at the Lobero Theatre, where I ran into

Figure 37. Pepe with his first wife, Kristine, on her birthday in 2024.

Kristine. Even though I was very drawn to Charlene, a strange force made me tell Charlene that I had to go. So, I took her home and then went to Kristine's parents' house. We stayed up talking until the sun came up! And by the morning, she was my girlfriend. Her father and I became and remained very close friends. He was a magnificent baritone singer. He had volunteered for service in World War II, and he fought in the Battle of the Bulge. After the war, now with a wife and baby, he taught voice for quite a few years at USC; in fact, our tenures there overlapped, and I cherished him as both a colleague and a friend. But he always regretted not having pursued a career on the stage, which was his first love.

After Kristine and I married in 1965, she wanted me to follow her father's lead and stay home rather than tour. She thought I could make a very good living by teaching at USC, as well as giving private lessons. But like her father, my first love was actually the stage. I wanted to perform, so conflict was inevitable. As was divorce. Yet, I retain a great love for Kristine. I think that we were probably too young when we got married, as we were both just 21 years old. But had we waited, perhaps we would never have married at all, because it turned out that we were quite different in almost all of our philosophical ideas. I was politically liberal, while she was very conservative. And when it came to raising children, I tended to be rather permissive, while she was much more strict. In short, we had very different personalities, and in the end, that led to divorce. But we remain very close.

***

Q. You finally found someone with whom you were very compatible, Carissa. How did that come about?

A. In the 1970s, I started leading two very separate lives: I had a life at home, and then I had the touring life. In the latter life, I could explore the sort of absolute freedom, both mental and physical, in which I could be with a woman and satisfy her completely, without any conflict. There was no commitment, no obligation. And then I found myself once again in Houston, where I was engaged to teach a master class at St. Thomas University. It was a hot summer day in 1973, and when I arrived at the class, there was a young lady sitting at the table collecting the entrance fee from the students who came just to audit the masterclass. She was quite attractive, her hair was up, and I couldn't resist the impulse to come up behind her and kiss her on the neck. She quickly turned around and said, "Oh, brother!" And yet, there was something immediate that caught me. I thought she was very beautiful, though I didn't yet know her name, much less that she would one day be my second wife: Carissa.

The class was being presented by Susan Gaschen and her husband, Terry, and they held a party at their guitar shop after each session. I met all sorts of interesting people at those get-togethers, including Abel Carlevaro, Sergio Abreu, and Leo Brouwer. But on that evening a platonic friendship between Carissa and me started, and it would last seven years. I remember saying to one of the students, Robert Wetzel, "Robert, if you don't marry her, I will!" But this was before I had spoken two words to Carissa, and we both just laughed. Carissa was always at the masterclasses, and we become good friends, though she soon became Robert Wetzel's girlfriend. On one occasion, she accompanied him to California, and we spent

LOVE RELATIONSHIPS

Figure 38. Pepe with his second wife, Carissa, in Moscow, December 1991.

some quality time together. She eventually became my absolute best friend and confidant. Carissa accepted and understood me as I was, leading my double life with a wife and family in Del Mar and then being on the road and straying from my marriage vows.

However, it was not possible to keep my two lives in separate compartments. I was slated to perform in Houston, and Kristine decided to fly out from San Diego to attend the concert. She wanted to see what was going on there. I was so upset by this that the concert that evening was one of the worst I've ever played. I felt so emotional that I made a lot of mistakes.

***

Q. I can't imagine you playing a concert and making a lot of mistakes!

A. Well, that's how it felt. When you're on the hot seat, mistakes may seem much bigger than they are. Even a near miss feels like a big mistake! In any event, it was not a concert in which I felt at peace and was in the best state of mind to perform.

I thought I would never get divorced because as a Catholic, that was not an option—even for a non-practicing Catholic like myself. That was simply the tradition in which I was raised and how I viewed the institution of matrimony. Kristine and her family attended the Christian Science Church, though we were married in the Episcopal Church. Later on, she joined Self-Realization Fellowship, founded in 1920 by Paramahansa Yogananda, author of *Autobiography of a Yogi*. This inspired her to become a vegetarian and to embrace sexual abstinence except for the purpose of procreation. I respected her decision, but it did nothing to ameliorate our marital problems. Anyway, I continued to cultivate relationships outside of my marriage, some of them quite serious. Then one day in early 1980, I got a call from Susan Gaschen, who invited me to Houston to celebrate my thirty-sixth birthday! What persuaded me to go was the opportunity of spending my birthday with Carissa, who at that time was still just my friend. But I had a great attraction to her as a companion, as somebody I wanted to be with. At that point, we had known one another for about seven years.

We met at the party, and she noted that I had been doing a lot of touring lately, which was true. Then she made a kind offer: "Why don't I take your clothes, wash them, and bring them to you in the morning before you leave?" That was an offer I couldn't refuse, and she fetched my clothes for cleaning. I now felt a completeness with Carissa, emotionally and spiritually, and it was as if an atomic bomb had exploded inside of me. That very evening, we consummated our relationship—and here we are, forty-four years later! She was raised in the Protestant Reformed Church, a very conservative denomination, and her family did not approve of our relationship. In fact, they had made Carissa stop dancing ballet when she was a young teenager because it was too sensual! But love conquers all, and our love overcame all religious obstacles, whether Protestant or Catholic.

Kristine and I finally divorced in 1986, though it didn't become final until the following year, and it was in same year of 1987 that Carissa and I were married. We have remained happily married since. She has made my subsequent career possible, taking on the day-to-day tasks so that I can devote myself to music. For instance, I'm not much of a businessperson, and in the drawers of my desk, she found several uncashed checks from USC, which she promptly cashed! She soon became my spokesperson and my manager,

LOVE RELATIONSHIPS

making travel arrangements and minding my schedule. She dealt with the record companies and various managers in the different countries. We became and remain a very successful team. Since she was 23 years old, Carissa has dedicated herself wholeheartedly to being my unwavering partner, muse, manager, and collaborator. She has done a mountain of work, providing me with support, time, energy, inspiration, and encouragement not only on my journey with the guitar and music but also so that I could be a better son, father, brother, friend, and all that I needed to be and feel like a complete person. I shall be forever grateful and forever in love with my eternal beloved, Carissa.

Her parents eventually accepted our relationship, and I became very close friends with them. I should also mention that Kristine and I kept our commitment to the children, i.e., to never say anything negative about one another to them. And now they're old enough to understand. My four children, Tina, Angelina, Susanna, and Pepe—what a blessing they have always been to me! They went through the hardship of separation anxiety while I was on tour during much of their lives as children. They went through the tremendous hardship of my divorce. They are connected to divine love, and our relationship as father and children has never faltered. They have chosen to celebrate our joy of togetherness, which they have passed onto our grandchildren. Throughout my children's lives, they have always given and received love for their mother, Kristine, for me, and for Carissa. I am so fortunate and love my children and grandchildren so much!

***

Q. Does the guitar's shape remind you of a human being? Whether it's "male" or "female," love relationships have clearly affected your life as a guitarist, and vice versa.

A. No, I've never thought of the guitar as a man or a woman. I think of the guitar as a spirit. And I know that many people see a resemblance between the shape of the guitar and the shape of a human body, but for me, that idea has never influenced how I think and feel about the guitar. As for the second part of that question, yes, relationships impact your career and the way you play, because they are so connected to who you are as a human being, to your feelings, be they happy or sad. When you think with clarity or when your

Figure 39. Pepe (*center*) with his children (*left to right*): Pepe Jr., Tina, Angelina, and Susanna, at Christmas 2023.

thinking is turbulent, all of that affects your career, and your career in turn impacts your relationships. I have found that the guitar is the greatest counselor, because when you play, you go to the depths of your spirit. And from there, the real feelings come.

And if I think about the people with whom I have had an emotional or sexual relationship as a result of the guitar, of music, I can say that I have nothing but good feelings about each and every one of them. I have gained acceptance of the things that bothered me at the time. Those conflicts have been completely defused, vaporized, and eliminated, so that only the good memories remain.

***

Q. What do you hope for the futures of all the people you have loved?

A. That the dreams we shared for however long it was will come true in some way or another. I hope that they will all find peace and true love.

16

GIVING 100%

Q. It appears that whatever you do, you give 100% of yourself. What are the various challenges that you have faced, especially health challenges?

A. I think that the first challenge is time, i.e., time versus ambition. That has been the greatest challenge that I have faced from the time I started playing. My ambition has been to learn music and to play it as well as I can. I am like a horse with a carrot in front: no matter how far and fast I go, I still can't reach the carrot. And yet, on the other side, I am not frustrated by that fact. Perfection is a very blurry concept because it exists only in one's mind and desires. So, I have always tried to play better, and therefore I'm always working against my limits.

A long time ago, I was given some great advice by one of our managers at Columbia Artists, Carl Dahlgren. I was still a young guy, and he told me, "Pepe, when you're thinking about your career, be like the horses that have blinders on. The reason they have the blinders is so that they don't get spooked by any other horse. Every artist needs to have blinders so that they think only of the race they are running. Don't worry about anybody else." So, I've never, ever been competitive. How could I be competitive with my own father? I could not possibly compete with my idol, who was to me and continues to be larger than life. How could I compete with that which is the essence and foundation of everything I have done? I could never compete with him. I would have lost the battle before it even began.

But on the other hand, I have always remained conscious of my own abilities. I'm very grateful that I have them and fortunate that I recognized that I had them. I was given the gift of musical talent, which means not only my sense of hearing and technical facility but also my experience of the wonderful things that happen inside my

Figure 40. Pepe with his ultimate idol, Celedonio, in 1996, the year of his passing.

consciousness when I am exposed to music, as either a listener or performer. And most of all, I have the will to develop my abilities to the maximum; however, I have never felt competitive with anyone else. I have always been highly competitive only with myself.

***

Q. What does it mean to give 100%? You mentioned perfection, but you stated that perfection is something we cannot achieve.

A. I strive for it. I give 100% in striving for perfection, through all of my efforts. And the first effort is being able to recognize the difference between what I desire, how I hear the music, how I conceive it, and how I'm able to do it, how close I am to being completely satisfied with the results. And for that reason, I would say that I've consistently given 100% of my efforts in the pursuit of taking the music as close as I can to what was the composer's inspired moment.

That is my goal: not to stand in the way but rather to allow the music to flow directly from the composer's muse to the ears of the listeners. That muse dances its way through the craft and gift of the composer into my craft and gift as a performer, without any interference. That requires not only technical but also philosophical and spiritual work, so that the muse flows through me into the ears and souls of those who listen.

In my recordings, I've always tried to position myself at the receiving end of the process, by making sure that I am playing directly into the body, mind, and spirit of the person who may be listening to it years later. I want whoever listens to the recording to have direct contact with what is happening musically. What I don't want is for my self-conscious mind to tarnish the music with anxiety about making a mistake. Even if the playing is flawless, that fear would still affect the musical outcome.

I feel that when we practice, we are mining our hearts for emotions. We have a mine, and we go mining for love. That is the main ingredient of which our music is made: love. First, we mine our hearts for emotion, and then we craft it into a sort of sonic jewelry that we give to the public. This requires openness to the feelings that we mine and with which we subsequently imbue the music. And that's why I think musicians need to receive love. We need it to exist, we need it like we need oxygen, we need to receive that same love that we dig out of our own souls to give to the public.

For me, the process of practicing is very mysterious and wonderful. Because every time I play a piece that I love, it goes deeper inside my consciousness, inside my spirit. And it provokes profound feelings that are essentially variations of love. The piece is then "dressed up" not only with what the composer put in it but also with the love that it has elicited from me. After having practiced it many times, I go out onto the concert stage or into the recording studio to share that love with the public. I am thereby connected to those people who hear and now possess a love that is very private and very special to me.

So, giving 100% has meant mental and spiritual preparation, as well as completely surrendering myself to receiving the music, whether listening to someone else perform, performing it myself, or learning it, and then of course the physical preparation of giving my undivided attention to what I am practicing. In the development of technique, giving 100% means never practicing something without having a goal in mind, something to achieve, and making sure that when you focus on one aspect, you don't ignore the others. I can focus on one thing, perhaps the choreography of the left-hand fingers, but I must not lose peripheral awareness of what my right hand is doing. When I look at my left hand, I can still see in my mind's eye what the right hand is doing.

Awareness is a word I keep coming back to: awareness that it sounds and feels good. It is much better to practice for ten minutes fully concentrated than for an hour while allowing all kinds of unwanted sounds and feelings to enter and become part of what you accept as normal. I devote 100% attention to what the composer has written, because the score they have left is a treasure map. My task is to learn as much as I can about that map, about what every symbol on that paper means, so that I know what the composer is telling me. And later, when I'm performing, I surrender myself to the moment, because everything I practiced and learned has become a part of me. At that point, I can no longer be trying to think and control: "Here is a dotted rhythm, and now there is a crescendo." No, I give away the controls and pay full attention to how the music is being sung *to* me, not *by* me.

The music is inside my head, inside my body. I feel that what my father used to call the Great Guitarist is playing it for me. In a sense, I'm playing along with the Great Guitarist, who is the same one who played through Giuliani, Sor, and Tárrega. We all were and are musicians, but in a moment of inspiration, it is the Great Guitarist playing through us. I have been very fortunate to feel that presence playing through me. That's what it means to give 100%: to be in tune with the Great Guitarist. When you surrender all your preparations, you place them at the service of the Great Guitarist, and you invite the audience to sit together with you at the feet of the composer and partake of the great gifts that they have given us.

**

Q. Giving 100% implies that there are obstacles that you have overcome. What are some of the obstacles that you have had to overcome?

A. Dyslexia was a big obstacle, though I believe that every obstacle is a gift. Dyslexia made it very difficult for me to read. I had to go very slowly, which meant I had to be extra careful. I had to read everything two or three times to make sure that I had it right. I may not be able to sight-read as fast as most people, but every obstacle comes with a gift, and every gift comes with an obstacle.

One of the great obstacles faced by any musician who has the gift is time management: working with great conductors, getting to know great composers, not to mention socializing, traveling, practicing, rehearsing, and performing. All of that is very demanding on your time, and for me it has been a constant challenge. I cannot multitask, so whatever I'm doing receives 100% of my attention. When I was sitting in the garden with Rodrigo smoking a Havana cigar, I was giving 100% to enjoying a moment that was going to be very meaningful to me for the rest of my life. When I was sitting in my house, learning one of his pieces, I was giving 100% to that. I found that I was always short of time with the guitar in my hands, learning and practicing the music.

So that need to get ready for whatever was coming up triggers a sense of urgency. When I cannot practice, for instance during a long plane trip, then I do a lot of mental work, reading through the music and hearing it in my head from start to finish. I recall the emotions associated with it, the positions and choreography of the left hand on the fingerboard, the feeling of the right hand, in my arms, and of the guitar. That is something I have been forced to do because of innumerable hours spent traveling from one place to another in air-planes, trains, and cars. And it all boils down to time management.

***

Q. But there have been physical problems and illnesses that have made it more difficult for you to give 100%. When you were young, you faced the obstacle of polio. And more recently you have experienced some physical challenges. But you continue to give 100%. Can you say more about that?

A. I have enjoyed very good health throughout most of my life, but there have been setbacks there as well. The first was a car accident going over the Rockies near Loveland, Colorado. I was fortunate to survive, but as a result of it I developed some problems with my back, which made it difficult for me to sit for a long time. So, I had to do a lot of physical therapy and be very careful of my movements. That was the first time I had ever felt that a physical problem might threaten my guitar playing; fortunately, I fully recovered and continued to practice and perform, soon thereafter making my first recording for Philips.

Years later, in 1986, I had a second car accident, about the same time that the space shuttle Challenger exploded, and that resulted in a herniated disk in my neck. I now had to be very careful to sit in just the right position when I played, in order to avoid aggravating the injury. If I sat incorrectly, my hands would start to fall asleep! That only lasted for a short time, and it wasn't an impediment to my playing as long as I sat properly. I just had to make sure that the flow of the energy from the neck into the arms was not impeded by any kind of weird position.

If I held the guitar in a casual position, my fingers would start to tingle and the pain in my neck became horrendous. I remember once being in Salzburg teaching and I could not sleep because of the neck pain resulting from that bulging herniated disc. I went to a spinal doctor in Salzburg, who gave me daily injections into my shoulder to numb the nerves. These were not pleasant and went on for the month I was there. Then I went to Málaga and was visiting my friend Ángel Luis Cañete, a wonderful flamenco guitarist and guitar collector. This was at the same time that my father received the Gold Medal of the City of Málaga, and all kinds of tributes were being paid by Málaga to him. When I went to Ángel's home, I found that he was in bed with terrible back pain, and I consoled him at his bedside.

Then I left to play some concerts, and when I came back a week later, he was completely fine. That's when he told me about this *curandera* (healer) in Arcos de la Frontera, a small village between Ronda and Cádiz. She had healed him, and now I wanted to visit her as well. So Ángel drove Carissa and me to her, and we had a memorable journey. We stopped for breakfast at an incredibly picturesque restaurant in Ronda, which is one of the most beautiful Andalusian towns and one where my father had concertized early in his career. Then we made our way to Arcos de la Frontera and the home of Teresa de los Huesos (Teresa of the Bones), as she was known there. She was an illiterate country woman, but in order to be able to practice healing, she had to have a medical license. So, her daughter became a doctor, and that way she could practice under her daughter's license. When it was finally my turn to go in, she instructed me to take off my shirt and lie down. And the next thing I noticed was her assistant entering the room with a barber knife! I had no idea what was going to happen, but this was just to shave the hair on the place she was going to treat and over which she would place bandages.

Then the treatment started. She was not even touching me, but I could hear my bones cracking and the pain leaving me, followed by feelings of peace and comfort. When she finished, she put a bandage over the affected vertebrae and where I had the herniated disc. And then she explained to me, "Okay, you will be fine. Just don't take this off for a week to ten days. You will be okay for about a year, and after that, you may need another treatment."

Sure enough, I was absolutely perfect for about a year and a half. And then when I was in Salzburg, all of a sudden the pain returned. When my class ended, Carissa suggested that I go back for a second treatment. We booked a flight to Spain and then returned to Teresa, who fixed it completely. So, despite the pain and inconvenience, my playing was not harmed, and the bulging disc eventually disappeared. In addition to Teresa, I was seeing Nikolaos Polyxiadis, a physical therapist, whenever I was in Madrid. And with his therapy every week whenever I went to Madrid, by the end of the 1980s, I was in great health and enjoying completely trouble-free guitar playing.

PEPE ROMERO

***

Q. Was that the end of your health ordeals?

A. Well, yes, until April 30, 2022, when I performed *Medea* by Manolo Sanlúcar in Long Beach. It is a very difficult piece to play, but I immensely enjoyed preparing it. And I felt great about the performance. But the next day, I got sick and soon tested positive for COVID. About this same time I started taking Crestor for cholesterol. My cardiologist thought that my numbers were okay, but he wanted to lower them a bit with medication. I was soon over COVID, but I had difficulty regaining my strength, and this affected my technique. It couldn't have happened at a worse time, as I had a lot of concerts booked, and I increasingly felt that I was fighting against an invisible enemy. I performed in Madrid, Zaragoza, Berlin, and then Granada, where I gave my first performance of Rodrigo's *Sones en la Giralda* for harp and orchestra, which I had transcribed for guitar.

It went well, and the reviews for those concerts were phenomenal. Probably the best reviews I've ever had. But I was not at 100%, and my abilities continued to diminish until my right hand was completely paralyzed. My arm had no strength whatsoever. Even before I reached that point, I noticed a serious decline. Celin and I were signing autographs, and I said to him, "I'm having trouble writing my name. I can't write my name the way I used to." Writing became really difficult, and I didn't have even enough strength to shave or brush my teeth. I completely lost the use of my right arm and hand. Thank goodness that happened during a time when I was not performing. I had finished my all of my concerts and was "off duty." But for me, that was a very sad way to live. My joyful and fruitful life was put on pause, and I now set off on a journey to find my way back to the way things had been.

So, I went immediately to my good friend Dr. Richard Brown, an outstanding surgeon, and he referred me to a neurologist, who examined the condition of my nerves. Then I went to physical therapy in Del Mar, where they discovered that my neck was perfect and there was no obstruction of the nerves there. But somehow the nerves had been hit by a virus, and when I told them that I had had polio as a child, they suspected that that virus had been revived by COVID, which had been awakening different viruses.

However, I then went to my regular doctor, a general practitioner, for a normal checkup. He didn't believe that I had polio, and he put me on a regimen of taking lots of vitamins to revive the nerves. And sure enough, my sense of feeling started to return. I now had enough energy to produce sounds on the guitar, and it was a very exciting process for me to teach my right hand how to play, all over again. I started to rebuild my technique on the guitar, just as I had done in my youth! Fortunately, I never lost the memory of the sense of touch. I still remembered not only how it's done but also the feeling of doing it well.

My doctor pointed out to me that COVID attacks the motor nerves the same way that it does the sensory nerves of smell and taste. His diagnosis was correct, and the nerves were now recovering sufficiently for me to be able to play. I gave two concerts in Dallas, and I was probably at 50%. But that was a lot better than zero, which was where I had been a few months earlier.

However, there were further revelations. A cardiologist friend of mine was talking to me about his own health problems. And just magically, as we were having a glass of wine one night in Granada, he told me to get off Crestor because a side effect was harming my muscles. Was that the reason I was still was having trouble getting out of bed and that I was unable to regain 100% of my technique? Evidently it was. After consulting with my cardiologist here, I stopped taking Crestor, which is a statin drug. Within three days, I started feeling better.

By early 2024, I felt that I had recovered 100% of my technique. I could play everything, even the most challenging works, to my absolute satisfaction. And I feel that my brain is as free and as easy as it ever was. I recently played the *Concierto de Aranjuez* in Athens, Greece, with the great Christoph Eschenbach conducting. It was one of my favorite performances ever of that work. I am so grateful to God for the miracle of giving me back something I love so much. I feel so grateful to everyone who's helped me find my way back. I'm so thankful for the patience to be able to peacefully retrace my steps, to reclaim the gift that I was given and for which I am so grateful, which is the freedom of being able to do on the guitar whatever I hear in my head, whatever I feel in my heart.

***

Q. Was it the Crestor all along? Or do you think it was a combination of things?

A. It was clearly a combination of things. Crestor did not affect the nerves at all, so that was COVID and definitely not polio. But after I gave up Crestor, my right hand returned to normal. I could now play scales and arpeggios faster and longer. And then my left hand regained its former agility as well. So, my technique is now back to 100%. I can no longer blame technical deficiencies on illness. Anything I do wrong now is the fault of my mind, not my technique.

***

Q. So, are *you* now back to 100%?

A. Yes. Or at least striving 100% for perfection, without the handicap of any health issues. I've always tried to enjoy life 100%. This includes accepting and overcoming the obstacles to becoming a better musician and person. Without the obstacles, we don't grow, and growing is what life is all about. So, now that I feel back at 100%, I'm starting to think of how I want to bring my career to an end. For as I said, I have always wanted to cease concert touring at the height of my abilities. I believe that I want to stop on my eighty-first birthday, though that does not mean that I will end my journey with the guitar. That journey will only end when my life itself comes to an end. It does not mean that I will never play another concert. Yes, I will play concerts, but I will play them only when it feels like the right thing to do. I will not commit to any tours, though I will continue to record, for there are many pieces inside of me that I have not yet recorded. And I shall continue to do that for as long as I can.

***

Q. Are there any final thoughts you would like to share with your readers?

A. I have followed my destiny, with music as my companion. Yesterday, I was a child prodigy. Tomorrow, I will be a memory. But the music I have felt will be eternal. I believe that God created music so that we can find our true soul and come back to God. I further believe that luck is simply opportunity coming to those who are prepared to receive it. It's very important to put forth your best effort and then surrender it into the unknown. We have been given the gift to play beautiful music, so that people can enjoy it and so that we can glorify God, so that there can be a moment of forgetting the day's troubles and problems and just enjoy not only listening to music and having a good time, but also the feeling of togetherness and connection with our fellow human beings.

We are like chefs who carefully prepare a feast of music in our kitchen/studio and then share it with love. It seems to me that when we walk off of the stage, that's when we know our job is done. I believe in the power of music, of drama, of love, and of expression. For me, music is the ultimate expression of human feelings and the best vessel for exploring one's innermost self. It connects us to the Creator of all things, to the Great Player that plays through all the musicians that surrender with total trust into the arms of the Muses. For those who play the guitar, let the Great Guitarist take over your hands and sing into your ears and out of the guitar, suspending all who witness this miracle in a sea of vibration. That is music. I wish that for all the musicians who play with love, work hard, glorify God, and bring joy to those who listen.

APPENDIX 1

CHRONOLOGY

Year	Event
1944	José Luis (Pepe) Romero born March 8.
1946	Angel Romero born August 17.
1954	The Romeros meet Evelyn and Farrington Stoddard, who will assist them in moving to the U.S. First, the family moves to Seville.
1957	The Romeros finally succeed in arranging their escape from Spain, with help of the Stoddards and highly placed officials in the U.S. government. Leave from Lisbon for U.S. on TWA flight to New York and then Los Angeles. Settle in Santa Barbara, California, with Stoddards.
	Pepe Romero performs first live concert in U.S. at "Fiesta" at entrance of the Old Mission Santa Barbara.
1958	Celedonio gives his debut recital in the U.S., at Santa Barbara's Lobero Theatre on June 13. Family moves to Hollywood and establishes guitar school there.
1960	Quartet makes first appearance, Lobero Theatre in Santa Barbara. Earliest recordings made with Contemporary Records. Celin completes active duty and enters U.S. Army reserve.
1961	Romeros present themselves at Wilshire-Ebell Theatre in Los Angeles, January 21. Go on to perform with manager James Lucas in San Francisco, Chicago, Boston, and New York. Appear on *Jack Paar* television show.
1962	Quartet appears again at Town Hall in New York. Quartet record first three recordings for Mercury.
1963	Romeros' manager James Lucas retires and now they are managed by Columbia Artists.
1965	Quartet appears on the *Tonight Show.* Pepe marries Kristine.

216 APPENDIX 1

1967	Quartet appears on the *Ed Sullivan Show*. Death of Farrington Stoddard. Premieres Rodrigo's *Concierto andaluz* with San Antonio Symphony.
1970	Celedonio builds home in Del Mar, CA, and his sons find houses there as well.
1971	Quartet performs at the Nixon White House prior to a State Dinner for President Tito of Yugoslavia and other dignitaries.
1979	Quartet performs at Carter White House for President Park of South Korea.
	Quartet premieres Torroba's *Concierto ibérico* in Vancouver.
1970s to present	Pepe and Celin hold a variety of teaching positions, at University of Southern California, San Diego State University, University of California, San Diego, California State University, Los Angeles.
1983	Pepe premieres Rodrigo's *Concierto para una fiesta.*
1984	Celedonio is admitted as a knight to Orden de Isabel la Católica.
1986	Quartet plays for Pope John Paul II in the Vatican.
1987	Pepe marries Carissa.
1988	Celedonio's knighthood is upgraded to Comendador de Número.
1994	University of Victoria confers honorary doctorate on Pepe in June.
1996	Celedonio dies on May 8.
1999	Angelita dies on March 10. Death of Joaquín Rodrigo, July 6.
2000	Celin, Pepe, and Angel are admitted as knight commanders to Orden de Isabel la Católica (knighted by King Juan Carlos of Spain), February 11.
2001	PBS airs documentary on Romeros on September 14.
2004	German Norddeutscher Rundfunk airs documentary about Romeros on October 30.
2007	Romeros receive President's Merit Award from the Recording Academy (Grammys) on February 8.
2011	San Francisco Conservatory of Music confers honorary doctorate on Pepe in May.

APPENDIX 1

2012   Pepe's recording of Ernesto Cordero's *Concierto Festivo*, with I Solisti di Zagreb, nominated for Latin Grammy.

2017   In May, Pepe receives Premio Huella Cultural from Club Rotario de Málaga.

2018   Pepe receives "la Medalla de Honor" de la Real Academia de Bellas Artes de Granada, Nuestra Señora de las Angustias

Publication of *Los Romeros: Royal Family of the Spanish Guitar.*

2020   Pepe records and sends live videos from his home in Granada.

Pepe receives the "Orchestra Award for Artistic Achievement" given by the International Classical Music Awards (ICMA).

Pepe performs live-streaming concert (without audience) from the Patio de los Arrayanes in the Alhambra as part of Digital Granada Festival 2020.

Pepe performs live streaming recital from his home in Del Mar for Austin Classical Guitar Society.

2021   Pepe and the Romeros perform with hundreds of other guitarists in a virtual performance of his composition, "Malagueñas de Jotrón" celebrating the sixtieth anniversary of the Romero Guitar Quartet.

2022   Pepe is the first recipient of the "Premio Alhambra Internacional" from the Fundación Alhambra Guitarra (Spain).

Pepe celebrates the first Pepe Romero Guitar Festival Málaga.

2023   Pepe premieres the guitar concerto "Wayfaring" by David Leisner.

2024   Pepe receives a Lifetime Achievement Award from the Los Angeles Guitar Festival.

Pepe and Walter complete the manuscript of this memoir.

APPENDIX 2

AWARDS

Year	Award
1991	Los Romeros received the "Prix de Martell," created to recognize classical music's champions and an outgrowth of the Martell Cordon Bleu Concert Series. Previous honorees included Maestros Georg Solti, Zubin Mehta, and Leonard Slatkin, former opera star Robert McFerrin, pianist Horacio Gutiérrez, musicologist Dr. Samuel Floyd, and "Live from Lincoln Center" director Kirk Browning.
1993–95	Pepe Romero as performing artist in the documentary *Shadows and Light: Joaquin Rodrigo at 90* (released September, 1993)

Wichita Symphony, USA, 2002: Invited to take part in Symphony's Concert Series

Guitar Foundation of America: International Convention and Competition, California, USA, 2001

Shadows and Light screened at the Museum of Contemporary Art

Gemini Awards, Canada, 1995

> Gemini—Donald Brittain Award—Best Documentary Program

> Gemini—Best Direction in an Information/Documentary Program

> Gemini—Best Sound in an Information/Documentary Program

International Television Festival, "Golden Prague," 1994: Golden Prague (First Prize)—Joint prize with *Concierto de Aranjuez*

The Chicago International Film Festival, 1994: Silver Hugo Award—Arts/Humanities

APPENDIX 2

International Emmy Awards, 1994: Nominated—Best Arts Documentary

Columbus International Film and Video Festival, USA, 1994: Honorable Mention

National Educational Film and Video Festival, USA, 1994: Gold Apple—Performing Arts: Music—Profiles of Artists

The Banff Television Festival, Canada, 1994: Nominated— Rockie, Arts Documentary

Concierto de Aranjuez—(released September, 1993)

Gemini Awards, Canada, 1995

> Gemini—Best Sound in a Comedy, Variety, or Performing Arts Program

> Nominations—Best Direction in a Variety or Performing Arts Program;

> Best Performing Arts Program; Best Photography in a Comedy, Variety, or Performing Arts Program; Best Picture Editing in a Comedy, Variety, or Performing Arts Program

International Television Festival, "Golden Prague," 1994

> Golden Prague (First Prize)—Joint prize with Shadows and Light: Joaquin Rodrigo at 90

Columbus International Film and Video Festival, USA, 1994

> First Prize—Chris Award—Arts and Culture

San Francisco International Film Festival, 1994: Certificate of Merit—Arts and Humanities

National Educational Film and Video Festival, USA, 1994: Silver Apple—Performing Arts: Music

Festival International du Film sur l'Art, Canada, 1994— Selected—Trajectories

1994   Pepe Romero received "Diapason d'or" from France for his Philips recording (438 016-2) of *Concierto de Aranjuez, Fantasía para un gentilhombre*, etc. with Neville Marriner conducting.

Pepe Romero received "Premio Andalucía de la Música" given by the Consejería de Cultura de la Junta de Andalucía.

Pepe Romero received the degree of Honorary Doctor of Music from University of Victoria, British Columbia.

2000	Pepe Romero (along with Celin and Angel Romero) was admitted with the knight's cross to the Order of Isabel la Católica by King Juan Carlos.
2002	Los Romeros received for their recording included in "Homenaje a Joaquín Rodrigo" won the best classical music album award in the sixth "Premios de la Música" [Music Prizes Competition] organized by the Academia de Artes y Ciencias Musicales [Academy of the Arts and Musical Sciences].
2003	Pepe Romero received the "Humboldt Plaketten" given by the municipality of Berlin-Reinickendorf (Germany).
2005	Pepe Romero received the "Profesor Visitante ad Honorem" from the Muncipalidad de Montes de Oca, Universidad de Costa Rica.
2006	Pepe Romero received the "Premio Trujamán de la Guitarra" from the Jornadas Internacionales de Guitarra de Valencia (Spain).
2007	Los Romeros received the "President's Merit Award" from the National Academy of Recording Arts and Sciences (in recognition of the Romero Quartet's extraordinary artistic accomplishments and strong commitment to educating the next generation).
2009	Celin and Pepe Romero received "Lifetime Achievement Awards" from the Koblenz International Guitar Festival and Academy (Germany).
2010	Pepe Romero received the "Artistic Achievement Award" from the Guitar Foundation of America.
	Pepe Romero received the "Isaac Stern International Award" given by the American String Teachers Association.
2011	Pepe Romero received the degree Doctor of Music, honoris causa from San Francisco Conservatory of Music.
2017	Pepe Romero received the honor of "Málaga en el Corazón" given by the Asociación Malagueña de Escritores "Amigos de Málaga."
	Pepe Romero received the "Premio Huella Cultural" from the Rotary Club Málaga.
	Pepe Romero received a "star" on the Adelaide Festival Centre's Walk of Fame after being the 2014 recipient of Adelaide Festival Centre Trust Choice.

APPENDIX 2

2018   Pepe Romero received "la Medalla de Honor" de la Real Academia de Bellas Artes de Granada, Nuestra Señora de las Angustias.

2020   Pepe Romero received the "Orchestra Award for Artistic Achievement" given by the International Classical Music Awards (ICMA).

        Pepe Romero received the "Premio Reconocimiento Honorifico" from the European Guitar Foundation.

2022   Pepe Romero was the first recipient of the "Premio Alhambra Internacional" from the Fundación Alhambra Guitarra (Spain).

2023   Pepe Romero received an honor from the city of Granada.

APPENDIX 3

DISCOGRAPHY

¡Flamenco Fenómeno!	Contemporary LP	S-9004	Recorded 1959
¡Flamenco Fenómeno!	Contemporary CD	CCD 14070-2	Re-release 1993
¡Flamenco Fenómeno!	Decca	485-4015	Re-release 2023
Flamenco! Pepe Romero, Guitar	Mercury Living Presence	MG-50297	Recorded 1962
Flamenco! Pepe Romero, Guitar	Decca	485-4015	Re-release 2023
The Royal Family of the Spanish Guitar Celedonio, Celin, Pepe and Angel Romero	Mercury	MG-50295	Recorded 1962
The Royal Family of the Spanish Guitar Celedonio, Celin, Pepe and Angel Romero	Decca	485-4015	Re-release 2023
The Romeros: Spain's Royal Family of the Guitar, Baroque Concertos and Solo Works	Mercury	SR-90417	Recorded 1965
The Romeros: Spain's Royal Family of the Guitar, Baroque Concertos and Solo Works	Decca	485-4015	Re-release 2023

An Evening of Flamenco Music: The Romeros, The Royal Family of the Spanish Guitar	Mercury	SR-90434	Recorded 1965
An Evening of Flamenco Music: The Romeros, The Royal Family of the Spanish Guitar	Decca	485-4015	Re-release 2023
The Romeros: The World of Flamenco	Mercury	SR2-9120	Recorded 1967
The Romeros: The World of Flamenco	Decca	485-4015	Re-release 2023
Los Romeros: Die Könige der Spanischen Gitarre	Philips CD	422 164-2	Recorded 1967, released on CD
The Romeros: Spain's Royal Family of the Guitar, Vivaldi Guitar Concertos (San Antonio Symphony, V. Alessandro)	Mercury	SR-90487	Recorded 1968
The Romeros: Spain's Royal Family of the Guitar, Vivaldi Guitar Concertos (San Antonio Symphony, V. Alessandro)	Decca	485-4015	Re-release 2023
Rodrigo: First Recording: Concierto Andaluz for four guitars and orchestra, the Romeros; Concierto Andaluz for four guitars and orchestra, Angel Romero (San Antonio Symphony, V. Alessandro)	Mercury	SR-90488	
	Philips CD	434 369-2	Recorded 1968
Rodrigo: First Recording: Concierto Andaluz for four guitars and orchestra, the Romeros' Concierto de Aranjuez for solo guitar and orchestra, Angel Romero (San Antonio Symphony, V. Alessandro)	Decca	485-4015	Re-release

(continued)

Title	Format	Catalogue	Notes
Giuliani Guitar Concerto, Op. 30 (Pepe Romero) Rodrigo: Concierto Madrigal for two guitars, Angel and Pepe Romero (Academy of St. Martin-in-the-Fields, Neville Marrier)	Philips LP	6500.918	Recorded 1974
Rodrigo: Fantasía para un gentilhombre, Giuliani: Introduction, Theme with Variations and Polonaise, Op. 65 (Pepe Romero, Academy of St. Martin-in-the-Fields, Neville Marrier)	Philips LP	9500 042	Recorded 1975
Famous Guitar Music including Tárrega: Recuerdos de la Alhambra/Albéniz: Asturias/Villa Lobos/ Lauro/Sagreras/Sor, Pepe Romero	Philips LP	9500 295	Recorded 1976
The Romeros Play Classical Music for Four Guitars	Philips LP	9500 296	Recorded 1976
Giuliani Guitar Concertos Op.36 & Op.70 (Pepe Romero, Academy of St. Martin-in-the-Fields, Neville Marrier)	Philips LP	9500 320	Recorded 1976
Mauro Giuliani: Guitar Concertos (Op.30, Op.36, Op.70, Op.65) (Pepe Romero, Academy of St. Martin-in-the-Fields, Neville Marriner)	Philips LP (set of 2)	6770 012	Re-release as box set
Giuliani Complete Guitar Concertos: Gran Sonata Eroica and other solo works (Pepe Romero, Academy of St. Martin-in-the-Fields, Neville Marriner)	Philips CD (set of 2)	454 262-2	Re-release on CD
Works for Guitar from Renaissance to Baroque Sanz, Milán, Mudarra, Narváez, Pisador, Valderrábano, Pepe Romero	Philips LP	9500 351	Recorded 1976

Works for two Guitars: Diabelli, Giuliani, Carulli. Pepe and Celedonio Romero	Philips LP	9500 352	Recorded 1976
Giuliani: Handel Variations, Op.107, Gran Sonata Eroica, etc., Pepe Romero guitar	Philips LP	9500 513	Recorded 1977
Flamenco / Pepe Romero guitar	Philips LP	9500 512	Recorded 1977
Los Romeros—Telemann/Bach/D. Scarlatti/Loeillet/Dowland	Philips LP	9500 536	Recorded 1977
Rodrigo: Concierto de Aranjuez, Pepe Romero: Concierto Andaluz, Los Romeros (Academy of St. Martin-in-the-Fields, Neville Marriner)	Philips LP	9500 563	Recorded 1978
Joaquín Rodrigo: "Concierto Madrigal" "Concierto Andaluz," Los Romeros (Academy of St. Martin-in-the-Fields, Neville Marriner)	Philips CD	400 024-2	Re-release on CD
Joaquín Rodrigo: Conciertos Aranjuez, Madrigal, Andaluz, Para una fiesta; Fantasía para un gentilhombre (Academy of St. Martin-in-the-Fields, Neville Marriner)	Philips CD (set of 3)	412 170-1	Re-release as CD box set
Rodrigo: Concierto de Aranjuez; Fantasía para un gentilhombre; Concierto Madrigal (Academy of St. Martin-in-the-Fields, Neville Marriner)	Philips CD	432-828-2	Re-release on CD
Joaquín Rodrigo Conciertos: Aranjuez, Madrigal, Andaluz, Para una fiesta, Fantasía para un gentilhombre, and works for guitar solo (Academy of St. Martin-in-the-Fields, Neville Marriner)	Philips CD (set of 3)	432 581-2	Re-release as CD box set

(continued)

Title	Format	Catalog No.	Notes
Rodrigo: Complete Concertos for Guitar and Harp (includes Concierto de Aranjuez, Concierto Madrigal, Concierto Andaluz, Concierto para una fiesta, Fantasía para un gentilhombre)	Philips CD (set of 2)	462 296-2	Re-release on CD
Sor: Guitar Sonatas/Guitarrensonaten Op.22 & 25, Pepe Romero	Philips LP	9500 586	Recorded 1978
Boccherini Guitar Quintets Nos. 4,5 & 6 (Academy of St. Martin-in-the-Fields' Chamber Ensemble)	Philips LP	9500 621	
	CD	420 385-2	Recorded 1978
Torroba: "Concierto Ibérico"—Los Romeros "Diálogos," Pepe Romero First recording	Philips LP	9500 749	Recorded 1979
Boccherini Guitar Quintets Nos. 3 & 9, "La ritirata di Madrid" (Pepe Romero, Academy of St. Martin-in-the-Fields' Chamber Ensemble)	Philips LP	9500 789	
	CD	426 092-2	Recorded 1979
Boccherini Guitar Quintets Nos. 1,2 & 7 (Pepe Romero, Academy of St. Martin-in-the-Fields' Chamber Ensemble)	Philips LP	9500 985	Recorded 1980
Boccherini: The Guitar Quintets (Pepe Romero, Academy of St. Martin-in-the-Fields' Chamber Ensemble)	Philips LP (set of 3)	6768 268	Re-release box set
Boccherini: The Guitar Quintets including "La ritirata di Madrid" & "Fandango" (Pepe Romero, Academy of St. Martin-in-the-Fields' Chamber Ensemble)	Philips CD (set of 2)	438 769-2	Re-release as CD box set
Joaquín Rodrigo/Pepe Romero guitar (solo works)	Philips LP	9500 915	Recorded 1980

APPENDIX 3

Title	Format	Catalog No.	Recorded
Pepe Romero: Bach Partita BWV 1004 & Suite BV 1009	Philips LP	6514 183	Recorded 1981
	CD	411 451-2	
Famous Spanish Dances—Albéniz, Falla, Granados; Pepe and Celín Romero	Philips LP	6514.182	Recorded 1981
	CD	411 432-2	
Carulli 2 Sonatas: Diabelli Sonata Op. 68, Grande Sonate brilliante Op. 102 (Pepe Romero, Wilhelm Hellweg, fortepiano)	Philips LP	410 396-1	Recorded 1982
Jeux Interdits, Recuerdos de la Alhambra, Asturias; Pepe Romero	Philips LP	6514 381	Recorded 1982
	CD	411 033-2	
Rodrigo: Concierto para una fiesta Romero/Torroba: Concierto de Málaga (Pepe Romero Academy of St. Martin-in-the-Fields, Neville Marriner)	Philips LP	411 133-1	Recorded 1983
	CD	411 133-2	
Vivaldi Guitar Concertos, Los Romeros (Academy of St. Martin-in-the-Fields, Iona Brown)	Philips LP	412 624-1	Recorded 1984
	CD	412 624-2	
Bizet Carmen Suite—Falla Dances: Moreno Torroba Sonata— Los Romeros	Philips LP	412 609-1	Recorded 1984
	CD	412 609-2	

(continued)

Villa-Lobos, Castelnuovo-Tedesco Guitar Concertos; Rodrigo: Sones en la Giralda (Pepe Romero, Academy of St. Martin-in-the-Fields, Neville Marriner)	Philips LP	416 357-1	Recorded 1985
	CD	416 357-2	
Pepe Romero Guitar: Albéniz/Tárrega/Moreno Torroba/Romero	Philips LP	416 384-1	Recorded 1985
	CD	416 384-2	
Villa-Lobos: Five Preludes, Étude No.1: Suite populaire brésilienne, Pepe Romero	Philips LP	420 245-1	Recorded 1987
	CD	420 245-2	
Pepe Romero: Flamenco: Chano Lobato, Maria Magdalena, Paco Romero	Philips CD	422 069-2	Recorded 1987
Carulli, Molino: Guitar Concertos, Mozart: Adagio KV 261, Rondo KV373 (Pepe Romero, Academy of St. Martin-in-the-Fields, Iona Brown)	Philips CD	426 263-2	Recorded 1989
La Paloma: Spanish and Latin American Favorites, Pepe Romero	Philips CD	432 102-2	Recorded 1990
Vivaldi Guitar Concertos: I Musici, Pepe Romero, Massimo Paris	Philips CD	434 082-2	Recorded 1991
Rodrigo: Concierto de Aranjuez: Fantasía de un gentilhombre, Cançoneta, Invocación y danza, Trois petites piéces (ASMF, Neville Marriner, Agustín León Ara)	Philips CD	438 016-2	(recorded 1992)
	Laser CD	070 263-1	

(also released as Laser CD-Video disc and VHS cassette in *Shadows and Light: Rodrigo at 90*, a film by Larry Weinstein and Rhombus Media)	NTSC/VHS	070 263-3	Recorded 1992
Noches de España: Romantic Guitar Classics: World premiere recording Sor Fantasie, Pepe Romero	Philips CD	442 150-2	Recorded 1993
Los Romeros: Spanish Guitar Favorites (Celedonio, Celin, Pepe, Celino Romero)	Philips CD	442 781-2	Recorded 1993
Opera Fantasy for Guitar: Pepe Romero	Philips CD	446 090-2	Recorded 1995
Songs My Father Taught Me: Pepe Romero	Philips CD	456 585-2	Recorded 1998
Boccherini: Quintetti con chitarra n.2,6,7,4 (Pepe Romero with Quartetto Stadivari)	UNICEF	DC-U31	Recorded 1998
The Romeros: Generations	CPA Hollywood Records		Recorded 2000
Homenaje a Joaquín Rodrigo	RTVE	65136	(Recorded 1997, live performance at the Alhambra)
Los Romeros con Orquesta Sinfónica de RTVE		OSyC-022	
Homenatge a Montsalvatge Metamorfosi de concert (Pepe Romero, Orquesta de Cadaqués, Gianandrea Noseda)	Tritó	TD 0010	Recorded 2002
Chihara: Guitar Concerto (Pepe Romero, London Symphony, Neville Marriner)	Albany Records	TROY724	Recorded 2004

(*continued*)

Title	Label	Catalog number	Notes
Giuliani Guitar Concerto No.1, Rodrigo Concierto Madrigal	PentaTone	PTC 5186 141	Re-release 2004 on super audio CD
The Art of Pepe Romero	Philips	475 6360	Re-release 2005-2 CD set
The Rodrigo Collection	Philips	475 6545	(Re-release 2005 - CD/DVD, including "Shadows and Light" film)
Corazón Español Pepe Romero	CPA Hollywood Records		Recorded 2003
Classic Romero Pepe Romero	CPA Hollywood Records		Recorded 2005
Guitarrenmusik: Bach, Sor Pepe Romero	Philips Classics Eloquence Label	470 363-2	Re-release on CD
Recuerdos de la Alhambra: Spanische Gitarrenmusik, Pepe Romero, Los Romeros	Philips Classics Eloquence Label	473 746-2	Re-release on CD
Aita Madina (Concierto vasco para 4 guitarras y orquesta. Euskadiko Orkestra Sinfonikoa/Los Romero/Mandeal	Claves	CD 50-2517/18	Recorded 2005
Palomo: Andalusian Nocturnes, Spanish Songs (Pepe Romero, guitar, Maria Bayo, soprano. Seville Royal Symphony Orchestra, Rafael Frühbeck de Burgos)	Naxos	855713	Recorded 2000

Los Romeros: Golden Jubilee Celebration. 50th anniversary re-compilation	DECCA	478 0192	
Palomo: My Secluded Garden / Madrigal and Five Sephardic Songs, Concierto de Cienfuegos (Los Romero, Pepe Romero, Maria Bayo, Seville Royal Symphony Orchestra, Rafael Frühbeck de Burgos)	Naxos	8572139	Recorded 2001, 2008; released June 2009
The Romeros: Celebration	Sony RCA Red Seal/NDR Kultur	88697458272	Recorded 2008, released 2009
Cordero: Caribbean Concertos for Guitar and Violin (Pepe Romero, Guillermo Figueroa, I Solisti di Zagreb) Nominated for 2012 Latin Grammy "Best Classical Album"	Naxos	8572707	Recorded May 2010, released December 2011
Pepe Romero Plays Concierto Festivo with I Solisti di Zagreb	Mel Bay	MB22202DVD	DVD recorded May 2010, released May 2011
Christmas with Los Romeros Pepe, Celin, Lito, Celino and Angel Romero *Concerto Málaga*, Massimo Paris	Deutsche Grammophon	417 9365	Recorded at Santa Maria Cristina, Málaga. Recorded April 2010; released Germany, November 2011, USA October 2012

(*continued*)

Pepe Romero: Spanish Nights All Spanish repertoire—not previously recorded World premiere recording of *Suite madrileña*, No.1 by Celedonio Romero	Deutsche Grammophon	479 0073	Recorded December 2010, released June 2012
Pepe Romero: Live in Granada DVD	CPA Hollywood Records-Caja Granada		Recorded May 21, 2010, released Aug 2012
Ultimate Classical Guitar: the essential masterpieces. 5 CD set (3 entire CDs are Pepe Romero)	DECCA	478 0217	(re-release compilation 2008)
Pepe Romero: Master of the Guitar. 11 CD set celebrating Pepe Romero's 70th birthday	DECCA	478 5669	(re-release compilation 2013)
Torroba Guitar Concertos vol I: Concierto en flamenco (Pepe Romero), *Diálogos entre guitarra y orquesta* (Vicente Coves), *Aires de la Mancha* (Pepe Romero), *Suite Castellana* (Vicente Coves), Málaga Philharmonic, Manuel Coves, conductor	NAXOS	8.573255	(recorded 2013, released 2015) 1st recording in a complete collection of Torroba Guitar Concertos
Rafael Frübeck de Burgos conducts the Danish National Symphony Orchestra: Featuring Beethoven Symphonies, Concierto de Aranjuez, Pepe Romero. 6 disc DVD collection of live concerts (only recording of Pepe Romero conducted by longtime friend and collaborator Frühbeck de Burgos)	DACAPO	2.110417-22	Recorded 2012-2014

*Torroba Guitar Concertos vol 2 : Homenaje a la seguidill*a (Pepe Romero), *Tonada concertante* (Pepe Romero), *Concierto de Castilla* (Vicente Coves), Extremadura Symphony Orchestra, Manuel Coves, conductor. 1st recording of Tonada concertante written and dedicated to Celedonio Romero	NAXOS	8.573503	Recorded 2015
Aloha España: Pepe Romero and Daniel Ho	Daniel Ho Creations	80133	Recorded 2016
David Chesky: España. Includes Concerto for Two Guitars and Orchestra Concerto de Lucia"with Angel and Pepe Romero	Chesky Records	JD422	Recorded April 2019–June 2019

BIBLIOGRAPHY

The newspaper articles cited below are not meant to be comprehensive but are simply those found in the Romero family archive, now available for consultation at UC Riverside Libraries' Special Collections: http://www.oac.cdlib.org/findaid/ark:/13030/c8057mh2/

Albright, William. "Music: Guitarist Pepe Romero." *Houston Post*, December 6, 1975, 7F.

Anderson, Rex, and David Kennedy. "Pepe Romero Masterclass." *Guitar: The Magazine for All Guitarists* (October 1983): 13–15.

Baines, Charles. "Pepe: Spain's Prince of Strings." *Sunday Morning Post* (Hong Kong), December 13, 1992, 12.

Christ, Jürgen. "Mein Vater und Ich, Wir Sind ein Gitarrist." *Gitarre und Laute* (March 1999): 61–64.

Clark, Walter Aaron. *Enrique Granados: Poet of the Piano*. New York: Oxford University Press, 2006.

——. *Isaac Albéniz: A Research and Information Guide*. New York: Routledge, 2015.

——. *Isaac Albéniz: Portrait of a Romantic*. Oxford: Oxford University Press, 1999.

——. *Joaquín Rodrigo: A Research and Information Guide*. New York: Routledge, 2021.

——. *Los Romeros: Royal Family of the Spanish Guitar*. Urbana Champaign: University of Illinois Press, 2018.

——. "Rodrigo's *Concierto para una fiesta*. Its Genesis and Interpretation: An Interview with Pepe Romero." *Soundboard: The Journal of the Guitar Foundation of America* 47/4 (December 2021): 15–20.

Clark, Walter Aaron, and William Craig Krause. *Federico Moreno Torroba: A Musical Life in Three Acts*. New York: Oxford University Press, 2013.

Davila, Ana María. "Pepe Romero: 'para hacer arte, has de saber dónde están las raices.'" *El Mundo*, November 4, 1995, 60.

Duarte, John. "Pepe Romero." *Gramophone* (December 1981): 856.

González Mira, Pedro. "O el amor por la guitarra." *Ritmo*, no. 640 (February 1993): 8.

Hentschel, Horst. "Pepe Romero—the Virtuous Stylist." *Classical Guitar* (November/December 1983): 23–25.

Horsley, Paul. "Pepe Romero Has Never Known Life without the Guitar." *Kansas City Star*, September 24, 2000.

Ineck, Tom. "Orchestra to Premiere 'Zareh': Guitarist Pepe Romero Will Play Tjeknavorian Concerto." *Lincoln Journal-Star*, November 20, 1988, 1H.

Kozinn, Allan. "Pepe Romero: Member of Los Romeros Solo Classical Artist." *Guitar Player* (January 1981): 32–36.

Lawson, Michael. "World Class Guitarist Pepe Romero Strums to Classical Beat." *San Diego Sun*, February 24, 1994, D&E, 1.

Muñoz, Virginia. "Pepe Romero, el mago que embruja con una guitarra." *Sur* (Málaga), August 25, 1988, 8.

Ornish, Laurel. "The Soul of the Land: For Classicist Pepe Romero, It's Feelings, Not Notes." *Dallas Observer*, August 22–28, 1996, 70.

Romero, Pepe. *Guitar Style and Technique*. New York: Bradley Publications, 1982.

——. *La Guitarra: A Comprehensive Study of Classical Guitar Technique and Guide to Performing*. Malvern, PA: Theodore Presser Publications, 2012.

Russomanno, Stefano. "Pepe Romero: 'Si la guitarra no está feliz, algo estamos haciendo mal.'" *Scherzo: Revista de Música* 37/386 (July–August 2022). https://shcerzo.es/pepe-romero-si-la-guitarra-no-esta-feliz-algo-esta (accessed October 5, 2022).

Saltzman, Joe. "Pepe Romero's Guitar: In a World of Its Own." *Los Angeles Times*, September 30, 1982, 6.

Smith, Frederick. "Coming from Guitarist Family a Pleasant Burden for Pepe Romero." *The Ledger* (Lakeland, Florida), February 11, 1994, 6.

Suárez-Pajares, Javier, and Walter Aaron Clark. *A Light in the Darkness: The Music and Life of Joaquín Rodrigo*. New York: W. W. Norton, 2024.

Tennant, Scott. *Pumping Nylon: The Classical Guitarist's Technique Handbook*. 2d ed. Van Nuys, CA: Alfred Music, 2016.

Tenorio, Sue. "Pepe Romero Conducts Master Class." *El Extra News* (Hartford), October 17, 1997, 14.

Wager, Greg. "Music Is Nonstop for Pepe Romero." *Los Angeles Times*, December 4, 1987, VI-6.

Windeler, Diane. "Pepe Romero: Guitar Was My 1st Language." *San Antonio Light*, November 16, 1984.

INDEX

Abbado, Claudio, 143
Abreu, Sergio, 91, 173, 198
Academy of St. Martin-in-the-
Fields, 111, 119, 152, 161
Aguado, Dionisio, 188
Alba, Felipe, 66
Albéniz, Isaac, 49, 131, 171, 174, 177,
185
Albert II, Prince of Monaco, 145–46
Albuquerque Orchestra, 113
Ali, Muhammad, 149–50
Alix, Antonio, 136
Alix, José, 136
Almeida, Laurindo, 66, 152, 174
Alonso, Odón, 158, 159f
Álvarez, Antonio, 26, 34
Amaya, Carmen, 149, 172
ambition, 203
American Sinfonietta, 93, 94f, 106,
129
Anderson, June, 113, 115
Angarola, Anisa, 44
Ángeles, Victoria de los, 167, 188
anxiety, 31–32
Araiza, Francisco, 167, 168f
Arcas, Julián, 29, 127, 188
Argento, Dominick, 136
Arizona State University, 45
arpeggios, 28
Arrau, Claudio, 143
Assad, Sergio, 137, 173
athletics, 8
audience, 32–33
Avery Fisher Hall, 88
Ávila, Paco, 11, 35, 84
awareness, 206

Bach, Johann Sebastian, 28, 49–50,
92, 132–33, 179, 187, 192
Ballesteros, Luis, 15

Banderas, Antonio, 12
Barbeyto, María Victoria, 149
Barcelona, Juan, 43
barré, 28
Barrios, Agustín, 127
Barrios, Ángel, 127
Barrón, Mayita, 107f
Barrón, Miguel, 107f
Barrueco, Manuel, 91, 172–73
Bayo, María, 170
Beethoven, Ludwig van, 132–34, 161
Behrend, Siegfried, 173
Bender, Kenneth, 45
Benedict XVI, Pope, 143–44
Bernabé, Paulino, 67
Bernal, Alfonso, 67
Binder, Perry, 142
Blöchinger, Edmund (Edi), 47, 50,
51f, 58–59
Boatwright, McHenry, 85
Boccherini, Luigi, 123–24, 127, 151
Boney, Nick, 42
Bream, Julian, 54, 87, 118, 122, 174,
191
Brendel, Alfred, 93
Bretón, Tomas, 131, 185–86
Brouwer, Leo, 91, 103, 175, 198
Brown, Iona, 124, 126f

Caballé, Montserrat, 70, 169
Cadaqués Orchestra, 51
Calcraft, Raymond, 77
Cameron, Tom, 63
Cañete, Ángel Luis, 208–9
Cansino, Eduardo, 148–49
Capella, Sebastian, 148
Carcassi, Mateo, 7, 28–30, 37
Carlevaro, Abel, 91, 198
Carnegie Hall, 78
Caron, David, 91

Carson, Ann, 87–88
Carson, Johnny, 148
Carter, Jimmy, 141–42
Carter, Susan, 91–92
Carulli, Ferdinando, 126–27
Casals Orchestra, 113
Castelnuovo-Tedesco, Mario, 36
Celedonio Romero Guitar Institute, 40
Cervantes, Miguel de, 45, 173
Chapí, Ruperto, 186
Charles III, King of United Kingdom, 146
Chavalote, 42–43
Chen Gang, 133
Chihara, Paul, 51, 110
Chopin, Frédéric, 144, 189, 191
Civil War, 6, 9, 18, 34, 64
Colburn, Dick, 111
colombianas, 191
composers, 183–92
composition, 134–38
Contreras, Manuel, 59, 67, 69
Contreras, Pablo, 59
Cook, Jean, 146–47
Cook, Joan, 195–96
Cordero, Ernesto, 112–14
Coves, Manuel, 42, 116, 159*f*
Coves, Vicente, 42, 96, 96*f*, 159*f*
Coves Castellano, Vicente, 159*f*
Cuba, 137
Cuéllar, Pepe, 67
Cuenca, 97

Dahlgren, Carl, 87, 203
Dalai Lama, 144
Dallas Classic Guitar Society, 90
de Visée, Robert, 45
Dearman, John, 44
Delgado, Candelario, 65–66, 68
Delgado, Pilo, 68
Denman, Matt, 40
Deutsche Oper, 169
Diabelli, Anton, 127
Díaz, Alirio, 171
Diemecke, Enrique, 160

Dimitri Mitropoulos International Conducting Competition, 107
Domínguez, Francisco, 9–10, 62
Domínguez, Pepe, 10
Don Quixote (Cervantes), 18, 19*f*, 21, 45, 173, 193
Dunn, Alex, 44–45
Dutoit, Charles, 157
dyslexia, 105–6

Eddy, Kristine Meigs, 195
Eddy, William, 146–47, 163
education, early, 13–21
Elman, Amparo, 164–65
Elman, Mischa, 164
Émile (Rousseau), 13
Entremont, Philippe, 170, 170*f*
Ephesus, 78
Eschenbach, Christoph, 211
Eschig, Max, 108
Escudero, Mario, 115

Falla, Manuel de, 131, 157, 166, 185, 190
Fiedler, Arthur, 162
Figueroa, Guillermo, 113–15
Fine, Wilma Cozart, 86–87
fingering, 26–27
flamenco, 11, 16, 35, 109, 115–16, 127–28, 134, 172, 194
flexibility, in guitar, 48
Fortea, Daniel, 28–30, 189
Fox, Herbert, 87–89, 89*f*, 91–93, 132, 144
Fox, Tim, 90
Fox, Vicente, 144
Frühbeck de Burgos, Rafael, 50, 75, 95, 107, 146
Funke, Hans Werner, 95

Gaab, Tom, 42
Garzo, Gabriel, 138
Gaschen, Susan, 92, 198, 200
Gaschen, Terry, 91
Gates, Steven, 87–89
Geller, Nancy, 120

INDEX

geometry, 16–17
Ghiglia, Oscar, 173
Gido, Julius, 68
Giménez, Gerónimo, 131
Giuliani, Mauro, 29, 48, 93, 106,
   112–13, 117–23, 127, 136, 161,
   167, 174, 178
Giussani, Gioachino, 53, 174
God, 82–83, 213
Godunov, Boris, 85
Goldberg, Phil, 164
Gómez, Vicente, 174
González de Vega, Sonsoles, 95–96,
   136
Gould, Morton, 163*f*, 190
Goya, Francisco de, 165
Granados, Enrique, 131, 185, 191
Griffin, Merv, 148
Guardia Civil, 6
Guitar Foundation of America, 45
guitar makers, 9–11, 49–50, 61–71
guitarists, 171–80
guitars, 47–58, 90, 201–2

Haitink, Bernard, 143
Hamburg, 79
Hartmann, Audrey, 87, 89
Hauser, Hermann, III, 70–71
Hauser, Hermann, Jr., 50, 54*f*, 63, 67,
   69, 91, 174
Hauser, Hermann, Sr., 47, 53–54, 65,
   69, 173
Haydn, Joseph, 145
Hays, Brian, 103–4, 137–38
Hayworth, Rita, 148–49
He Zhanhao, 133
hearing, 27
Heck, Thomas, 118, 120
Heifetz, Jascha, 165
Hellweg, Wilhelm, 123–25, 125*f*,
   126–27
Hernández, Santos, 49, 56, 58,
   64–65, 174
Hurok, Sol, 87–88

improvisation, 128–29, 134

Iturbi, José, 164

Jeffery, Brian, 118, 123
Jiménez, Luz Ángela, 175
John Paul II, Pope, 142–43, 143*f*
Jordan Hall, 78
jota, 185
Juan Carlos, King of Spain, 145

Kakefu, Motomi, 45
Kanengiser, Bill, 41, 43
Kenny, Elizabeth, 10
King, John, 108, 118
Kinnell, Henrietta, 67
Kostelanetz, Andre, 110, 162
Kottke, Leo, 178–79
Krause, Bill, 45
Kreisler, Fritz, 191
Kreitzer, David, 147
Kressin, Jacob Romero, 136

Lagoya, Alexandre, 108
Lalo, Éduard, 190
LaMarchina, Robert, 109
Lamborghini, Susan, 91–92, 178, 180
Lawrence, Harold, 86
Lee, David, 99, 133
legato, 28
Lehmann, Lotte, 37, 163
Leinsdorf, Erich, 167
Leisner, David, 93, 103–4
Lincoln Center Philharmonic Hall,
   88
Liszt, Franz, 188
Llobet, Miguel, 127, 131
Long, Mary, 137
Long, Richard, 28, 108, 123–24, 137
López Cobos, Jesús 146, 161
López del Valle, Josefa, 43
López-Ferrer, François, 161
Lorimer, Michael, 54–55
Los Angeles Chamber Orchestra,
   110, 117
Los Angeles Guitar Festival, 36–37
Los Angeles Guitar Quartet, 43–44
love, 193–202, 205–6

INDEX

Lucas, James, 85–87
Lucena, Paco de, 188
Lucía, Paco de, 26, 178

Ma, Christina, 99
Macaluso, Vicente, 42
Madina, Francisco de, 93, 103, 109, 110f, 162, 186
Málaga, 11–12, 34
Malats, Joaquim, 62, 174
managers, 84–99
Marcus, Jonathan, 42
Markos, Lajos, 146, 147f
Marote, 149
Marriner, Neville, 51, 106, 111, 116, 119, 127, 156f, 157, 161, 164, 174
Marshall, Jack, 42
Martí, José, 20–21
Martín, Raul, 149
Martínez, Miguel Ángel Gómez, 158f
master classes, 37–39, 39f, 42
Masters, Martha, 45
mathematics, 16–17
Matthiesen, Heike, 45, 169
Mattingly, Robert, 42, 64, 68
Mena, Juanjo, 162
Merlin, José Luis, 178
Mertz, Johann Kaspar, 44, 188
Meyerson Hall, 78
Miklaucic, Tim, 50
Milán, Luis de, 187, 192
Molino, Francesco, 126–27
Molledo, Luis, 16–17, 146
Montoya, Ramón, 188
Montsalvatge, Xavier, 50–51
Morente, Enrique, 172
Mozart, Wolfgang Amadeus, 45–46, 113, 127, 133, 168, 183
Mudarra, Alonso, 187
Munich, 79
Munich Symphony Orchestra, 170f
Music Academy of the West, 37

Narváez, Luys, 187, 192
natural playing, 29–30
neck, of guitar, 48, 65

Nelson, Willie, 146
Nixon, Richard, 142
Nogales, José, 12
Norman, Jessye, 75, 143, 166

Obando, Miguel, 64, 66
Ober, Fritz, 50
Oistrakh, David, 92, 167
Oklahoma City University, 40
Ollcot-Bickford, Vahdah, 66
Orán, Humberto, 95–96
Orchestra of Guayaquil, 96–97
Oribe, José, 37, 68
Ormandy, Eugene, 162
Orpheus Chamber Orchestra, 113

Paisiello, Giovanni, 117
Palau de la Música Catalana, 78
Palmer, David, 39
Palmer, Michael, 39–40, 93, 94f, 108, 129
Palomo, Lorenzo, 95, 103, 156f, 161, 186
Park, Yoon Kwan, 98f
Parkening, Christopher, 36
Pass, Joe, 134, 178, 179f
Patapoutian, Ardem, 144–45
Pele, 150
Peña, Paco, 178
perfection, 205
performance anxiety, 31–32
Peris, José, 145
Picasso, Pablo, 12
Pidgeon, Charlene, 196–97
Pidgeon, Larry, 196
Pile, Randy, 44
Pisador, Diego, 187
polio, 10
Polyxiadis, Nikolaos, 209
Ponce, Manuel, 160
practice, 28, 206
Prada, Amancio, 178
premieres, 103–27
Presti, Ida, 108
Puccini, Giacomo, 183–85
Puebla, Niña de la, 191
Puerto Rico Orchestra, 113

INDEX

Pujol, Emilio, 127
Pulpón, Jesús Antonio, 84

Quartz Mountain Music Festival, 39–40
Quasthoff, Thomas, 167, 169*f*
Quesada, Enrique de, 96–97
Quesada, Ernesto de, 95
Quesada, Ricardo de, 95

Rainier III, Prince of Monaco, 145–46
Ramirez, Alexander, 45, 62
Ramírez, Amalia, 59
Ramírez, José, 63–64, 67, 91
rasgueado, 29
Ratzinger, Joseph, 143–44
reincarnation, 5–6
Rejto, Alice, 93
Rejto, Gabor, 37, 40, 93, 151, 165
Residencia Kempis, 109, 110*f*
Ressendi, Baldomero Romero, 18
Reveles, Nicholas, 40–41
Revueltas, Silvestre, 160
revivals, 118–27
Rheingau Festival, 61
Ricardo, Niño, 134
Robert Schumann Conservatory, 45
Robledo, Josefina, 127
Rodrigo, Cecilia, 157
Rodrigo, Joaquín, 18, 45, 92, 95, 103, 106, 108, 112, 122–23, 129–30, 134, 135*f*, 158, 160–61, 167, 187
Rodríguez, Manuel, 66, 68–69, 91
Rodríguez, Miguel, 49–51, 52*f*, 56, 66, 70
Rodríguez, Miguel, II, 51, 52*f*
Romanillos, José Luis, 59
Romero, Adolfo, 4
Romero, Angel, 7–8, 52*f*, 54, 54*f*, 69, 86*f*, 99, 112, 116, 132, 160, 177*f*
Romero, Angelina, 31, 63, 141, 169, 190, 201, 202*f*
Romero, Angelita, 3, 5–7, 13–21, 20*f*, 63, 89*f*, 110*f*
Romero, Bernardo, 60–61

Romero, Carissa, 42–43, 50, 77, 97–99, 114, 138, 168, 198–99, 199*f*, 200–201
Romero, Celedonio (father), 3–7, 18, 49–50, 55–57, 62, 64–65, 86*f*, 103, 110*f*, 172, 204*f*
Romero, Celin (brother), 3–4, 7, 13–14, 40, 54*f*, 65, 76*f*, 85, 86*f*, 88, 119, 121, 136, 145, 147, 158, 160, 177*f*
Romero, Celino, 40, 76*f*
Romero, Federico, 186
Romero, Juanillo, 6
Romero, Kristine, 63–64, 141, 195–98, 197*f*, 200
Romero, Lito, 40, 76*f*
Romero, Maximino, 4, 14
Romero, Pepe (images), 20*f*, 38*f*–39*f*, 51*f*–52*f*, 54*f*, 58*f*, 76*f*, 86*f*, 89*f*, 94*f*, 96*f*, 98*f*, 105*f*, 107*f*, 125*f*–26*f*, 135*f*, 143*f*, 156*f*, 158*f*–59*f*, 163*f*, 168*f*–69*f*, 177*f*, 179*f*, 184*f*, 197*f*, 199*f*, 202*f*, 204*f*
Romero, Pepe, Jr., 50–51, 55–60, 58*f*, 67–68, 106, 202*f*
Romero, Susanna, 201, 202*f*
Romero, Tina, 63, 106, 201, 202*f*
Romero Quartet, 75, 76*f*, 85, 86*f*, 130–31, 138
Romero School of Guitar, 35–36
Ros-Marbà, Antoni, 185
Rousseau, Jean-Jacques, 13
Royal Danish Orchestra, 157
Rubinstein, Arthur, 92, 144, 161
Rubinstein, Erna, 37
Russell, David, 173

Sabicas, 26, 115–16, 134, 149, 172
Saffer, Darryl, 38, 38*f*, 90
Sagreras, Julio, 29
Sainz de la Maza, Regino, 78, 171–72
Salas, Pepe, 9–10
Sánchez, Carlos, 43
Sánchez, Francisco, 178
Sanlúcar, Esteban de, 191
Sanlúcar, Manolo, 134, 176, 210
Sanz, Gaspar, 127, 188

scales, 28, 30
Schäffer, Martina, 45
Schang, Frederick Christian, 87, 89
Scheit, Karl, 173
Schleswig-Holstein Music Festival, 94
Schlote, Hans, 92–95
Schlote, Joachim, 93
Schubert, Franz, 166, 168–69, 189–90
Schumann, Robert, 7–8, 30, 191
Scully, Rodney, 144
Segovia, Andrés, 54, 87, 95, 103, 127, 158, 172, 175, 188–89
Sender, Ramón, 148
Seville, 8–9, 11–12, 17–18, 34–35, 66, 193
Shaw, Guillermo Fernández, 186
Shaw, Harold, 88–89
"Sicilienne" (Schumann), 7
slurs, 28
Smith, Erik, 119
Smith, Jim, 42
soccer, 8
Sophia, Queen of Spain, 145
Sor, Fernando, 7, 44, 48, 121, 123, 127, 180, 188
Spanish National Orchestra, 75
sports, 8
staccato, 28
stage fright, 31–32
Stoddard, Farrington, 84
strumming, 28–29
students, 36–37
Switzer, Mark, 38*f*

Tamianka, Henri, 151, 164
Tárrega, Francisco, 28–29, 127, 131–32, 188–89
Tashiro, Motomi, 45
teaching, 34–46, 38*f–39f*
Teatro Lope de Vega, 8–9
technique, 25–33
Tedesco, Tommy, 42
Tennant, Scott, 29, 41, 43
Tezanos, Mariano, Jr., 59
Tjeknavorian, Loris, 104, 105*f*

Tjeknavorian, Zareh, 104
Torres, Antonio de, 49–50, 61–62
Torroba, Federico Moreno, 42, 82, 95, 103–4, 115–17, 119, 158, 159*f*, 161, 167, 171–72
touring, 57, 63, 75, 77, 80–82
Traphagen, Dake, 56
tremolo, 26, 28, 31, 175
Trintschuk, Julia, 45
tuberculosis, 10
Tucker, Larry, 90–91
Tureck, Rosalyn, 132
Turina, Joaquín, 45–46

University of California, San Diego (UCSD), 40–41, 44
University of Southern California (USC), 40–41, 43–44

Valencia, 66
Vargas, Iván, 42–43
Vargas Larios, Manuel, 42–43
Velázquez, Diego, 17, 165
Verdi, Giuseppe, 183
Villa-Lobos, Heitor, 28, 32, 93, 103, 108
Vivaldi, Antonio, 133

Wagner, Richard, 132
Walters, Barbara, 148
Wetzel, Robert, 198
Widauer, Helene, 45
Wilford, Ronald, 87–88
Williams, John, 175
Williams, Len, 175

Yepes, Narciso, 171–72
Yogananda, Paramahansa, 200
Young, Chris, 90

Zannini, Nancy, 166
zarzuela, 53, 131, 154, 185–86
Zearott, Michael, 93, 103, 106–7, 107*f*, 120, 148, 162
Zeltins, Yuris, 56, 66, 71
Zorrilla, José, 15
Zurbarán, Francisco de, 17

Printed in the United States
by Baker & Taylor Publisher Services